Elizabeth

The Industrialization of São Paulo, 1880–1945

Latin American Monographs, No. 17
Institute of Latin American Studies
The University of Texas at Austin

The Industrialization
of São Paulo
1880-1945

Warren Dean

PUBLISHED FOR
THE INSTITUTE OF LATIN AMERICAN STUDIES
BY THE UNIVERSITY OF TEXAS PRESS
AUSTIN & LONDON

Standard Book Number 292–70004–0
Library of Congress Catalog Card No. 73–96435
Copyright © 1969 by Warren Dean
All Rights Reserved

Type set by G&S Typesetters, Austin
Printed by Capital Printing Company, Austin
Bound by Universal Bookbindery, Inc., San Antonio

For Judith

ACKNOWLEDGMENTS

It will be noticed by the reader that the author is intellectually indebted to certain scholars of the Faculty of Philosophy at the University of São Paulo. In particular a great deal more is owed to professors Fernando Henrique Cardoso, Juárez Rubens Brandão Lopes, Paulo Singer, Gabriel Bolaffi, and Florestan Fernandes than can be declared in footnotes. To their sophisticated analyses of the Brazilian industrial system this work may be considered an historical appendix containing a few amplifications and revisions. The author wishes also to thank professors Nícia Vilela Luz, Ciro Berlinck, Alice Canabrava, and Bernard Rosen, who offered valuable insights and assistance while his research was carried out in São Paulo. Appreciation is also owed to those who supervised the original version of the text, especially Professor Lyle McAlister, and to those who read and commented on later versions, professors Thomas McGann, Boris Fausto, and Stanley Stein.

Unfailing cooperation and assistance were encountered at libraries and archives in São Paulo. In particular the author is obliged to those at the Biblioteca Roberto Simonsen, the Departamento Estadual de Estatística, the British Chamber of Commerce, the Sindicato Patronal das Indústrias Textis do Estado de São Paulo, the Arquivo do Estado de São Paulo, the Instituto de Administração, the Associação Comercial de São Paulo, and the Biblioteca Municipal. Many Paulistas offered kindnesses and hospitality that were very much appreciated by the author and his family, who wish especially to thank Gabriel and Clélia Bolaffi, José and Jô Barbosa da Silva, and Simon and Ana Bal.

The Foreign Area Training Program and the Graduate School of The University of Texas provided funds that made this study possible. Of course, neither these institutions nor the persons cited above are responsible for its defects.

WARREN DEAN

Austin, Texas

CONTENTS

TABLES

A NOTE ON BRAZILIAN CURRENCY

The standard of currency in Brazil was, until 1942, the *milreis*. One milreis was written 1$000. The fractional currency was the *real* (plural *reis*), 1,000 to the milreis. Thus two hundred reis would be written $200.

The *conto* was used in quoting large sums of money. It equaled 1,000 milreis and was written 1:000$000.

In 1942 the milreis was renamed the *cruzeiro*.

Abbreviations Used in the Text and Footnotes:

CIFTSP   Centro dos Industriaes de Fiação e Tecelagem de São Paulo

JCSP   São Paulo (state). Junta Comercial de São Paulo

NA-DS   U.S. National Archives, Department of State

RRIAB   U.S. National Archives, Records Relating to the Internal Affairs of Brazil

SPITESP Sindicato Patronal das Indústrias Textis do Estado de São Paulo

The Industrialization of São Paulo, 1880–1945

CHAPTER I

The Coffee Trade Begets Industry

The industrialization of São Paulo depended from the beginning upon the demand generated by the growing overseas market for coffee. The cultivation of coffee started in that state well after the first plantings in the mountains above Rio de Janeiro in the beginning of the nineteenth century. For fifty years the trade gained ground in Europe and stimulated the establishment of new plantings further and further to the west. By the 1850's the wave of coffee groves had crossed to the Paulista side of the Paraíba Valley and been introduced to the region of Campinas, beyond the provincial capital. As the almost unknown interior of São Paulo came to be penetrated, it was discovered that the future of coffee lay there, for along the highland ridges between the tributaries of the Paraná River, far inland, were to be found the soils most suitable for its cultivation.

Toward the end of the nineteenth century the market for coffee began to expand more quickly. Demand in the United States and Europe was growing as industrialization increased productivity; Brazil's coffee was low-grade, suitable for consumption by the masses. Transport became cheaper and more reliable as iron-hulled steamships entered the South Atlantic sea lanes. The commercial system became more effective and extensive as undersea cables were laid and as importing houses and overseas banking operations were established. São Paulo began to experience the same euphoric prosperity that was overtaking other parts of Latin America at the same time.

Certain circumstances accelerated still further the sudden growth of the coffee trade. First, in Ceylon, São Paulo's principal rival, a blight was ravaging the coffee groves, drastically cutting output. Second, slavery was abolished in Brazil in 1888, opening the way to a more efficient and more viable labor force of free European immigrants. Third, the overthrow of the senescent emperor by the military in 1889 led to the institution of an extremely decentralized economic and political structure that allowed the state government of São Paulo to encourage the trade without hindrance and to retain all the profit from it within the state.

These external and internal stimuli produced spectacular results: shipments of coffee from Santos, São Paulo's seaport, more than doubled in each decade after 1870. In 1892 Santos exported $40,000,000 worth of coffee; by 1912 its exports totaled $170,000,000. State population grew from 837,000 in 1872, to 2,283,000 in 1900, to almost 4,000,000 by the outbreak of World War I—an increase of more than 14 per cent per year. Meanwhile the capital grew even more rapidly. A village of 23,000 in 1872, its inhabitants numbered 580,000 by 1920.[1]

Coffee was the basis of domestic industrial growth first of all because it provided the most elementary prerequisite of a factory system —a money economy. Without a crop for export, the landowners of São Paulo had little need for cash or for credit. Before the introduction of coffee, farms were typically devoted to subsistence agriculture, even when they were large enough to require slave labor or sharecropping. The planters prided themselves on self-sufficiency; all they needed from the outside world was "gunpowder and salt." In all of Brazil the circulating currency in the 1870's and 1880's amounted to a mere fifteen to twenty milreis per capita ($7–$15). In São Paulo there were

[1] São Paulo (state), *Anuario Estatística de São Paulo* (1898), II, 282, and (1940), p. 89. "São Paulo" will invariably be used to refer to the state, "the capital" to refer to the city.

only two banks before 1872, both of them branches of Rio firms. Once the planters encountered a cash market for their produce, however, the volume of money in circulation and of bank credit increased. One result of this trend was the installation of a few textile mills in the province in the 1870's. These mills turned locally grown cotton into rough, unbleached material that was sold to planters to clothe their slaves. Before then, planters had dressed their fieldworkers in homespun; by 1875 sales of coffee were beginning to provide cash to buy the cloth and to discourage employing the slaves in handicrafts.[2]

With the arrival of free labor the use of money spread to the mass of the population. In areas of Brazil beyond the export-producing system, abolition did not greatly increase the need for money in wage payments, because the freedmen remained unpaid sharecroppers.

In São Paulo the planters found it impossible to attract workers from Europe without payment of wages in money. They discovered, furthermore, that wage payments were to their advantage. The most economical employment of their laborers' effort was in coffee production, not in subsistence crops, therefore the *colonos*—immigrant workers—were prohibited from growing anything except coffee, once the coffee trees reached maturity. This also obliged them to buy their necessities at the plantation store. The store itself was a source of profit to the capitalistic planter, who either sold the concession or operated it himself.

Other effects of the more widespread use of money are harder to evaluate, but must have been significant. The land itself acquired money value and became a volatile factor of exchange. It could be sold to obtain capital, perhaps to buy agricultural machinery or shares in a commercial firm; or a merchant could buy land, or foreclose a mortgage, to gain entry in the coffee business. The new banks, whose funds were originally invested in short-term coffee transactions, might use some of their credit-creating capacity to finance manufacturers. The planters became more concerned with the commercial and financial

[2] *L'Empire du Brésil*, pp. 477–484; Brazil, Instituto Brasileiro de Geografia e Estatística, Conselho Nacional de Estatística, *O Brasil em números*, p. 71; Alice P. Canabrava, *O desenvolvimento da cultura de algodão na Província de São Paulo, 1861–1875*, pp. 282–285. Dollar values that follow quotations in milreis are based on the average exchange rate of the year in question.

aspects of their business; they lived more frequently in the cities and some turned to real estate, banking, railroad promoting, and exporting.[3]

Coffee planting was a kind of matrix that defined the possibilities of the entrepreneur. The structure of the plantation system was quite simple. Land ownership was highly concentrated. A few hundred extended family groups owned vast holdings subdivided into plantations of 100,000 to more than 1,000,000 trees. A freeholding lower class existed in São Paulo before the beginning of the coffee trade, but coffee tended to exterminate it. Coffee required capital and influence to buy slaves, to attract the railroad, to obtain credit, and to validate land claims. Those who did not possess these resources lost their lands to those who did and either began afresh, squatting on land beyond the coffee frontier, or accepted employment on the plantations.[4]

The labor system was based on the European immigrant. Those who went to the plantation were invariably of peasant origin. They worked the coffee groves for money wages, as tenants on yearly contracts. There was some small hope of eventually owning land, because older estates whose trees were beginning to lose their fertility were occasionally subdivided. It was more common, however, for the *colono* to change employers frequently and to return to his homeland either when he had accumulated some savings or after he had lost all hope of doing so. The scale of consumption in the rural areas was limited by the low wages offered by the planter, who managed to retain a very large share of the coffee income as profits; one informed report mentioned an 80 per cent return on capital even in the bad years of the mid-1890's. (The coffee workers never organized, but there were many rural strikes.) It was also limited by the high propensity of the *colonos* to hoard their earnings in order one day to return to their homeland.

Remittances to Italy via the São Paulo branch of the Bank of Naples averaged $1,000,000 a year in the first decade of this century. In years when coffee prices fell, the discouraged peasants left in such

[3] Pierre Monbeig, *La croissance de la ville de São Paulo*, pp. 27–31.
[4] Lucila Herrmann, "Evolução da estrutura social de Guaratinguetá num período de trezentos anos," *Revista de Administração* (March–June 1948), pp. 123–127; Pierre Monbeig, *Pionniers et planteurs de São Paulo*, pp. 84–85.

numbers, either for their homeland or for Argentina, that net immigration was close to zero. From 1902 to 1910 more than 330,000 Europeans arrived in Santos, but so many re-emigrated that the net gain was only 16,667 for the entire nine years.[5]

The demand of so depressed a mass market was restricted in volume and narrow in range. Travelers have described the furnishings of the *colonos'* one-bedroom houses: a frame bed with coarse cotton sheets, chairs and a table, pots and pans, candles, a *santo*, and religious or patriotic chromos. The immigrant and his family wore cotton drill, felt or straw hats, and leather shoes or canvas clogs. They produced their corn and beans and most of their meat and bought wheat flour, lard, salt, cod, soap, *pasta*, and sometimes beer, canned meat, and kerosene. All else was lacking, and all else, it may be presumed, was consumed only in the cities, as part of a luxury trade, and hence principally satisfied by imports: printed matter, medical and optical goods, drugs, printed textiles, linoleum and oilcloth, plumbing fixtures, electrical hardware, and many other objects already commonplace in industrialized Europe and America.[6]

It appears that productivity in coffee culture did not improve through the entire period of its geographical expansion except in three respects: transport, processing, and commercial organization. Domestic manufacture contributed in some degree to the first two improvements. For the rest, new investment in coffee was applied to the opening of new land rather than to the intensification of production on existing estates. This practice meant that productivity would at best merely remain stable and that the real wages of the rural laborers would increase only if the selling price of coffee improved in the international market.

The structure of the coffee-producing system, with its extreme polarity of planter and *colono*, and the general stagnation in technique,

---

[5] Jornal do Commercio, *Retrospecto Commercial* (1896), pp. 4–5; Salvatore Pisani, *Lo stato di San Paolo nel cinquantenario dell'immigrazione*, p. 1076; *Anuario estatistico de São Paulo* (1914), I, 108.

[6] Vicenzo Grossi, "Gl'italiani a São Paulo," *Nuova Antologia* (September 16, 1896), pp. 231–260; Eugenio Bonardelli, *Lo stato di San Paolo del Brasile e l'emigrazione italiana.*

which resulted in unchanging factor proportions, influenced manufacturing in many ways. It depressed aggregate demand, which was condemned to rise no faster than the increase in population. The pattern of demand also remained the same. The great mass of the population was able to buy only basic necessities of low quality and of a sort they were accustomed to consume in Europe. The agricultural worker required only the simplest of tools: hoes, the picturesque coffee sieves, cotton sacks, and little else.

The coffee trade not only generated a demand for industrial production, it also paid for much of the economic and social overhead necessary to make domestic manufacturing profitable. Railroad construction was entirely a function of the coffee expansion. The lines were built either by planters with their profits or by foreigners with the expectation of hauling coffee. The port of Santos, so important to early manufacturing because of the need for imported raw materials such as jute and wheat, was likewise a coffee venture. The earliest factories were powered by steam engines fueled with charcoal or imported coal, but later machine production depended on the installation of urban hydroelectric power systems. The electric companies were often organized by planters eager to adorn their inland towns with modern devices. The plants that provided the greatest share of power, those at São Paulo and Sorocaba, were built by European and American interests whose hope of profit was founded at least indirectly on coffee, that is, on the urban growth functionally dependent on the coffee trade. The largest of these infusions of capital was that of the São Paulo Tramway, Light and Power Company, incorporated in 1899 with $10,000,000 in capital to provide an electric trolley system. Gradually, as a subsidiary of the Canadian-incorporated Brazilian Traction, Light and Power Company, it absorbed other local power, telephone, and gas companies and installed the thermal and hydroelectric capacity needed to power industry as well as utilities.[7]

The first factories also benefited incalculably from the social transformation already wrought by coffee, most notably from the presence

[7] Frederick Mulqueen, "A Canadian Enterprise Abroad," *Canadian Banker* (Winter 1952), pp. 34–55.

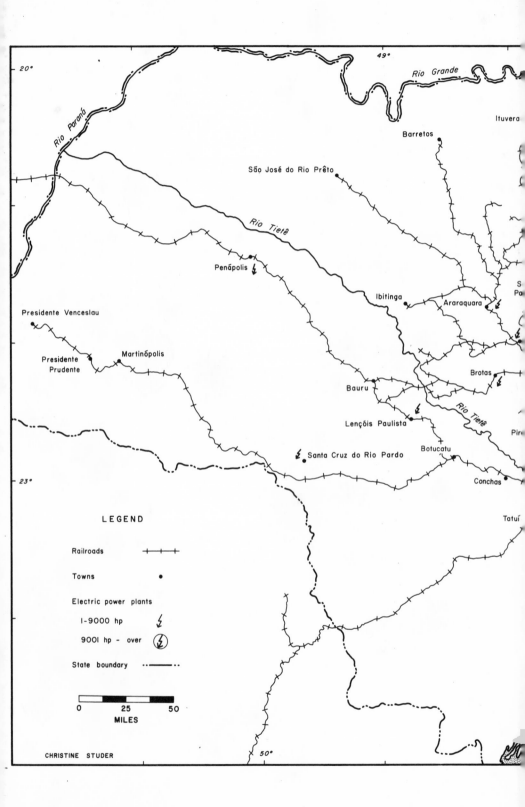

LEGEND

Railroads   +—+—+—+

Towns   ●

Electric power plants

1-9000 hp

9001 hp - over

State boundary   ··—··—··

0   25   50

MILES

CHRISTINE STUDER

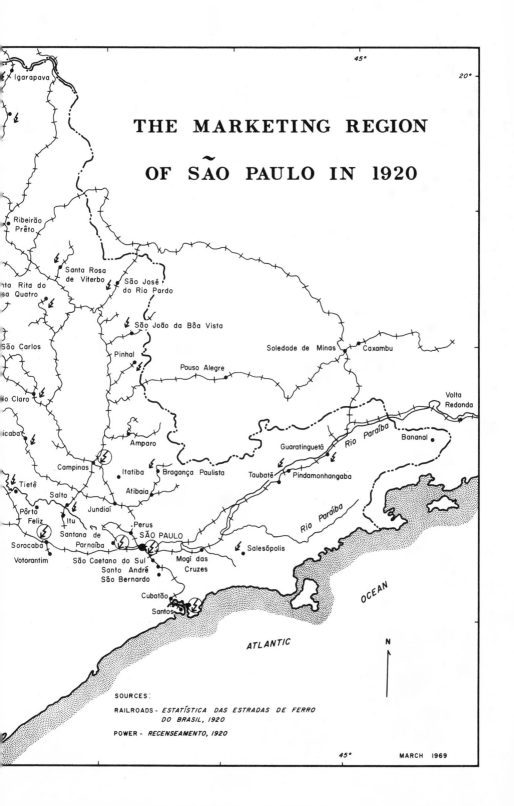

THE MARKETING REGION

OF SÃO PAULO IN 1920

Igarapava

Ribeirão Prêto

Santa Rosa de Viterbo

São José do Rio Pardo

nta Rita do sa Quatro

São João da Bôa Vista

São Carlos

Pinhal

Soledade de Minas

Caxambu

Pouso Alegre

io Claro

Volta Redonda

icaba

Amparo

Guaratinguetá

Rio Paraíba

Bananal

Campinas

Itatiba

Bragança Paulista

Taubaté

Pindamonhangaba

Tietê

Salto

Atibaia

Rio Paraíba

Pôrto Feliz

Jundiaí

Itu

Perus

SÃO PAULO

Santana de Parnaíba

Sorocaba

Salesópolis

Votorantim

São Caetano do Sul

Santo André

São Bernardo

Mogí das Cruzes

Cubatão

Santos

OCEAN

N

ATLANTIC

SOURCES:

RAILROADS - *ESTATÍSTICA DAS ESTRADAS DE FERRO DO BRASIL, 1920*

POWER - *RECENSEAMENTO, 1920*

MARCH 1969

of a work force, both immigrant and native, already inured to the necessity of steady labor, but also of a cadre of technicians and foremen hired in Europe to tend plantations or build railroads or trained in São Paulo's new institutes of higher learning. Besides the law school founded in the 1830's, new schools of engineering, commerce, medicine, and biology were created before World War I.

These sudden developments in the São Paulo region in the 1880's and 1890's, if they are considered all together, as a whole, were in a more profound sense the cause of industrialization. For the coffee boom provided that movement "along a broad front" that Gerschenkron believes is necessary if industrialization is to take hold, and if resistances inherent in stagnant economies are to be overcome.[8]

A rapidly expanding and buoyant export trade does not necessarily lead to a domestic industrial plant of any consequence, however. Indeed, surveying the other instances of export-oriented economies in Latin America before World War I, it seems that São Paulo's development was rather unique. How can its uniqueness be accounted for? Analyses of the beginnings of industrialization usually center on the question of the degree to which domestic manufactures are able to supplant imports. This is indeed an important subject, but it is not particularly relevant to the earliest stages of industrial development, if São Paulo is a typical case. The very first products to be manufactured there were those whose weight-to-cost ratio was so high that even with the most rudimentary technique they cost less to produce than to buy from Europe. At least until the 1920's the Paulistas were producing, with very few exceptions, only goods that were quite bulky and intrinsically low in value. Furthermore, these products were, with few exceptions, fashioned either from local raw materials or from imported materials which would have been much bulkier if fully transformed before shipment. The resource endowment of São Paulo can be seen quite clearly to have influenced the pattern of this early development. The most important activities employed local agricultural materials, notably cotton, leather, sugar, cereals, and lumber, or

---

[8] Alexander Gerschenkron, *Economic Backwardness in Historical Perspective*, pp. 10–11.

nonmetallic minerals, especially clay, sand, lime, and stone. The lack of significant iron deposits, on the other hand, meant that the metallurgical industry was to remain a small-scale operation, producing spare parts, specialized machines, or equipment made to order.[9]

Even so rudimentary a stage of industrialization as that of São Paulo before the 1920's involved a wide range of goods. It is impossible to conceive of an export product so lucrative that it would pay for the importation of bricks. Along with bricks, almost every kind of construction material was domestically produced by 1920: tiles, cement, nails, ceramic pipes, lumber, and even plate glass and plumbing fixtures. Other obvious examples are beer and soft drinks (and bottles to put them in), shoes, boilers, coarse textiles, furniture, stonework, flour, pots and pans, and hats.

It should be pointed out that at this early stage the industrial sector was quite marginal within the export-oriented economy. As long as the only customers of Paulista manufacturers were the planters and their tenants, manufacturing remained a venture even more speculative than planting. The manufacturers and the planters were equally dependent on coffee prices to cover their production costs, but the planter was far less dependent on foreign exchange for his survival. He needed very little imported machinery and no imported raw materials at all. Indeed, when coffee prices fell, the planter was indifferent to the consequent decline in the value of the milreis, because he could pay almost all of his expenses without resort to foreign currencies.

Furthermore, industrialization did not enjoy the support of an operational ideology of development that seems to be so often a motivating force behind the growth of manufacturing in undeveloped areas, and which was, indeed, a force behind the expansion of the agricultural sector. The spread of coffee cultivation was held to be intrinsically worthwhile, the key to material progress, and effective state support was mobilized in its behalf. Until the late 1930's, however, the replacement of imports by domestic manufactures was not the result of sympathetic or even conscious official encouragement,

[9] The products made by Paulista shops have been culled from newspaper and magazine advertising, especially *O Estado de São Paulo* and the *Jornal do Commercio (São Paulo).*

except in very special cases. The identity of political and plantation elites only partly explains this aspect of marginalism. To some degree it was the result of a general lack of acceptance of the products the manufacturers were offering. The Paulista entrepreneur produced, in the beginning, the simplest and cheapest of consumer goods. This was necessary, even inevitable, because the new manufacturer had to acquire technique gradually. At the same time he found more profit in goods whose weight-to-cost ratio afforded him the greatest advantage over imports. The result of this strategy was an unavoidable association, on the part of the consumer, between low-quality goods and domestic manufacture.[10]

The merchant, furthermore, had either to offer domestic goods for sale at a price lower than the comparable foreign items or disguise the origin of the domestic product. This he sometimes did, as a kind of reverse contraband, since the margin of a product made in São Paulo could be much higher than that of an imported article on which the tariff had been paid, once its origin was falsified with a borrowed label or container. The costs of this perhaps inevitable prejudice against local manufactures were high. Paulista industrialists insisted with reason that tariffs, in order to protect them, must be set high enough not merely to permit equality of prices, but to give them an advantage of 10 per cent or more, since an import with the same price tag would always be preferred. The Brazilian economy has paid dearly in royalties for labels that often had no relation to contents, but guaranteed consumer acceptance.[11]

Some of these obstacles were present in the unusual case of the Engelberg coffee huller. This was a highly efficient machine invented in São Paulo by a mechanic named Evaristo Conrado Engelberg sometime in the 1880's. Realizing that the world market for such a machine was very large and that the possibility of producing it in quantity in Brazil or of distributing it from there was unpromising, Engelberg

[10] *Brasil Economico* (September 1, 1928), p. 5.

[11] *Retrospecto Commercial* (1895), p. 6; *Monthly Journal of the British Chamber of Commerce* [São Paulo] (October 1918), p. 411; Jorge Street, *Carta aberta ao exmo. sr. dr. Araujo Franco, presidente da Associação Commercial do Rio de Janeiro*, pp. 12–13.

and his partners sold the world rights in 1888 to a group of Americans who formed a company to manufacture it. This firm, located in Syracuse, New York, and named after Engelberg, was extremely successful in marketing the machine in coffee-producing areas all over the world.[12]

Although the original agreement with the American group seems to have excluded rights to sell in Brazil, by 1904 the huller was being imported into São Paulo by F. Upton and Company with the help of some of Engelberg's original backers. By this time there were several other Paulista companies producing hullers, one of them managed by Engelberg, but the American-made machine was competitive and sold well in São Paulo for many years. Apparently neither local inventiveness nor local resources were sufficient to exclude foreign incursions in a market that was both in fact and psychologically dependent on Europe and North America.[13]

The first factory in São Paulo, it appears, was the iron works at Ipanema, founded in 1810 with a royal subsidy. In 1811 the first cotton textile mill was built, in the capital, employing water power and slave labor. In 1836 the first plant to use steam power, a sugar refinery, began operations in Santos. The official report of the provincial president in 1852 mentions only five factories: a cotton mill in Sorocaba, a potash plant in Bananal, a foundry, a glassworks (in decline), and a candle factory. A hat factory was built the next year. In the 1870's more textile mills and a few sawmills were established. At the time of a parliamentary inquiry in 1885 concerning tariffs, there were thirteen cotton mills and a woolen mill, at least four foundries, a match factory, and an unknown number of sawmills. The earliest count of industrial firms that pretended to completeness, a government report dated 1895 which included only the capital of the state, reported 121 firms using mechanical power. Of these, only fifty-two were really industrial firms. Eleven employed more than a hundred workers: three textile mills, a

---

[12] *Brasil Economico* (February 15, 1928), p. 8; Letter, John T. Schenck, President, Engelberg, Inc., to author, November 23, 1964; The Engelberg Huller Co., price list, 1892.

[13] F. Upton e Cia., "Catalog A."

brewery, three hat factories, a match factory, a foundry, and two railroad machine shops.[14]

In 1901 A. F. Bandeira, Jr., attempted to survey industries all over the state, in order, he said, to publicize local manufacturers who suffered unfair competition from the more aggressive businessmen of Rio de Janeiro. He discovered 170 factories, of which 50 employed more than 100 workers. Seventeen of these were textile mills and seven were foundries. In addition to the factories mentioned six years before, Bandeira listed plants making bricks, cement, sugar, wheat flour, drugs, glassware, shoes, ready-made clothing, and paper. Neither survey was in any sense complete. The census of 1920 counted 293 surviving firms founded between 1850 and 1900. It is impossible to know, therefore, anything certain about the earliest manifestations of the factory system in São Paulo. It is likely that the only steam-powered plant founded before 1870 which was still in existence at the turn of the century was the hat factory of A. Schritzmayer. From 1870 onward, the installation of factories continued at a fairly steady pace. By 1907, when the Centro Industrial of Rio de Janeiro carried out another survey, the number of Paulista factories had grown rapidly. There were more than 24,000 industrial workers and 326 firms in the state. However, this, too, was an incomplete census.[15]

From these modest beginnings the regional economy of São Paulo grew even larger. By 1920 it had replaced the area of Rio de Janeiro and the federal capital as Brazil's most important industrial center. By the 1940's the state undoubtedly possessed the largest agglomeration of manufacturing capacity in Latin America.

This phenomenon deserves historical study. It is clear this late in the twentieth century that economic development is not an automatic process in the underdeveloped world. It may stop, and it may even be reversed. The coffee boom, which supplied the initial market for Paulista manufacturers, became progressively less significant to the

---

[14] Eugênio Egas, *Galeria dos presidentes de São Paulo*, I, 204; Antônio de Toledo Piza, *Relatorio Apresentado ao cidadão Dr. Alfredo Pujol*, Appendix.

[15] Antônio Francisco Bandeira, Jr., *A industria de São Paulo em 1901*; Centro Industrial do Brasil, Commissão d'Expansão Economica do Brasil, *O Brasil*, vol. III.

growth of industry. In what terms, then, can its continuation be explained? The following chapters consider this question mainly from the point of view of the industrialists themselves. Their decisions may be said to have caused industrialization in the most direct sense of the word "cause," whether or not one accepts the centrality of the entrepreneur in Joseph Schumpeter's writings.

This study will try to deal with three related and sequential aspects of the entrepreneurial role. Part One considers the origins of the entrepreneurs; what they did before they turned to industry, what social groups they came from, how they amassed their capital, and what kinds of production they first attempted. The cadre of entrepreneurs with which this study is concerned for the most part emerged before World War I; therefore Part One covers the period 1880 to 1914.

In Part Two growth of industry is related to historical circumstance and to business structure. In particular industrial growth is compared with the growth of the export sector in order to test the theory that manufacturing grew because the export trade declined. Part Two deals with the years 1914 to 1929, but also overlaps the 1930's somewhat.

In both parts One and Two the industrialists are discussed as a group, first as a bourgeoisie arising out of existing and *nouveau* elites, then as a new elite beginning to make its own demands upon society and inevitably coming into conflict with other economic sectors. In Part Three of this study, this conflict becomes the central concern. As domestic industry came to employ more workers and to supply a larger share of the market, the manufacturers began to reveal in words and behavior an outlook on society, conditioned by their origins and by objective conditions, which was a significant determinant of the next phase of industrialization. The manufacturers' attitude toward their workers, toward the middle class who were potential technicians and shareholders, and toward consumers in general are discussed for the period between the wars. With the onset of depression and the collapse of the old political structure in 1930, government began to take upon itself the solution of social conflicts and economic stagnation. Increasingly through the 1930's and into the period of World War II, therefore, the government reorganized the environment in which trade and manufacturing operated. The last part of the study concludes in 1945, when the government's role suddenly contracted.[16]

The historical perspective of this study is thus essentially sociological. The macroeconomic aspects of the economy are discussed as causes of industrial development, but it is assumed that they are not the only causes. No matter how suitable for industrialization the circumstances are, the decision to commit resources to that purpose will not be taken unless the perceptions and interests of the elite are favorably engaged. This condition is in turn the consequence of the composition of the elite and its relations with the society it manages. From this perspective the entrepreneur is not a cultural hero, the cause uncaused, but merely the representative of a new group that is groping its way to an arrangement with the other men of power within the society. That the industrialist has the power to restructure society utterly may be something even he does not understand.

[16] Entrepreneurship as cause of industrialization is discussed by Fernando Henrique Cardoso, in "Condições sociais da industrialização de São Paulo," *Revista Brasiliense* (March–April 1960), pp. 31–46; and "The Industrial Elite," in Seymour Martin Lipset and Aldo Solari, eds., *Elites in Latin America*, pp. 99–114. See also W. P. Strassman, "The Industrial Elite," in John J. Johnson, ed., *Continuity and Change in Latin America*, pp. 161–185.

PART ONE

●

ECONOMIC AND SOCIAL ORIGINS

OF ENTREPRENEURSHIP

1880–1914

CHAPTER II

The Economic Matrix: Importing

The coffee economy was at first almost destitute of industrial capacity to feed or clothe itself. In the early years of the coffee rush the importing business was at its zenith. From the crowded stores of Syrian cloth merchants on Twenty-fifth of March Street to the luxury shops on São Bento Street, the Paulista bought every product of Europe and America, from the most basic to the most superfluous. In 1910 São Paulo's imports equaled the output of the state mills and workshops. In 1915 the inflow of foodstuffs alone was insufficient to provide half a pound of food daily for each person in the state. The preponderance of imported goods in commerce was only a secondary consequence of the rapid growth of the export trade. Initially domestic capital must have been employed in the expansion of the coffee groves and in the attendant transportation and agroindustrial enterprises. The shortage of labor turned field hands from subsistence crops to coffee cultivation, and often subsistence crops were forbidden on the plantation. Hence importation massively supplied the new domestic market for consumer and industrial goods.[1]

[1] Data on imports to be found in São Paulo (state), *Mensagens apresentados ao Congresso Legislativo de São Paulo pelos Presidentes do Estado e Vice-*

Although imports were substitutes for products that could not be supplied locally in the early days of the coffee trade, the importing business was not an obstacle to the development of industry. On the contrary, it was clearly the progenitor of an industrial sector that grew up alongside the agroindustrial enterprises of the planters. Three sets of circumstances favored the involvement of importers in the creation of industrial enterprise. First, importing by nature required a number of locally performed operations. The installation of hydroelectric equipment, for example, or of textile mills or bascule bridges all required skills that the buyer generally left to the importer to exercise. The importer frequently had to complete locally the manufacture of goods that were too expensive to ship fully transformed, such as nails, beer, and boilers, but there were numerous other considerations besides weight and volume. Some goods, such as acetylene, were too dangerous to ship; some, like biscuits or *pasta,* were too perishable; others, like hardware and plumbing fixtures, would require too costly an inventory. Sometimes the finishing operations involved raw materials cheaper to obtain or make in São Paulo than to ship, and therefore the importer might invest in brick kilns, sawmills, or glassworks that contributed to the elaboration of his bridges, industrial machinery, or bottled products.

This sort of industrial activity, in essence an outgrowth of the importer's operations, was a phenomenon common to other economies oriented toward foreign trade. For example, in seventeenth-century Amsterdam the largest concentrations of industrial capital were those in the importer-owned factories that finished trade goods destined for reshipment, such as sugar refineries and textile dyeing and printing mills. In São Paulo these *verkeersindustriën* did not re-export, but were otherwise analogous in function. It should not be imagined that the importer's finishing operations were without real consequences for the process of industrialization. Once technicians and machinery were

Presidentes em exercicio desde a proclamação da Republica até ao anno de 1916, p. 626; *Anuario Estatistico de São Paulo* (1900–1920); São Paulo (state), Secretaria de Agricultura, Indústria e Comêrcio, Directoria de Estatística, Indústria e Comêrcio, *Commercio de cabotagem pelo Porto de Santos* (1919); *Revista de Commercio e Industria* (September 1916), pp. 254–255.

imported to perform these limited tasks, the importer might well set them to work at more elaborate projects in order to keep them fully employed. Thus the Swedish importing firm of Holmberg Bech was one of the first to produce steel in São Paulo, after being long involved in the installation of heavy machinery and fabrication of spare parts.[2]

A second explanation of the transition from importing to manufacturing is to be found in the importer's strategic position in the structure of commerce. The importer, and no one else, possessed all the requisites of a successful industrialist: access to credit, a knowledge of the market, and channels for the distribution of the finished product. The scarcity of capital in the Paulista coffee trade was matched by a scarcity of credit for commercial purposes. Apparently all credit derived ultimately from overseas, either through European manufacturers or distributors or through local branches of European banks closely associated with manufacturers and trading houses overseas. Credit advances from importers allowed a substratum of wholesalers (*atacadistas*) to operate, and importing firms extended credit to country stores and packtraders (*mascates*). Importers whose merchandise included machinery financed manufacturers as well as traders. In the decade before World War I, when overseas trade was encouraged by several European governments, generous credit was available to importers for the installation of industrial equipment. Thus one German importing house sent salesmen through the Paulista interior offering to set up hydroelectric plants on easy terms to any planter who wanted to modernize his *fazenda* (plantation), his factory, or the neighboring county seat. Because of the scarcity of credit outside the importing business, however, the emergence of entrepreneurs elsewhere was unlikely. Eventually they would have to accept finance from an importer, which meant control, or they would have to absorb an importing house to gain direct access to overseas credit.[3]

[2] Violet Barbour, *Capitalism in Amsterdam in the 17th Century*, p. 67; *O Estado de São Paulo* (December 25, 1921); "Sweden's Aga in Brazil," *Brazilian Business* (December 1957), pp. 26–28.

[3] Stanley Stein, *The Brazilian Cotton Manufacture*, pp. 69–77; U.S. Department of Commerce, Bureau of Foreign and Domestic Commerce, *Banking and Credit in Argentina, Brazil, Chile, and Peru*, pp. 48–49.

The importer's knowledge of the market was, within the circumstances of the frontier market, a matchless advantage. The calculation of the relative cost of domestic manufacture implied a familiarity with the vagaries of the tariff and its application beyond the reach of the wholesalers or any other potential industrial entrepreneur. In the 1890's, before any of the ports of Brazil published even the most rudimentary classification of goods passed through customs, the "attack on the import list" could only be mounted by someone whose business routine included this kind of intelligence. Since the importer was rarely a specialist, but was most often a dealer in the widest imaginable line of goods, from calico to locomotives, this knowledge was likely to be fairly close to omniscience.

The importer was as valuable to the manufacturer for his outlets as for the credit he could supply. The domestic manufacturer typically distributed his products through importers, not through wholesalers. He could not supply the wholesalers with the short-term credit they needed if they were to buy his goods; the importer could and was willing to absorb the risks involved. He had private sources of credit information when that kind of commercial service was not yet available. The importer, furthermore, had sometimes risen through the distributive system from packtrader or country store owner to city wholesaler to importer. In this case he knew the business from the ground up.

In one other way the position of the importer was strategic as potential industrialist. Countless times the importers converted their sales agencies into licensed factories. This phenomenon appeared only more recently, however, as the process of industrialization began to affect the importation of complex machinery protected by patents, and as the standards of consumption began to increase the demand for superfluities like alcoholic beverages, proprietary drugs, and cosmetics.

It was likely, then, considering their resources and experience, that the importers would grasp the opportunities presented by the shifting pattern of trade and would themselves encourage domestic manufacturing. The importers were after all simply merchants; if they bought from French, German, and English manufacturers, why not from Brazilians?

From one point of view it might seem strange that importers would invest in domestic manufacturing. Manufacture is, after all, an activity competitive with importing. Might not the importer fear the growth of an economic interest capable of replacing him in the domestic market? Much historical writing has asserted that a conflict is inevitable. Humberto Bastos, for example, who has written several monographs on the development of Brazilian industry, insists that "Commercial capitalism is subsidiary, in general, to foreign enterprises and banks. Living from the importation of consumer goods all of its effort is directed to facilitating the entrance of these goods in the semi-colonial markets." Furthermore he quotes Maurice Dobb to the effect that commercial capitalism supports the traditional structure of society to this end. Although it seems indeed true that economic elites tend always to support one another, the refusal of the importers to perceive the eventual advantages of diversification would seem to be limited to rather specific circumstances. First, it might happen that the overseas suppliers of trade goods, the manufacturers or exporting companies, might discourage the importer from buying domestic goods by cutting off his credit. Second, it might happen that the importer may decide that the manufacturer could eventually bypass him as a distributor.[4]

In Rio the first of these potential conflicts of interest was actual during the nineteenth century. There the large English importing houses that controlled the greater part of the city's commerce were forced by their suppliers in England to deal exclusively in English goods. A Brazilian knitting mill that had dared to offer its line of stockings to one of them in the early 1880's was almost run out of business. But with the arrival of the submarine cable and the development of competition with Germany and France, the wholesalers who had been buying from the English importing companies were able to place their orders directly with a variety of foreign suppliers. Some of these wholesalers, mainly Portuguese immigrants, thereafter specialized in importing and, with their freedom to buy where they wished, soon overshadowed the English. This struggle had been won by the independent Rio importers at least a decade before São Paulo emerged as a

[4] Humberto Bastos, *O pensamento industrial no Brasil*, p. 84.

market for imported goods. In São Paulo the compromised English importer never possessed a significant portion of the trade. Instead, independent immigrant importers shared the market with several large mercantile companies run by German nationals, whose European operations were scattered enough to prevent control by their suppliers. Even the English firms seem to have changed their policy in this regard by then. Edward Ashworth and Company, for example, a Rio firm, was heavily involved in financing and distribution for three textile mills in São Paulo.[5]

Of course, once the importer was strong enough to defy his overseas source of supply, he might behave just as fecklessly. A very early example of the domestic sales agent turning upon his foreign creditor was Antonio Sánchez, who represented the New York Life Insurance Company in Rio de Janeiro from 1882 to 1893. In that year Sánchez opened an insurance company of his own, Sul America, and blandly destroyed his former patrons by lobbying through a bill in the federal legislature that made all policies effective as soon as they were written. Since New York Life refused to allow its representatives so large an authority, the company left Brazil. Of course, it was easier to manage such a coup in services than in manufacture, but analogous methods are possible. Designs, parts, labels, then whole machines, can easily be copied without license or royalty in a place so remote. The frequent complaints about this practice in United States consular correspondence can indicate only that it was still more common.[6]

The possibility that the manufacturer might at some point bypass

---

[5] Stein, *The Brazilian Cotton Manufacture*, pp. 70–71; Stein, "Brazilian Cotton Textile Industry," in Simon Kuznets, Wilbert E. Moore, and Joseph J. Spengler, *Economic Growth: Brazil, India, Japan*, p. 434. Ownership of importing houses derived from various directories, including British Chamber of Commerce of São Paulo and Southern Brazil, *Importers and Manufacturers in the State of São Paulo*; Brazil, Ministério de Trabalho, Indústria e Comércio, *Sociedades mercantis autorizadas a funcionar no Brasil, 1808–1946*. The registry of corporations located in the Junta Comercial de São Paulo (hereafter JCSP) has been used extensively to determine date of organization, directors, capital, and multiple ownership.

[6] U.S. National Archives, Records Relating to the Internal Affairs of Brazil [hereafter RRIAB], 832.5064/orig., May 6, 1924.

the importer and sell directly to the wholesaler or retailer could not become actuality for, at least, the first thirty years of industrialization. The importer was strong enough in his control over credit and the distribution system to discount such an eventuality. In some cases his financial interest in the manufacturer bought him the right of exclusive distribution. In other cases the identity was complete: the importer was himself the industrial entrepreneur. Even when the importer owned no share at all in the firms for which he acted as distributor, he was generally unconcerned about the eventual consequences of domestic manufacture. Therefore, when local manufacturers applied to the federal government for tariff relief, importers did not raise objections against a higher tariff per se. They were certain enough that they would be the middlemen for the product, whether it was foreign or domestic, to abstain from complaint unless they believed the domestic petitioner was not, in fact, capable of meeting the demand. When the Companhia Brasileira de Cimento Portland requested tariff increases for Portland cement, the principal cement importers of Brazil appointed a commission, not to condemn the request, but merely to find out if the factory owned by the company was really able to replace the imported product, in quantity and quality.[7]

One importer turned manufacturer, Oscar Reinaldo Müller Caravellas, has written memoirs that demonstrate how importers applied their experience and their knowledge to manufacturing. Müller, a third-generation immigrant whose father had settled in São Paulo, was apprenticed to various importers and eventually became a manager for the Zerenner-Bülow importing house. After World War I he became intrigued with the idea of manufacturing: "Given the low level of the monetary exchange, that would never return to its former rates, and the evident and progressive elevation of the customs duties, quoted in gold, already various foreign factories, with quite varied products, were coming to open factories here."[8] He cast about for a product he could manufacture and finally hit upon toothpaste tubes. "The consumption, in Brazil, of toothpaste and similar products . . . was con-

[7] *Boletim Official da Associação Commercial* (August–December, 1926), p. 406.

[8] Oscar Reinaldo Müller Caravellas, *História de uma indústria*, pp. 75–85.

tinually growing. The importation was already considerable, with a tendency to increase." He decided that foreign companies could be persuaded to come to Brazil to make the paste if a tube factory were already in place. His importing experience also helped him find the machinery he would need. "Versed as I was in the hardware business, it wasn't difficult for me to orient myself in the research on my subject." He consulted European machinery catalogues and technical journals "and ended up sending letters of inquiry to various of my customary correspondents abroad." Interestingly enough, most of his financing came from his father-in-law, a retired bank manager, rather than from his father, who was a small-scale manufacturer of water heaters. Müller was critical of his father's lack of interest in modernizing the heater or in expanding his line, a failing he attributed to traditionalism and inability to understand the market. As it turned out, the technical problems of tube making were quite difficult for the young Müller to solve, but eventually he succeeded in setting up his plant and in attracting German and American toothpaste manufacturers to come to São Paulo.

Müller's case illustrates the usefulness of import experience but not the actual transfer of capital or the expansion of existing importing houses into manufacturing, since he did not own any share in such a company or obtain any financing from them. Yet this transfer did take place and on a large scale. A list of sixty-five importing firms compiled from business directories and newspaper advertising for the years before World War I contains at least thirty-seven that engaged in, or invested in, manufacturing activity (Table II-1). Of the thir-

TABLE II-1. **List of Importers,** *Circa* 1910

Name of Firm	Manufacturing Interests
Afonso Vizeu	textile mill
Almeida, Lisboa	. . .
Antenor de Camargo	. . .
Assumpção & Cia.	textile mill
Augusto Rodrigues	ready-to-wear
Avelino Souza	. . .
Brasital	textile mills

TABLE II-1 (*Continued*)

Name of Firm	Manufacturing Interests
Bromberg, Hacker	textile mills, vegetable oils
Byington & Cia.	textile mills
C. P. Vianna	woolen mill
Carlos Urban	metallurgy
Casa Nathan	matches, candy, textile mill
Cássio Muniz	. . .
Cia. Paulista de Importação	. . .
Costa Siqueira	. . .
Davidson Pullen	matches
Dodsworth & Cia.	. . .
Edward Ashworth	sandals, shoes, canvas
Elias Calfat	textiles (later date)
Evaristo Ramos	. . .
F. de Siqueira	. . .
F. S. Hampshire	. . .
F. Upton	metallurgy
Fracalanza & Cia.	wicker furniture
Franca Pereira	. . .
Freitas, Lima Nogueira & Cia.	. . .
General Commercial Co., Ltd.	. . .
Giorgi Picossi	. . .
H. Stolz	milling, beer, nails, hardware
Haupt & Cia.	metallurgy
Hugo Heise & Cia.	. . .
Holmberg Bech	acetylene, steel
Irmãos Jafet	textiles
João Jorge, Figueiredo	nails, soap, oils
João Reynaldo, Coutinho	textiles
Jorge Fuchs & Cia.	. . .
Krüger	metallurgy
Krug & Cia.	. . .
L. Perroni	. . .
Lee & Villela	wire, enamelware
Lion & Cia.	. . .
Lupton Co.	metallurgy
M. Almeida	. . .
MacDonald & Cia.	acetylene, oxygen

TABLE II-1 (*Continued*)

Name of Firm	Manufacturing Interests
Mappin & Co.	. . .
Martins Ferreira	hardware, nails
Mesbla	. . .
Naumann, Gepp	carriages, beer, liqueurs
Nelson Bechara	ready-to-wear
Noschese	tubs, enamelware, hardware
Reichert Irmãos	toilette articles, biscuits, candy
Richard Wichello	. . .
Salgado & Cia.	cigarettes
Schill & Cia.	machinery, foundry
Serva Ribeiro	. . .
Soares de Sampaio	. . .
Souza & Cia.	glassware
August Tolle	mineral water, candy, biscuits
A. Trommel	. . .
Theodore Wille	textiles, steel, metallurgy, stockings, weighing scales
Werner, Hilpert	silk and textiles
Whately & Cia.	metallurgy
Wilson Sons	. . .
Victor Isnard	. . .
Zerenner-Bülow	beer, ice

SOURCES: JCSP, index; British Chamber of Commerce of São Paulo and Southern Brazil, *Importers and Manufacturers in the State of São Paulo*; Brazil, Ministério de Trabalho, Indústria e Comércio, *Sociedades mercantis autorizadas a funcionar no Brasil, 1808–1946*; *Commercial Encyclopedia, Third Sectional Issue, South America*; Monte Domecq' et Cie., Société de Publicité Sud-Americaine, *O Estado de São Paulo*; Empreza Editora, *São Paulo moderno; Erstes Jahrbuch für die deutschsprechende Kolonie im Staate São Paulo, 1905.*

teen cotton mills built before the turn of the century in São Paulo, eleven, by 1917, were controlled by importing firms or by entrepreneurs who had started out as importers. During the same period twenty-one more mills had been constructed, and of these sixteen were importer-controlled.[9]

[9] Ownership recorded in JCSP, index, and in São Paulo (state), *Diário Oficial* (1900–1920).

By the mid-1920's the industrial activities of importers and importers-turned-manufacturers were impressively varied and sophisticated, including holdings in all phases of textile manufacture, in milling, beer and liquor bottling, hardware manufacture, steel and brass forging, metal plating, aluminum stamping, cast iron enameling, papermaking, vegetable oil refining, and all sorts of machinery made to order —elevators, boilers, ovens, pumps, scales, and milling equipment.

The Paulista importers, much more than the Rio houses, tended to lose their identities as importers and to become manufacturers. This was partly because the Paulista houses had so much larger a share in creating and expanding the mills. The historical context was also significant. The importers of Rio had grown slowly in a regional economy that owed as much to vegetative population increase and to the growth of the federal bureaucracy as to the coffee cycle. They had been importers a long while before they acquired shares in industrial concerns. The Paulista importers had hardly established themselves before they found it necessary to adapt to the decline in coffee's capacity to pay for goods from abroad. It is interesting to note that while the importers of São Paulo turned to industry as importing became more difficult, those of Rio sold out their industrial interests and retreated to their original occupation, that of mere wholesalers. This was the fate of Sotto Maior and Company. Founded in 1865 by a Portuguese immigrant, as a wholesaler of goods imported by English firms, it became the greatest of the importers at the turn of the century, controlled half a dozen Rio mills, then returned to wholesaling by the 1930's and sold out all its factory shares.[10]

Those Paulista importing houses that retained their identities as importers continued to influence the growth of the industrial sector. Through their ability to mobilize credit they began to act as factors for manufacturers. Some Rio importers in the mid-1930's were financing textile manufacturers without actually taking part in the distribution of the cloth. Some of the importing houses in São Paulo, in spite of the relative decline of the importing sector, managed to increase their

[10] Interview with Oswaldo Costa, director of Sotto Maior e Cia., Rio de Janeiro, September 4, 1963; *Commercial Encyclopedia, Third Sectional Issue, South America*, p. 493.

business by acquiring wholesaling and retailing functions, such as the Cássio Muniz and Mesbla houses. Thus they became imposingly large outlets for local goods as well as foreign. By keeping pace with the sophistication of the market, importers such as Lion and Company and Mesbla became major suppliers of capital goods. Frederick Upton, an early example, was an American immigrant who adapted to the growth of Paulista industry by specializing in more complex manufactures. Before 1903 he had imported wheat flour, lumber, phosphates, cement, lubricants, and kitchenware. In that year he reorganized and began to sell automobiles, tractors, motors, and agricultural machinery. This realignment paralleled the change in exports from the United States, Upton's principal source, whose machinery was beginning to enter foreign markets.[11]

The men who, like Müller Caravellas, learned importing and then employed their experience in manufacturing were more important in the long run to the increasing industrialization of São Paulo than the importers who invested in manufacturing. Only a few of the first industrial entrepreneurs did not start their careers as merchant-importers: Simeon Boyes, Felix Guisard, and John Kenworthy were technicians who came to Brazil to run cotton mills and later founded mills of their own. George Craig arrived in 1880 to contract to a foundry as a machinist and later started his own foundry. One immigrant who chose to trade in the interior became an industrialist before he ever had contact with the importing business. This was Nicolau Scarpa, who gained control of some cotton mills through his cotton-broking business.[12]

The other larger entrepreneurs all possessed importing experience. Francisco Matarazzo arrived in Rio with a stock of lard he hoped to sell. He opened a country store in Sorocaba and rendered lard as a sideline, but his first large-scale business was the importing of lard in cans, wheat flour, and rice. It was not until 1900, nineteen years after he arrived in Brazil, that he began his first industrial venture, a flour

[11] Arno S. Pearse, *Brazilian Cotton*, pp. 40–41. *Commercial Encyclopedia*, p. 480.

[12] *Twentieth Century Impressions of Brazil*, pp. 406, 410; Monte Domecq' et Cie., Société de Publicité Sud-Americaine, *O Estado de São Paulo*, p. 659; JCSP, index.

mill. The four Jafet brothers, who settled in São Paulo between 1887 and 1893, did not decide to enter textile manufacturing until 1906. They had spent long years, first as wholesalers, then as importers of cloth. An anecdote, possibly apocryphal, had it that some of the funds they were later able to transfer to other lines of manufacturing came from a windfall in importing: an order for aniline dyes placed by their firm shortly before the outbreak of World War I contained two ciphers too many, so that one hundred times more dye arrived than was needed, at the moment that the price of anilines soared.[13]

Rodolfo Crespi came to São Paulo as an agent for a Milan firm that had begun to export to Brazil. Pereira Ignácio worked for importers in São Paulo in Rio, then engaged in trading on his own account in Sorocaba for many years. Ernesto Diederichsen was manager of the Theodore Wille trading company. These men later owned some of the state's largest textile mills. Egydio Gamba and the brothers Puglisi Carbone were both importers of flour and other foodstuffs before they went into flour milling. The Klabins and Weiszflogs both sold imported paper for a considerable time before they began to produce it.

The significance of the importing function did not lessen for the entrepreneur after he had committed himself to manufacturing. Once Scarpa was entrenched in cotton ginning and textiles in Sorocaba, his firm began to import a variety of construction materials, machinery, chemicals, and fuels for resale. Alexandre Siciliano, who had opened a foundry in São Paulo which he expanded into the state's largest producer of machinery and metal products, absorbed the Lacerda Camargo importing company. An advertisement for Siciliano in 1917 listed the equipment he imported: locomotives, rails, coal, steel, iron, cement, oils, asphalt, pipes and tubing, electrical equipment, steam engines, autos, and army and navy stores. Roberto Simonsen, who started as a building contractor in Santos, acquired interests in a packing plant and a brick and tile factory and then absorbed an importing house, Casa Baruel.[14]

13 Antônio Jafet, *Vida e obra de Basílio Jafet*, pp. 32–39.

14 *Jornal do Commercio (São Paulo)* (January 9, 1917); Roberto Capri,

The industrialists continued to be importers for several reasons. First, they needed raw materials from abroad when taking advantage of tariff rates that increased the cost of the finished product without increasing the cost of the materials needed to produce it. Even when they did not employ foreign raw materials, they still relied on foreign machines, parts, lubricants, and finishing materials like dyes, bleaches, paint, and so forth. Whenever he could, the industrialist ordered directly, on a large scale, to avoid the commissions of middlemen. From importing on his own account it was only a step to importing for resale. Materials that the industrialist ordered for his own purposes might be overstocked, or he might buy them in larger quantities than he needed in order to obtain discounts. Finally, he might need foreign-made goods to round out his line, or he might acquire dealerships merely because he had connections abroad that seemed to offer something profitable. The Jafets were still importing finer textiles in the late twenties; Matarazzo possessed dealerships for automobiles, lubricants, and motion picture films; Pereira Ignácio sold imported cotton thread, and Noschese, a plumbing fixture manufacturer, resold sewing machines.

For all these reasons the functions of importing and manufacturing were regarded by the entrepreneurs not as conflicting but rather as complementary. Francisco Matarazzo, the most successful of Brazil's entrepreneurs, insisted in 1928 that the question of tariffs did not enlist his opinions on one side or another: "If I am an industrialist, as indicated by the generosity of my friends in making me president of the Center [of industrialists], I'm also a merchant, an importer on a large scale, and a farmer in this state. I feel myself quite at liberty, therefore, concerning this question." Matarazzo was exaggerating his lack of commitment to industry, since his agricultural and most of his importing operations by 1928 served merely to feed his factories with raw material. Nevertheless his statement was serious in its implication that he would as soon import as manufacture, if there was more

---

O Estado de São Paulo e seus municipios, pp. 141–152; *Twentieth Century Impressions of Brazil*, p. 696.

profit in it. It was this spirit that initially led him and many others to manufacturing.[15]

It was the same spirit that motivated succeeding generations of importers who turned to manufacturing as Brazil's economy diversified. The only Brazilian company to respond to the challenge of the administrative order that closed the country to foreign-made automobiles was a former Studebaker importer. The Nôvo Mundo group, essentially a banking and importing organization controlled by Domingos Fernandes Alonso, shopped in Europe for an automobile to produce under license after Studebaker decided not to build a plant in Brazil. From the German Auto-Union it acquired rights and technical assistance for their models of sedans, jeeps, and station wagons. No private Brazilian manufacturing group risked such a venture, not even one of those already producing heavy machinery.[16]

Still more remarkable is the case of Sotema, a company founded in 1934 to sell construction materials and machinery, which has institutionalized the process of import substitution. Beginning with a number of important agencies, such as Allis-Chalmers and Bucyrus-Erie, they began, during World War II, to produce their own materials, starting with railroad wheels and axles. With later expansion into tractors, asphalt, agricultural equipment, and bulldozers, the company developed the policy of forming subsidiaries for production "when a sector is ripe for the industrial phase." Through such organizations the importing function continued to be an important agency for the promotion of industrialization.[17]

[15] Interview in *Folha de Manhã*, June 12, 1928, transcribed in *Brasil Economico* (August 1, 1928), p. 16.

[16] "Organizações Nôvo Mundo–Vemag Enters Automobile Industry," *Brazilian Business* (May 1957), pp. 16–19.

[17] "Aliam a técnica ao comércio," *Visão* (October 16, 1964), pp. 37–38.

CHAPTER III

Social Origins: The Plantation Bourgeoisie

Those who initiate one stage of economic growth often seem incapable of transferring their capital and talents to more complex forms of production. For this reason Henri Pirenne has insisted that for each stage of economic history "there is a distinct and separate class of capitalists." In particular Latin-American landowners are considered to be so committed to the manorial existence and the ministrations of an abject peasantry that they refuse to preside over a risky transformation of their societies. Several theoretical models of economic development have been built, therefore, which assign the innovative role to subordinate groups or to an elite that has suffered a loss of status. If these theories are generally applicable, the planters of São Paulo would appear to be an extraordinary anomaly. The landowners as a class have not merely survived but have directed the passage from a routine cultivation of sugar cane early in the nineteenth century to a complex industrial system in the mid-twentieth.[1]

[1] An earlier version of this chapter appeared in the *Hispanic American Historical Review* (May 1966). Henri Pirenne, "The Stages in the Social History of Capitalism," *American Historical Review* (Winter 1914), p. 494; Everett E. Hagen, *On the Theory of Social Change*, pp. 185–217; Bert F. Hoselitz,

A few studies of the origins of the coffee planting elite tend to show that most of them owned land for several generations. The original estates were not highly concentrated and were set out to subsistence crops as well as sugar. The spread of coffee represented an opportunity principally to those planters who had been most successfully engaged in growing a cash crop. Only they could afford to buy the slaves needed to clear more land. These planters then began to buy up the properties of their shorthanded neighbors, who hired out as foremen or moved farther into the forest. In its beginnings, therefore, coffee planting involved the renovation of an existing elite. Some of the new group of landowners were originally dealers in cattle, mules, or slaves, or army officers who had held commands in the province. They soon married into the older clans.

The creativity of the coffee planters is evident in two major achievements: the construction of railroads and the shift to a free labor system. The most important of the rail connections, the Santos-Jundiaí, which had to climb the three-thousand-foot coastal escarpment, was built with English capital, but it was conceived in São Paulo, subsidized by the provincial legislature, and organized by a group of Paulistas led by the Baron Mauá. As soon as the Paraguayan War ended, four trunk lines to potential coffee-producing areas of the interior were built by different groups of planters.

More difficult to remedy was the scarcity of labor caused by the end of the slave trade. Slavery represented more than a mere technical or financial challenge; it was the social basis in Brazil of three hundred years of agricultural exploitation. Nevertheless, in contrast to the elites of other plantation systems, the Paulistas eventually realized that they must actively foster the conversion to a free labor system if the export economy were to continue to grow. In 1871 the provincial assembly voted a subsidy to companies formed to transport Italian peasants. They saw as well the necessity of abolishing slavery quickly in order to encourage the flow of free labor. The assembly sought in 1878 to tax the interstate trade in slaves, but was thwarted by the court for several

"Entrepreneurship and Economic Growth," *American Journal of Economics and Sociology* (October 1952), pp. 104–105.

years. In 1886 a new immigration contract was signed that introduced ninety thousand Europeans in just three years. The planters devised a system of short-term wage contracts that provided sufficient incentive to maintain yearly arrivals of immigrants but at the same time cannily preserved ownership of the land in their own hands.[2]

The financing of the coffee trade remained a local business to a remarkable extent. The trade was divided into two parts: the brokers (*comissários*), who provided credit for the planters, and the exporters, who dealt with the brokers. The brokers were usually planters who had turned to financing their neighbors' crops. Some of them founded exporting houses or went into banking. Foreign dealers captured most of the export side of the trade by 1910, but some of the larger planter-owned houses survived. Although foreign banks gained the major share of the commercial discount business by the outbreak of World War I, the local banks managed to outlast their rivals and in time eclipsed them. Planters also became importers, partly because of their exporting experience. Commercial directories published before World War I include fifteen planters whose importing interests are specifically mentioned. An interesting case is that of the Companhia Lupton, an English house that had financed a sugar mill in Capivári. In 1890 it was incorporated with two of its erstwhile planter-creditors, Hermínio Moreira Lemos and Antônio de Souza Queiroz, as directors.[3]

It can be seen from these examples that, in order to valorize their holdings, the planters were led to engage in commercial and other activities on a large scale. The railroads and the banks were all joint-

---

[2] Nícia Vilela Luz, "A administração provincial de São Paulo em face do movimento abolicionista," *Revista de Administração* (December 1948), pp. 80–100; Pierre Denis, *Le Brésil au XXe siècle*, pp. 132–136.

[3] Brazil, *Coleção das leis*, Decree 989, November 8, 1890. Luciano Martins suggests that the fact of the industrialist, in some cases, coming from plantation families, is of little significance compared to his intermediate occupation, which was often "services," that is, importing. It is possible that Martins' data underestimate the amount of effort and capital transferred directly to manufacturing. Even if the extent of participation in commerce was very great, plantation origins ought not to be overlooked; they are extremely significant politically and economically. "Formação do empresariado industrial," *Revista Civilização Brasileira*, no. 13 (May 1967), pp. 91–132.

stock companies. The brokerage and import houses were partnerships of several plantation families. The spirit of association existed therefore, though often these combinations were reinforced by dynastic marriage or by political affiliations.[4]

The desire to render agricultural holdings more profitable was behind the first manufacturing ventures as well. In the 1880's several sugar-grinding mills were constructed in the Piracicaba area, again as joint-stock companies. Four of them fell into the hands of a French corporation that already owned mills in the province of Rio de Janeiro, but still others were built by planters in the Ribeirão Prêto area, farther to the north, probably with coffee profits. These eventually supplied the major part of the expanded internal market. The growing coffee trade called forth other industrial ventures. Coffee beans must be hulled, dried, and sorted to be marketable, and the shortage of labor stimulated experimentation with machines to perform these tasks. Although the mechanics who perfected the new equipment were often of immigrant origin, like Engelberg, the initiative and capital behind their workshops were Paulista. These same shops produced a great range of cast and machined equipment, principally for farm and railroad use, such as boilers, pumps, boxcars, and the like. The largest industrial employer in São Paulo in 1896 was the planter-owned Paulista Railroad. Its repair shops, with 703 employees, made railway carriages. By 1911 entire locomotives were being assembled there.[5]

Most important of the agricultural transformation enterprises, however, was the cotton spinning and weaving industry that was created in the wake of the modest cotton export boom of the 1860's. Some of the planters who had grown cotton, foreseeing the eventual return of the American South to the world market, wisely invested some of their profits in textile machinery. Of the nine mills erected in the 1870's and 1880's, all were sturdily profitable. Still more were built

---

[4] Genealogical information was gleaned from obituaries published in *O Estado de São Paulo* and *Correio Paulistano* and in current biographies such as *Personalidades no Brasil* and *Quem é quem no Brasil* (1948–1963).

[5] Henri Raffard, *A industria saccharifera no Brasil*, pp. 42–59; *Boletim do Ministério das Relações Exteriores* (April 1942), p. 321.

in the city of São Paulo. By 1903 there were thirteen mills employing 2,910 looms.[6]

Other plants for the transformation of agricultural or mineral resources built before World War I with coffee money included meat-packing plants, leather tanneries, corn and manioc mills, saw mills, lime and cement plants, and kilns for bricks, ceramic pipes, and glassware. In the 1920's even steelmaking was attempted on a small scale by two planter-owned companies. Occasionally the planters' interests extended beyond the manufacture of goods whose raw materials they could supply. They owned factories for making drugs, beer, gunpowder, enamelware, and sanitary fixtures. Counting the larger firms in São Paulo, in 1901 the planters employed, according to Bandeira, almost half of the workers engaged in manufacturing. Finally, there was much interest in urban improvements. Companies were formed to provide electric lighting, tramways, water supply, telephones, and to undertake pretentious public construction. Although the utilities and public buildings were intended to embody the civic pride of local planters, a good number of them represented useful economic or social overhead.[7]

Why were the Paulista planters so enterprising? Is it possible to maintain that there was in São Paulo, in the last quarter of the nineteenth century, a concentration of entrepreneurial ability more intense, or a capitalist mentality more highly developed, than in other parts of Brazil or Latin Amercia? Although the profit motive appears to have been more strongly evident in São Paulo than in other parts of Brazil, the capitalist spirit does not appear to have been more intense there at that time. Rather, it encountered historical circumstances more favorable to its wider employment than were to be found elsewhere.

The strongest evidence that factors not cultural were at work may be seen in the large number of Paulista landowners who did not shift from subsistence crops to coffee and in the even larger number of

[6] *Retrospecto Commercial* (1903), pp. 27–28; Alice P. Canabrava, *O Desenvolvimento*, pp. 282–285; Isaltino Costa, "As origens de cultura de algodão em São Paulo," *Revista de Algodão* (February 1935), pp. 5–11.

[7] Bandeira's list shows 5,530 out of 12,680 employed by planters. Ownership from JCSP.

Brazilians who migrated from other states to participate in the coffee boom. The latter came mostly from the states of Minas Gerais and Rio de Janeiro and the smaller numbers from Alagoas, Rio Grande do Sul, Pernambuco, and other parts of Brazil. A resident of the Ribeirão Prêto area in 1882 estimated that its population was 80 per cent mineiro. Still other planters were second- or third-generation immigrants: Portuguese (Vergueiro, Souza Queiroz), English (Whitaker, Simonsen), or German (Diederichsen). If entrepreneurial talent was not the monopoly of Paulistas, but was distributed more or less evenly geographically, then the large cultural differences among the various regions of Brazil were not relevant to entrepreneurial ability or to the tendency to reinvest. The increase in entrepreneurial activity in São Paulo may be better accounted for by the more intense operation of the market economy, that is, by the greater profitability of coffee and by the fuller use of money as a medium of exchange.[8]

It is also probable that the apparently greater entrepreneurial ability of the successful planters conceals pre-existing accumulations of capital. In the 1880's the coffee-growing area was not the locale of many rags-to-riches success stories. It is highly unlikely that planter families from the Paraíba Valley or from Minas moved to the Paulista West because of economic necessity. The new lands had to be bought. Therefore the newcomers must have been already prosperous families who were transferring assets from a region of declining fertility to one of potentially higher return. Stanley Stein's study of Vassouras contains the names of two families, Junqueira and Teixeira Leite, both merchants and both originally *Mineiros*, who seem to be the predecessors of plantation families in São Paulo. Aluísio de Almeida points to strong extraeconomic motives impelling the richest families toward the frontier: the desire to maintain their status, to provide stakes for all the family's male children, and even the desire to avoid political confrontations within counties already settled and structured. The families who sold their properties were often lacking not in capitalistic men-

[8] Luz, "A administração provincial . . .," p. 91; some other cases of immigration in Aluísio de Almeida, "Notas para a história de São Paulo," *Revista do Arquivo Municipal* (July 1952), pp. 18–20; Monbeig, *Pionniers et planteurs de São Paulo*, pp. 84, 237.

tality but rather in the capital to develop the land themselves. Thus the Count of São Clemente, who sold nine thousand acres of his patrimony to Schroeder, Gebrüder and Company of Hamburg, was capitalist enough to demand in return debentures, not cash, and a place on the board of directors of the new company.[9]

It has been suggested, nevertheless, that there was a difference in the degree of adaptability between the coffee planters of São Paulo and those of the Paraíba Valley and that the difference is to be attributed to cultural traits. Unlike the Paulista planters, those of the Paraíba Valley were unable to adjust to a free labor system. They resisted abolition and eventually lost their plantations, retreating to the professions and the bureaucracy. Was this difference due to a lack of capitalistic mentality on the part of Paraíban plantation families? Pointing to the avidity with which the planters of the older coffee-growing region sought patents of nobility and to the luxury of their mansions, Maria Isaura Pereira de Queiroz contends that the Paraíbans were would-be aristocrats who did not reinvest their profits but spent them on needless luxuries. The Paulistas, on the other hand, she says, were commercial bourgeois, frugal and adaptable, who were interested in organizing a new internal market.[10]

The contrast is greatly overdrawn. It can be seen that in São Paulo state, as in Rio, there were many families who failed to maintain their fortunes when their coffee trees declined in fertility. There were also Paraíban planters who managed to transfer their wealth to the newer areas in São Paulo. Persons of Paraíba Valley families prominent in the later development of São Paulo included Rodolfo de Miranda, Nazareth de Souza Reis, Gabriel Dias da Silva, and A. P. Rodovalho. The fondness for titles existed in both places but was not a necessary indication of an aristocratic mentality. There were barons in São Paulo as well as in the Paraíba Valley, though many of the former were at the forefront of the economic reorganization: the Baron of Piracicaba,

[9] Stanley Stein, *Vassouras, A Brazilian Coffee County*, pp. 17–18, 74; Almeida, "Notas . . .," pp. 18–20; *The Economist* [London] (June 12, 1897).

[10] Maria Isaura Pereira de Queiroz, "A estratificação e a mobilidade social nas comunidades agrárias do vale do Paraíba," *Revista da História* (April–June 1950), pp. 215–218.

the provincial governor who pressed for abolition; the Count of Álvares Penteado, builder of the largest textile plant, the Marquesses of Monte Alegre and São Vicente, organizers with Mauá of the Santos Railroad; and the Count of Prates, involved in finance, urban real estate, and factories.

The real difference between the planters of the Paraíba Valley and those of the Paulista West lay in the contrasting circumstances surrounding the beginnings of their separate development. Coffee production in the Paraíba Valley reached its apogee before 1860; in São Paulo is could not begin to increase until the Santos-Jundiaí railroad was completed in 1867. The Paraíba plantations, then, developed entirely in the shadow of slave labor. Even though the trade was banned in 1850, slavery remained viable for another ten years because the increase in the price of slaves after the end of the trade doubled the value of existing "stocks." During the 1850's and 1860's, therefore, profits in the Valley were reinvested in an expensive supply of new slaves. The Paulistas' experience was quite different. There were never enough slaves, and by the 1870's it was already apparent that they were a poor investment. In 1873 they formed only 19 per cent of the state population, having declined from 28 per cent in 1854. Once diverted from new slave purchases, profits were available in São Paulo for more productive purposes. The initial cost of European labor was trifling compared to the traffic with Africa. By 1900 the state program of subsidizing immigration had cost only seven million dollars and had brought in almost one million immigrants.[11]

It might be more easily argued that the shift to capitalist forms of land and labor utilization occurred at the beginning of the Paraíban coffee expansion rather than at its end. In the Paraíba Valley many of the early estates were assembled by merchants from the city of Rio or by men who had possessed mining interests to the north. By the second quarter of the nineteenth century their land acquisitions were greatly augmented as a result of laws in 1835 and 1850 which abol-

[11] Stein, *Vassouras*, pp. 65, 229; Samuel H. Lowrie, "O elemento negro na população de São Paulo," *Revista do Arquivo Municipal* (1938), pp. 5–56; *Anuario estatistico de São Paulo* (1906), p. 163.

ished primogeniture and substituted cash payments for grants in the distribution of crown lands.

The willingness to shift to free labor, however, did not necessarily imply a more rational or humane approach to its utilization on the part of the Paulistas. Apparently they originally intended to deal with the new European workers as ruthlessly as they had with the slaves whom the immigrants replaced, but in time the constant shortage of labor forced the planters to relax their hold. A standard labor contract evolved, and the terms of payment expanded sufficiently to discourage debt servitude. To a degree, therefore, the free labor system stimulated a capitalistic outlook, rather than vice versa. In support of this interpretation one may contrast the pessimism of Max LeClerc's report of 1890, which found most of Antônio da Silva Prado's "colonists" in debt and declared the system unjust, with that of Pierre Denis in 1909, which found the terms of labor in the same region favorable to the workers.[12]

The nature of coffee cultivation, as it was practiced in Brazil, enhanced the selective effects of the market. Because land was very cheap relative to capital and labor, no effort was expended on prolonging its fertility. As a consequence the pattern of a hollow frontier developed, gradually moving westward and leaving behind land fit only for pasturage. Contrast this pattern with sugar cultivation, which enabled the landowners to remain on the same property for generations without any need to improve the land or the agricultural technique. The coffee planter was obliged to reinvest in new estates if he did not want to see his real worth decline. But to develop lands beyond the settled areas required real estate promotion, in its broadest sense, and on a grand scale. It meant railroads, urbanization, sawmills, and the successive waves of woodsmen, wage laborers, and merchants. Repeated dislocations of the *casa grande* must have weakened the planter's identification with his plantation. The past was hundreds of miles behind him; his

---

[12] The theory originates with Fernando Henrique Cardoso, "As condições sociais da industrialização de São Paulo," *Revista Brasiliense* (March–April 1960), pp. 31–46. Max LeClerc, *Cartas do Brasil*, pp. 82–90; Denis, *Le Brésil*, pp. 132–136.

future, or perhaps his son's, was still farther ahead, for an estate covered with thirty-year-old coffee trees would be but a meager inheritance.[13]

Another aspect of coffee cultivation may have been favorable to the transfer of plantation capital to commercial and industrial ventures. The heaviest capital investment came during the first year, with the clearing of land and the laying out of seedlings. From the fifth year to the thirtieth, depending on circumstances, the planter could expect to earn a profit. These profits were not continuously reinvested in new plantings, however. From 1890 to 1895 unfavorable coffee prices and a confused political situation retarded new investments. In the next five years, however, the number of coffee trees grew from about 300,000,000 to 660,000,000, absorbing, it is likely, almost all of the planters' profits. From 1900 to 1906 coffee prices were again depressed, and the planting of new trees was reduced. From 1906 until the outbreak of World War I the planters received excellent returns, but were reluctant to lay out new plantations and were constrained from doing so by state laws that sought to limit supply. There were, in 1915, only 47,000 more trees in São Paulo than there had been ten years before. It appears that much of the planters' profits during these years were transferred to other sorts of enterprise, particularly industry.[14]

In summary, the entrepreneurial success of the Paulista planters as a class may be attributed not to innate or to cultural endowments but to the operation of a profitable market which attracted outsiders and rewarded the capable, to capital brought from other places and other activities, to the necessity of conforming to the requirements of a market economy, particularly to free labor, and to the nature of coffee cultivation, which rewarded the capitalistic—that is, the reinvesting—planters.

In proposing explanations for the planters' entrepreneurial prowess, however, the obverse of the argument must not be overlooked: Why

[13] The paradoxically invigorating effects of soil exhaustion are hypothesized by Pedro Calmon, *História do Brasil*, IV, 385.

[14] *Boletim da Directoria de Industria e Commercio*, (January 1917), p. 3.

was there so little competition from other economic groups, internal and external?

One important reason is that the planters controlled the machinery of government and used it constantly and effectively to advance their own interests. It is not remarkable that this should have been so. Because of the confusions of the Brazilian landholding system, planters could not acquire large domains without some degree of political influence to legitimize claims. During their long struggle to promote the coffee trade they also used the provincial and imperial parliaments to press for government subsidies for immigration, the abolition of slavery, and the reduction of imperial powers over Paulista economic policy. When the overthrow of the empire in 1889 offered them an opportunity to improve their position, they advocated in the constituent assembly a political decentralization that gained for São Paulo all the essentials of sovereignty with few of its expenses: control of the imperial lands, the right to levy export taxes and to borrow abroad, and a state army. They also supported disestablishment of the Church and increased rights for naturalized citizens, partly from a desire to encourage immigration.

Perhaps it was because of their thoroughly politicized view of economic development that the planters restricted themselves largely to undertakings that the state government could concede as monopolies, such as railroads, utilities, and emission banks or projects that could be strongly assisted through government favoritism. The railroads received "privileged zones" and guarantees of profit, which by 1904 had cost the government of São Paulo the equivalent of forty million dollars. Similar guarantees were granted to sugar mills. Planter-backed companies secured contracts to build docks, water and sewerage supply systems, and public buildings. Others acquired the right to import agricultural or textile equipment or even raw materials free of tariffs. The resistance of local banks to the vast inflow of foreign capital may be ascribed to the fact that foreign branch banks were excluded from government favors and restricted to the commercial discounting business. Finally, if a particular project of the planters proved unprofitable, the government could be induced to buy them out. The resulting public

corporation invariably continued to be directed by members of planta- | ✔
tion families, presumably in the interests of their group.[15]

Some of the early planter-industrialists themselves held political
posts during the most of their careers. Rodolfo Miranda, who owned
several estates, in addition to an importing house and a textile mill in
Piracicaba, was a federal deputy and minister of agriculture. Eloy de
Miranda Chaves, also a federal deputy and protégé of Rodrigues
Alves, owned a textile mill in Jundiaí. Antônio de Lacerda Franco, who
administered vast family properties at Itatiba, fifty miles north of the
capital, and who founded a coffee brokerage house, was a federal
senator and an important figure in the Paulista Republican Party. When
the Republic was proclaimed he managed to obtain a concession for
a bank of emission and started an ambitiously large textile mill in
Sorocaba. He later founded another smaller mill in Jundiaí, a telephone company, and was a director of the Paulista railroad.

Antônio da Silva Prado, whose family had been at the forefront
of every significant development in the plantation system, had himself ✗
opened plantations in the Paulista West between 1866 and 1889. He
was one of the backers of Engelberg, a director and president of the
Paulista railroad, and the initiator of factories that produced glass
bottles, leather, and frozen meat. As a minister of the Empire he had
played an important role in encouraging immigration and railroad and
port development, and he sponsored the final act of abolition in 1888.
As mayor of the capital from 1899 to 1910, he presided over the
beautification of the city which involved vast outlays for public works.[16]

The government of the state ignored the needs of the landless as |

[15] Adolfo Augusto Pinto, *História da viação publica de São Paulo*, pp. 31–54, 182–185.

[16] Dunshee D'Abranches, *Governos e congressos da Republica dos Estados Unidos do Brasil, 1889 a 1917*, I, 180–181; II, 166–167; Monte Domecq' et Cie., p. 645; Richard Morse, *From Community to Metropolis*, pp. 170–171; *50 anos de vidro*, 1903–1953; Roberto Capri, *Album comemorativa, Companhia Vidraria Santa Marina*; Monte Domecq' et Cie., p. 661; A. d'Atri, *L'État de São Paulo et le renouvellement economique de l'Europe*, p. 44; Nazareth Prado, *Antonio Prado no Imperio e na República*, pp. 473–480.

effectively as it promoted those of the planters. It did not attempt to create a literate, stable, or skilled citizenry either in the towns or in the countryside. There was no public policy of land redistribution, universal education, or broadened political rights which might have eliminated the dependence on imported laborers and technicians or induced the immigrants to regard Brazil as a new homeland. State expenditures on primary education averaged sixty-five cents (three milreis) per capita a year from 1890 to 1900. As a result the landless classes of society were deprived of a principal avenue of upward mobility. On the other hand the educational opportunities of the sons of the elite were considerably expanded. Technical schooling abroad became fairly common, and new colleges of civil engineering, medicine, and agriculture were added to the traditional faculty of law. Entrance to these schools was limited because almost all the secondary schools were private.[17]

Nearly all Brazilian entrepreneurs came from the plantation elite. By 1930 there was not a single manufacturer of native-born lower- or middle-class origins, and only a very few appeared thereafter. This is in striking contrast with industrialization in other countries: Johannes Hirschmeier, for example, points out the importance of peasant and merchant participation in Japanese industrialization. In such circumstances only the urbanized European immigrants could challenge the hegemony of the planters.[18]

Historical circumstances largely account for the ability of the Paulista planters to develop the coffee economy without having to alienate most of their resources to foreigners. The Europeans and North Americans never intruded in the São Paulo area to the extent that they did in Cuba, Argentina, Mexico, or Chile for several reasons not connected with the degree of competition offered them by the planters. In the first place, unlike the foreign trade of other Latin-American countries, the control of Brazilian trade was divided. Most Brazilian coffee was sold to the United States and Germany, but the trade was

[17] Primitivo Moacyr, *A instrucção pública no Estado de São Paulo*, II, Appendix.

[18] Johannes Hirschmeier, *The Origins of Entrepreneurship in Meiji Japan.*

financed in England. The British did not drink much coffee, nor did they regard control of coffee as vital in their foreign trade. For these reasons they did not interest themselves in São Paulo as much as in Buenos Aires. Though the British held first place among suppliers of Brazilian imports, the Germans were aggressive competitors. The Americans, French, Italians, and Portuguese all supplied the Paulista market with goods and invested capital in banks and other businesses, although on a smaller scale than either the British or Germans. The Paulista market was never the private sphere of influence of a single country or a single financial combine.

Even so, if the European powers had not been discouraged repeatedly concerning the prospects of investment in São Paulo, or if they had not suffered the catastrophes of world war and depression, their inroads upon Paulista capitalism might have been far greater. During these recessions of European influence the Brazilians were able to work out their own solutions to the shortage of capital and imports and to buy up foreign interests at bargain prices. The English, for example, had options to extend the Santos railroad beyond Jundiaí but chose not to do so, thereby opening the way for Paulistas. On another occasion a group of British investors became unnerved at the revolutionary ferment of 1889 to 1893 and sold out the Rio Claro line to the Paulista Railway. World War I, as will be shown, proved disastrous to German investments.[19]

Even though the undertakings of the planters seemed ambitious and manifold, they were not a complete program of development. The role of immigrants in the growth of the Paulista economy was large, especially in the manufacture of consumer goods, for if the planters by their efforts created an internal demand, they did not do a great deal to satisfy it. The reasons why they ceded this sector, and the contrasting success of the immigrants, will be considered in the next chapter. It should be noticed, nevertheless, that the planters were in many cases the originators of firms that were bought up later on by immigrants and that the planters were never entirely without interests in the manufacture of consumer goods. Finally, as the state economy

[19] Pinto, *História da viação*, pp. 36–47, 199–201.

began to turn to capital goods industries in the 1930's and 1940's, the plantation families, better connected politically, obtained government development loans and re-entered the manufacturing sector very strongly.

In spite of the challenge of other interest groups, then, the planters maintained their position in the regional economy. They did not lose control of the land; instead they continued to open new regions to coffee and later diversified to other cash crops. Their banking, insurance, and commercial interests increased with time. Their manufacturing interests tended to grow along with the complexity of manufacturing processes. As an example of entrepreneurship, probably the most important one in Latin America, the planters seem to bear out those, like Louis Kriesberg, who have insisted that "entrepreneurial activity is not held in check by profound cultural process." The case of the Paulista planters demonstrates that the "situational processes," as Kriesberg calls them, are more significant. A change in the means of production does not necessarily require a change in the composition of the elite that controls and enjoys the new sources of wealth. The success of this elite is not due to a greater endowment of entrepreneurial skills, nor is the failure of other groups culturally pathological. Instead the major determinants have been historical-economic: (1) the advantages of prior successes, such as capital accumulation and possession of political power; (2) the objective economic stimuli, including potentially high profits and the challenge of the tasks involved, technological and organizational; and (3) factors discouraging competition from other groups.[20]

[20] Louis Kriesberg, "Entrepreneurs in Latin America and the Role of Cultural and Situational Processes," *International Social Science Journal* (1963), pp. 581–596.

CHAPTER IV

Social Origins: The Immigrant Bourgeoisie

The importers who complemented the planter-entrepreneurs in the development of Paulista industry were almost always immigrants. There were many importing houses that were owned by Brazilians—a few of them without plantation connections, although this cannot be known for certain—but not very many of them developed into manufacturing firms. It would be interesting to speculate on the reasons for this identification of one sector of the economy with a single social group.

Might not Georg Simmel's concept of the stranger or Robert Park's marginal man explain to some degree the tendency of the immigrant to take over sectors of the economy which were more risky and perhaps less prestigious than planting? In these terms the wanderer finds the land and the crafts closed to him. He must become the intermediary or he cannot survive. He is, furthermore, more successful than those who have not migrated, because he is free of the community and its values to a degree; he is both more objective and more opportunistic. Simmel's conception had as its prototype the European Jew, who was a stranger more in a psychological than a physical sense, yet the term has been extended by Manning Nash to the "Turco," the Syrian or

Lebanese who was so frequently the packtrader in São Paulo as well as other places in Latin America.[1]

Marginality, however, seems to be only partially applicable to the milieu of turn-of-the-century São Paulo. The economic opportunities available to the immigrants were limited only by the legal requirements of citizenship for the exercise of certain professions, and even this obstacle seems to have been occasionally waived. Landholding was not closed to the immigrant; indeed, vast quantities of land were for sale. In order to consolidate an estate political influence might be needed, at least on a local level, but this was readily acquired through citizenship, party affiliation, and informal agreements with the local political boss. The owner of the largest personal holdings of coffee lands was an immigrant, Francisco Schmidt, and other immigrants whose principal business was importing and industry acquired lesser interests in planting. Finally, it would be difficult to maintain that the immigrant entrepreneurs felt that they were excluded from more prestigeful occupations. As will be shown, the immigrants who came to engage in trade and industry were by origin *petit bourgeois*; their experience and training, it may be assumed, predisposed them to those pursuits.

The landed Brazilian families were similarly predisposed to agriculture. Whether coffee prices rose or fell, their efforts were most profitably employed in expanding the plantations. Those few members of the family who did not occupy themselves with agriculture operated interests that were closely associated with it. Nevertheless, it might be argued that the planters were relatively uninterested in manufacturing, especially that sector of it engaged in satisfying consumer demand. Superfluous members of the plantation families generally went into the professions, rather than trade or industry. Would this indicate that these pursuits lacked prestige in their eyes? An analysis of the circumstances surrounding the beginnings of industry in São Paulo, however, suggests other explanations.

The most obvious reason for the preponderance of immigrants in

[1] Georg Simmel, *The Sociology of Georg Simmel*, pp. 402–408; Robert E. Park, *Race and Culture*, pp. 350–356; Manning Nash, *Primitive and Peasant Economic Systems*, pp. 25–26.

trade, though it does not explain their propensity for manufacture, is the almost complete absence of a cadre of native Paulistas with an urban style of life. The population of the provincial capital in 1872, before the immigration companies were formed, was only 23,000. By 1920 almost two-thirds of its 580,000 residents were foreign-born or their offspring. The working class of this metropolis was for the most part immigrant, composed of men who had tried tending coffee trees but had not done well at it and of subsidized immigrants who had never signed contracts but had managed to stay in the cities. Their numbers were augmented by immigrants with industrial experience who had been contracted in Italian cities by Paulista factory owners, particularly textile mill operators, and by the freedmen who were at best unskilled day laborers, at worst a miserable *lumpenproletariat*.[2]

These people had little chance to rise out of the lower class; at best they might reach the level of the retail trade or craft shops. Those immigrants who acquired fortunes and came to equal the planters in social position were of quite different origins. Biographical data on the immigrant industrialists reveal that almost all were, in their homelands, city dwellers, of middle-class families, and the possessors of technical educations or at least of some experience in trade or manufacture. Many arrived with capital in some form: savings from a business in Europe, a stock of merchandise, or the intention of setting up a branch of their firm. Others had been contracted for work in planter-owned enterprises, just like the *colonos* and the textile workers, but in technical or administrative capacities. Therefore, although there were a very few immigrant entrepreneurs who began as factory workers or *mascates* (Dante Ramenzoni, a hat manufacturer, and Nicolau Scarpa, a milling and textile industrialist, are the only prominent names), as a rule the immigrant bourgeois came to São Paulo with resources that placed them far ahead of their fellows and practically determined a prefabricated class structure.[3]

[2] *Anuario Estatístico de São Paulo* (1940), p. 89; Richard Morse, *From Community to Metropolis*, pp. 175–177.

[3] Besides directories listed in Chapter III, there are many accounts by foreigners that provide information about their emigré compatriots. Otto Bürger, *Brasilien, Eine Landes- und Wirtschaftskunde für Handel, Industrie und*

A second explanation of the marked correspondence of importer-
directed industrialization and immigrant entrepreneurship lies in the
ready-made market that the rural and urban European-born masses
provided for those who were familiar with their tastes and habits.
Neither the plantation elite nor the native-born merchant group knew
very much of the dietary, sartorial, or architectural preferences of the
Europeans. A few planters built mills for grinding the manioc and
corn meal that they and their own lower classes were accustomed to
eating, but they did not appear in the wheat flour milling business.
Italian, Portuguese, and Syrian merchants imported the salt codfish,
felt hats, *pasta,* olive oil, beer, spices, and wine that Europeans were
fond of, and soon began to manufacture them, along with other products that had been too expensive to transport from Europe at all, such
as marble ornamental work and wooden furniture.

Occasionally they devised ersatz for products that could not be made
in São Paulo, such as cottonseed oil to substitute for olive oil. Although
the immigrants, as time went on, accepted Brazilian patterns of consumption to some degree, as in the use of manioc meal and straw hats,
the gradual assimilation of European standards by the native-born
population seems to have been much more widespread and offset any
loss of market. Humberto Bastos, for example, has discussed the
great desire of the Brazilians to imitate European patterns of consumption in furnishings, foodstuffs, and dress as marks of status.[4]

The immigrant masses were valuable to the immigrant entrepreneurs
in other less crucial, perhaps, but still significant ways. The *colonos*
provided a sizable contribution to the capital available for industrial
ventures through the savings they accumulated. Usually these savings
were deposited in local agencies established by banks operating in their
home countries. The immigrants apparently preferred these agencies
to Paulista banks because they were familiar with them and could
easily transmit remittances through them. These agencies were per-

---

Einwanderung; Eduard Dettman, *Das moderne Brasilien*; Paul Walle, *Au
pays de l'or rouge*; Alfredo Cusano, *Italia d'oltre mare*; Francesco Ruotolo and
Carlo Basile, *Il libro d'oro degli italiani nel Brasile*; and others cited below.
     [4] Bastos, *O pensamento industrial*, pp. 53–54.

quisites of the immigrant entrepreneurs. The first Italian fortune in São Paulo, that of Giovanni Briccola, was founded on banking. In 1885 Briccola, who had come to São Paulo as an engineer for the Paulista Railroad and later went into trade and banking, became the agent for the Bank of Naples. By 1911 he was worth five million dollars. Later Italian immigrants with banking agencies included Giuseppe Martinelli, a shipper and importer, Francisco Matarazzo, whose career will be described in some detail below, and Giuseppe Puglisi Carbone, whose banking contacts will be discussed in another connection. One observer estimated that the remittance business in 1903 totaled seven million dollars.[5]

Furthermore, the immigrant community was for the entrepreneur reciprocally, at different stages of his career, the helping hand up and the source of trustworthy assistants or promising young men worth investing in. Entrepreneurs tended to hire or back persons from their own countries, or even from the same towns in Europe. Thus Raul Carvalho Bastos, later the sales manager for Pereira Ignácio, mentions that he was hired by the Rio importer Affonso Vizeu chiefly because he was a fellow Portuguese. Francisco Schmidt, when in Santos, would meet ships from Germany to assist new arrivals. Matarazzo in his first years paid the passage for young men from his home town who had skills he needed. This cohesiveness seems to be an almost invariable characteristic of immigrant entrepreneurship everywhere.[6]

The usefulness of the immigrant community to the entrepreneur may be inferred from the much more modest success of Italian businessmen who became resident in parts of Brazil that did not possess any sizable Italian community. In Pará and Bahia there were Italian businessmen in considerable numbers, but no Italian communities and no great Italian fortunes. Of course, there was no coffee boom in those places either, but there was rubber and cocoa, and the occasional im-

[5] Cusano, *Italia d'oltre mare*, pp. 146, 149, 155; Ruotolo and Basile, *Il libro d'oro*, p. 80; *The Brazilian Year Book, Second Issue, 1909*, pp. 768–769. Domenico Rangoni, *Dopo un viaggio in Italia*, p. 93.

[6] Raul Carvalho Bastos, *Homens e fatos do meu tempo*, chapter entitled "Affonso Vizeu"; S. Pôrto, *Cia. Comêrcio Indústria "Antonio Diederichsen,"* 1903–1953, p. 28.

migrant fortune was not impossible in the North for there was the outstanding example of Hermann Lundgren, a Swede, the textile entrepreneur of Pernambuco.

Besides their urban background and their prior experience in trade, and besides the advantages provided them by a large market of compatriots, the immigrants possessed yet another superiority: the connections they could maintain with sources of capital in their home countries. It has been supposed that the industrial ventures of the immigrants were created gradually by reinvestment. In fact, the greater part of their original funds seems to have come from overseas sources. Obviously, as importers, they enjoyed lines of credit for the installation of equipment provided by their suppliers. But their opportunities were broader than that, for the immigrants were, in a sense, the chosen instruments of European financial and political interests in the commercial rivalry that preceded World War I.

The coffee trade awakened Europe to the possibilities presented by São Paulo for export and investment. Mauá and his associates, in the 1850's, had experienced great difficulty in persuading British capital to underwrite the Santos-Jundiaí railway, and up to the 1880's only a trickle of European, mostly British, capital flowed into the area. It paid for the erection of a gasworks and the establishment of a few plantations and importing houses. But the increase in São Paulo's exports caused a rapid expansion of foreign investment from 1895 onward. The coffee trade, until then operated by individual merchant-planters, was first captured by American, British, French, and German firms, then consolidated and nationalized. Companies like Brazilian Warrant, Ltd., absorbed warehousing and processing facilities, bought out brokers and planters, and acquired steamship agencies. By 1913 only two Brazilian firms ranked among the fifteen largest exporters in Santos.[7]

The federal and state governments, eager to underwrite public works projects of all kinds, furthered the penetration of European interests. Loans contracted there brought São Paulo under the financial tutelage of the Paris Rothschilds before the turn of the century. The

[7] Pierre Monbeig, *Pionniers et planteurs de São Paulo*, pp. 97–98; Emile Quoniam Schompré, *La bourse de São Paulo, 1911*, p. 237; *Importers and Manufacturers in the State of São Paulo*, p. 204.

valorization of the 1906 coffee crop increased the interests of the German-English Schroeder group and of the Disconto Gesellschaft-Norddeutsche Bank, both already represented by commercial and banking connections. The next year French and Belgian bankers took control of the only bank owned by the state, and with it much of the state's agricultural mortgage business.

Radiating concentrically from the financial epicenters of the Rothschilds, the German export banks, the Italo-German Banca Commerciale of Milan, the French *banques d'affaires*, and other minor investment banks, Belgian, Dutch, and Portuguese, were the specialized banking companies designed for overseas trade, such as the British Bank of London and South America, the Brasilianische Bank für Deutschland, and the Banco Francês e Italiano para America do Sul. These firms in turn financed the operations of trading and manufacturing companies operating in foreign markets. Theodor Wille, a Hamburg–São Paulo firm that engaged in coffee exporting, coffee planting, importing of machinery, financing of hydroelectric plants and numerous factories, and the operation of factories under its own name, was the leading example of this sort. Its financial connections were with the Brasilianische Bank (Disconto Gesellschaft–Rothschild) and the Deutsche Überseeische Bank (Deutsche Bank). There were others: E. Dell'Acqua & Company, the Société Financière et Commerciale Franco-Brésilienne, the Caisse Générale de Prêts Fonciers et Industriels, Wilson & Sons, Ltd., The Anglo-Brazilian Commercial and Agency Co., Ltd., Zerenner-Bülow & Cia., and the City of São Paulo Improvements and Freehold Land Company.[8]

Among all these firms there were numberless interconnections that make the financial structure of São Paulo as matted and impenetrable as a liana-festooned jungle. The statutes of the Banque Brésilienne Italo-Belge, a minor component of the Paulista financial system, show that its owners included not only Antwerp exporting houses and the Banque de l'Union Anversoise, but also the Credito Italiano, a promi-

---

[8] JCSP, index; Percy A. Martin, *Latin America and the War*, p. 81; E. Lloyd Rolfe, *Report on Brazil's Trade and Industry in 1918*; for general background see Herbert Feis, *Europe, the World's Banker, 1870–1914*, chapters 1–6; and Jacob Riesser, *The Great German Banks*.

nent planter of São Paulo, the British Bank of South America, and the Teuto-Argentine Bunge & Born group.[9]

To the European bankers the aim of trade expansion was not necessarily incompatible with the financing of Paulista industry. Some of the banks, the German particularly, were connected with industrial concerns producing capital goods. Therefore they readily permitted their overseas affiliates to advance credit for the installation of machinery. Occasionally the decision involved other considerations. The Banca Commerciale Italiana backed E. Dell'Acqua heavily in order to install a weaving mill in São Paulo that would employ thread spun by Dell'Acqua's Italian mills. A French bank financed a venture to mill wheat, since no French trading companies were involved in selling flour via Santos, and the same bank backed a sugar refinery, since there were four French grinding mills already located in the state. Although the home office of the London and Brazilian Bank was cool to an expansion of its interests in São Paulo, its local manager, the ebullient and optimistic F. C. S. Ford, between 1903 and 1923 financed a good part of the textile industry, possibly out of a desire to increase the importance of his own position.[10]

The immigrants appeared to the European trading companies to be the most dependable instruments for the advancement of their interests. Some were trained by the companies themselves and sent forth as salesmen or technicians; others enjoyed previous commercial or social contacts. Political considerations, or at least nationalistic sentiments, counseled the employment of fellow countrymen. German firms invariably hired Germans, English firms hired Englishmen, and so on. The convenience of a mutual language was also a consideration; immigrants, especially the German and the English, were customarily fluent in their forebearers' tongues, even to the third generation. Eugenio Bonardelli, an Italian consular official, lamented the rapidity with which the Italian immigrants forgot their language. The reason for it, he believed, was that the "practical utility" was lacking. "If

[9] *Statuts de la Banque Brésilienne Italo-Belge, Société Anonyme.*

[10] Stanley Stein, *The Brazilian Cotton Manufacture*, p. 40; Decree 3544, December 30, 1899; David A. Joslin, *A Century of Banking in Latin America*, p. 166.

effective action were taken to promote the economic wellbeing of our colony and to intensify the commercial ties with the home country, as a necessary consequence a feeling for the utility [of the language and culture] would grow. . . . It is not out of mere feelings of patriotism that the English and Germans preserve their language and nationality." The European firms were also anxious to avoid a dependence on natives because they generally regarded them, as will be shown further on, as innately inferior to fellow-Europeans.[11]

The immigrant-importers were more than the tools of European interests; they were willing collaborators. Indeed, in many cases the initiative was theirs. A very clear case is that of the Banco Commercial Italiano de São Paulo, founded in 1900 by Matarazzo, Giuseppe Puglisi Carbone, and some other Italian immigrants with 1,000 contos ($190,000). The bank was doubtless a useful complement to their trading activities. Matarazzo left the group sometime before 1906, but Puglisi Carbone remained. In 1906 the bank received a transfusion of funds, an additional three thousand contos from the Banca Commerciale Italiana of Milan. The bank's name was changed, and a European representative was placed on its board.[12]

From that point on Puglisi Carbone's fortunes soared. In three years he acquired what seem to have been controlling interests in a large flour mill, a silk-weaving mill, and a sugar refinery. In 1910 the bank merged with the local interests of the Banque de Paris et des Pays-Bas, whose capital in São Paulo totaled 25,000,000 francs ($4,825,000), and its name was changed to the Banco Francês e Italiano para America do Sul. By then the bank was apparently the source of funds for several other groups. Rodolfo Crespi, the cotton textile manufacturer, Henrich Trost, an importer, and Emgidio Falchi, a biscuit manufacturer, were on the board of directors, and there were second-degree connections with E. Dell'Acqua and Co., Alexandre Siciliano, the machinery maker, and Edward Wysard, a representative of the Société Commerciale. By 1912 the bank was clearly well connected politically. It obtained the right to lend the municipality of São Paulo ten thousand

[11] Eugenio Bonardelli, *Lo stato di San Paolo*, p. 116.
[12] *Brazilian Year Book, Second Issue, 1909*, p. 768; *O Estado de São Paulo* (November 20, 1921).

contos (three million dollars) at a profitable 7 per cent, with an option on all future loans until it was repaid.[13]

There were other kinds of investments by European financial and manufacturing interests which encouraged Paulista industrialization and specifically favored immigrant entrepreneurship. One kind was direct investment through firms organized in Europe to operate in Brazil, such as the Société des Sucreries Brésiliennes, the French company that had erected grinding mills in the state of Rio de Janeiro and then brought out four Paulista mills in the 1880's. Other foreign firms were branch operations, such as the Anglo-Argentine São Paulo Alpargatas, which made canvas and canvas-topped sandals, the Scotch-owned Clark shoe company, and J. and P. Coats sewing thread mill. Such companies, although their ownership was foreign and although they constituted but a small segment of the industrial sector before World War II, were nevertheless useful to the immigrant entrepreneurs. They contracted European technicians, thus providing the initial employment in some cases for future entrepreneurs. They supplied the immigrants with electricity, machinery, and semifinished materials. The multiplication of shoe factories in São Paulo, for example, begins with the establishment in Rio de Janeiro of a branch of the United Shoe Machinery Company.[14]

English, French, and Italian minority backers were probably as common as German. Pierre Duchen, a French immigrant biscuitmaker, sold a half interest in his business to a group of French financiers led by Germain Auroux. The partners of the Monzini Schiffini hat factory obtained 460,000 lire in 1900 to expand their business from the Milanese hatmakers G. B. Valere e Ricci in return for control. The cotton mill built by the Souza Queiroz family in Americana was taken over by Hermann Theodor Müller, an immigrant textile importer.

[13] *Brazilian Year Book, Second Issue, 1909*, pp. 772–774; Decree 8169, August 25, 1910; 8246, September 22, 1910, Cusano, *Italia d'oltre mare*, p. 149; Emile Quoniam Schompré, *La Bourse de São Paulo*, 1911, p. 227; São Paulo (state), Law 1536, April 30, 1912.

[14] U.S. Bureau of Foreign and Domestic Commerce, *Boots and Shoes, Leather, and Supplies in Brazil*, pp. 25, 40.

Müller had the help of Rowland Rawlinson, an English belting manufacturer he dealt with. Rawlinson took 150 out of 350 shares. Another sort of investment by foreigners was silent partnership. Immigrants sometimes obtained funds from Europeans—relatives, former associates, or trading partners. It is difficult to trace the application of foreign funds to minority interests and bondholding. Partnerships were very risky under Brazilian law for nonresident partners, so that there were few of them that involved foreign capital. Corporations, on the other hand, required no special permission to operate with foreign funds unless they were banks, insurance companies, or utilities, and so the source of capital is usually obscure. During World War I some of the firms that obtained funds from German sources were revealed when they appeared on the blacklists of the Allies.[15]

It is likely that there were many other cases of silent partnerships that do not appear in federal decrees or in the Registry of Contracts. Otherwise it would be difficult to explain how so many factories could have been constructed in the few years 1906–1913 and why in so many cases these factories did not expand for a decade after. It may be hypothesized that at least a part of the European capital attracted by the Valorization of 1906 found its way into the hands of immigrants to be applied to industrial development and that for a long time after they were fully occupied with repayment. The case of Rodolfo Crespi seems to have followed this pattern.

Crespi was a Piedmontese who had come to Brazil as a salesman for the Milanese textile manufacturing and exporting company of E. Dell'Acqua in 1893. His brother, Giovanni, had arrived earlier and had formed a partnership with the planter-importers Assumpção, Toledo and Company to operate the Labor textile mill. Rodolfo married the daughter of an immigrant named Regoli who was operating a put-out weaving business. Rodolfo left Dell'Acqua and formed a partnership with his father-in-law. In those first years, the new partnership

[15] Decree 6634, September 5, 1907; 3610, March 13, 1900; Interview, Francisco Müller Carioba, São Paulo, July 9, 1963; JCSP, index. On incorporations see Richard P. Momsen, *Legal Requirements for Operations of Foreign and Domestic Corporations in Brazil*, pp. 7, 8, 17.

supplemented its earnings by opening a restaurant on Cathedral Square.[16]

The partnership gradually acquired weaving sheds of its own, then a spinning section. In 1906 Regoli retired to Italy, and Crespi took another brother, Giuseppe, into the firm. Up to this point the business appears to have been modest: he was employing only 300 workers according to an observer in 1901; in 1903 there were only 150 looms and as yet no spinning frames. The total sales of this factory from its inception in 1897 to 1906 would have been about 12,500 contos ($3,130,000), counting an average work force of 300 and. average sales per worker (using the 1907 census report on Crespi's firm) of 4,840 milreis. Yet Crespi incorporated in 1906 at the equivalent of $2,000,000, a million each in capital and reserves. Besides this he had paid the departing Regoli 2,000,000 lire ($400,000) for his share in the business, and shortly afterward he bought into a cement plant, a hat factory, and a silk weaving plant, all belonging to Puglisi Carbone. Between 1906 and 1909 his factory was greatly enlarged; by the latter date it employed 1,300 workers, but in 1912 he reported the same capitalization of $20,000,000. In 1913 he added a wool spinning and weaving shed. For this sudden growth from 1906 to 1909 to have been financed by reinvestment, from 1897 to 1906 his profits would have had to amount to five times his fixed and operating costs, a most unlikely possibility. More likely is the deduction that Crespi had acquired most of the necessary capital from E. Dell'Acqua or the Banca Commerciale or, through their intercession, from some other source in Milan.[17]

As Antônio da Silva Prado is the model of the planter-entrepreneur, Francisco Matarazzo is the model of the immigrant-entrepreneur. Like Prado, Matarazzo was the most successful, hence not the typical case. There is some material surviving to enable one to piece together the man's career and even to understand something of his character.

[16] Alfredo Cusano, *Il Brasile, gl'italiani e la guerra*, p. 212; *Twentieth Century Impressions of Brazil*, p. 406; JCSP.

[17] Cusano, *Italia d'oltre mare*, pp. 152–153; JCSP; Antônio Francisco Bandeira, Jr., *A industria de São Paulo*; Centro Industrial do Brasil, *O Brasil*, III, Appendix.

Matarazzo was an immigrant from Calabria who created the largest industrial complex of South America. He was twenty-five when he arrived in 1881, already married, and with two children. He was of a modest middle-class family. His father, who died when Francisco was still a child, had been a civil servant in the town of Castellabate on the Gulf of Salerno. Francisco had attended grammar school and high school, then went into business, specializing in hogs and lard. Why he decided to come to America is not known; probably others from the town had gone before him and sent word of the possibilities in Brazil. Matarazzo arrived with a small stock of lard to sell, but the lighter that carried him to shore foundered.[18]

He appears to have gone immediately to Sorocaba, a town about sixty miles west of the capital, then important as a livestock market. In Sorocaba he was befriended by other Italian tradesmen, and opened a small store. He began to deal in hogs. The idea of manufacturing lard never left him. "Fats that came from the United States . . . were very expensive to buy, while in Brazil the pigs were swarming," he recalled. His fellow tradesmen supplied him with capital, and he began to render lard. By 1890 he had forty-six contos ($21,000) to invest in an importing house with two of his brothers. He moved to the capital and began to import wheat flour from the United States and from a cousin in Argentina and rice from Cochin China. Lard was Matarazzo's great success. American imports arrived in wooden kegs which the local manufacturers re-used to put up their own product. Matarazzo had seen lard arrive from the United States in cans as well and decided to attempt the same process. His brother, Giuseppi, had more to do with the manufacturing process than Francisco, for the plant was located in Rio Grande do Sul. The new product swept foreign competition from the market and was sold in Rio and the North as well as in São Paulo.[19]

During nine years of trade in the capital, Matarazzo achieved some important financial connections. He won the friendship of the director of the British Bank of South America by relieving him of a shipload

---

[18] *In memoriam, Conde Francisco Matarazzo,* p. 13; Conde Francesco Matarazzo, *Scelta di discorsi e interviste,* p. 121.

[19] *Scelta di discorsi e interviste,* pp. 122, 138; *In memoriam,* p. 157; JCSP.

of flour claimed for the debts of a bankrupt importer. By 1899 Matarazzo persuaded the banker to finance a wheat flour mill in São Paulo. São Paulo had no mills of its own, although a great deal of flour was imported from Rio, where mills had been in operation for many years. Matarazzo installed his new enterprise in 1900, with machinery from a Liverpool firm and a work force of seventy.[20]

From that point on Matarazzo's ventures grew swiftly. Two more flour mills were opened. He decided to make the sacking for the flour himself, erected a cotton mill for the purpose in 1904, and bought another in 1911. The first mill contained machines for printing the fabric, for Matarazzo realized that the farm wives used the sacking for dress material. He was probably the first to employ this innovation in Brazil, and his printing mill was the only one in São Paulo to operate profitably before World War I. He also decided to make his own crates for transportation and thereupon constructed a boxmaking plant. Rather than buy cotton from the ginners, he installed machines of his own and bought the cotton in the boll. The valuable cottonseed was pressed and used to make soap and glycerine. Since the lard business and the flour milling depended on raw materials imported from Argentina, Matarazzo bought some coastal freighters and shipped them himself.[21]

Some idea of the extent of his business can be gathered from the volume of lard and wheat entering Santos, since Matarazzo monopolized the former and processed at least a third of the latter. From 1910 to 1912 the average yearly value of lard imports was 4,800 contos ($1,520,000) and of wheat imports, 7,200 contos ($2,280,000). His two cotton mills employed more than a thousand workers and produced surplus goods for sale through jobbers in São Paulo and Rio.[22]

[20] *Al conte Francesco Matarazzo, gloria dell'ingegno e del lavoro,* p. 24; *In memoriam,* pp. 101, 612; Bandeira, Jr., *A industria de São Paulo.*

[21] Antonio Piccarolo and Lino Finocchi, *O desenvolvimento industrial de S. Paulo,* p. 113; *Boletim da Directoria de Industria e Commercio* (July 1912), pp. 310–311.

[22] Brazil, Ministério de Agricultura, Indústria e Comêrcio, *Anuario estatistico do Brasil* (1908–1912), pp. 127–131; *Anuario estatistico de São Paulo* (1911–1913).

It can be seen that one of Matarazzo's most important strategies was vertical integration. As time went on he also bought a cannery in São Paulo, a lithography shop for making labels, a sawmill to supply the box plant, and foundries and machine shops to repair his equipment. He built his own docks for the coastal fleet, kept a special contingency fund so that he would not have to buy insurance, and banked through the branch of the Bank of Naples that he directed. Matarazzo bought a large section of the Agua Branca district in the capital, grouped most of his industrial plant there, and subdivided the rest. As time went on he bought lands to grow sugar and raise beef cattle and developed both these ventures to the final products of refined sugar, beef, and leather. Matarazzo sold a factory on just one occasion, a match factory; it was the only one whose processes he could not control from start to finish.[23]

Most of the other manufacturers exhibit the same tendency to self-sufficiency to some degree at least. Vertical integration was not principally the result of a desire to absorb the profits of middlemen. Matarazzo and the other industrialists, operating in a frontier economy, were anxious above all to reduce the uncertainties of raw material supply and of transport and power. This motivation is seen most clearly in his building of separate docks for his coastal vessels. The construction must certainly have cost more than the use of the public Docas de Santos Company, but the latter were perpetually backlogged, and the losses from pilferage and breakage were exorbitant.

Similar considerations were important to Matarazzo in his policy of selling directly to retailers. An English technician he employed for many years, Donald H. Rust, remembered that Matarazzo had 45,000 accounts and that he preferred smaller companies to large ones. They were more loyal, and it was only a trifling loss to him if they failed. Other industrialists complained of the lack of credit information, but few were large enough to follow Matarazzo's example.[24]

The Industrias Reunidas Francisco Matarazzo (IRFM) benefited from his attention to detail. Rust mentioned Matarazzo's pride in his

---

[23] *O Conde Matarazzo aos oitenta annos*, p. 36; *In memoriam*, p. 16.
[24] *O Conde Matarazzo aos oitenta annos*, p. 39.

exchange speculations. His custom was to buy foreign currencies when the milreis was high and use them to pay off import accounts when the milreis declined. He or his son perennially set prices and made all the purchases. Matarazzo divided his time between the factories and offices and often worked seven days a week. He instituted a planning system for all his departments, so that future requirements could be forecast.[25]

The Paulista entrepreneurs operated in an environment of almost perfect laissez faire. Aside from import and export duties, neither the state nor the federal government concerned itself with the activities of private businessmen until the working class riots of 1917. Monopolies were arranged, working conditions in many of the mills were abominable, the quality of food products was unregulated. Local industries were subject to few taxes, and these were generally evaded. Entrepreneurs regularly plotted each other's ruin. Matarazzo, the biggest of the industrialists and perhaps the most efficient, for the most part avoided the unprincipled tactics of more marginal operators. His factories were safer and less disagreeable to work in, and his attitude toward his workers, if less than egalitarian, was not ruthless. His one monopoly, canned lard, was possibly the result of his headstart and superior organization. He refused to participate in cartels with other producers. Even so, some accounts of his early years, possibly apocryphal, suggest that his operations may have been less scrupulous than they were after he attained impregnable positions in the market. It is said, for example, that he was the only man in São Paulo to realize that the involvement of the United States in a war with Spain would curtail kerosene imports. He went from store to store buying every drop he could, until he had cornered the supply.[26]

Matarazzo was more highly regarded than most of the other industrialists, not only for the way he conducted his business, but also

[25] *Ibid.*; "Uma vida de animador," *Diario de São Paulo* (March 9, 1934).

[26] Factory conditions in *Boletim do Departamento Estadual de Trabalho* (1911), pp. 35–77; *A Gazeta* (May 1917); Paulo R. Pestana, "A Industria de banha," *Boletim da Directoria de Industria e Commercio* (October–November 1914), pp. 497–499. Prices of kerosene show, at least, that *someone* cornered the supply, *Retrospecto Commercial* (1899), p. 37.

because he was all accounts a very charming man. He disarmed acquaintances, fellow businessmen, even the hostile press, with his camaraderie, his simple ways, and his ability, when necessary, to be self-deprecatory. The interviewing reporter liked to hear him say, "I never studied anything, I'm ignorant." The corner grocer, who bought Matarazzo's flour by the barrel, could read in his newspaper, "I'm just a merchant of flour, salt cod, cotton, . . . I don't understand very much." He always wore a plain black suit and drank beer. But the dinner guest was served good wine, and a bottle to take home would be his if he complimented it. The graciousness and generosity had practical applications: along with his ability to charm others went an ability to size them up as credit risks.[27]

Matarazzo was a tough and energetic man as well as a charming one. Photographs of him reveal a proud, unsmiling face, its expression intelligent and self-conscious, as though he knew that his appearance impressed others as much as his wealth. He shaved his head as he grew bald, wore a small moustache, and always kept his strong athletic figure, so that he appeared to be a soldier rather than a businessman. He gained some of his first backwoods customers in Sorocaba while at his favorite sport, hunting on horseback. His drive and competitiveness were proverbial. "I want you to note that I have never had, nor ever wished to have *quello che si chiama padrone.*" He delighted in his feuds with Pinotti Gamba, Martinelli, and others and never bore them a grudge. Rust would find him on the couch at 4 A.M. smoking and reading machinery catalogues, dreaming of still bigger undertakings. The newspapers carried over and over his invariable advertisement, "The products of our factories . . . are processed by the most perfected mechanisms of the best and most reputed foreign manufacturers."[28]

[27] *O Conde Matarazzo*, p. 62–63; Piccarolo and Finocchi, *O desenvolvimento industrial*, p. 113.

[28] "What is known as a boss," *Scelta di discorsi e interviste*, p. 122; *O Conde Matarazzo aos oitenta annos*, p. 39. An extraordinarily interesting biographical study of Matarazzo has been written by José de Souza Martins. Employing social-psychological theory, the author seems to see Matarazzo as a member of a fallen elite in terms similar to Everett Hagen's explanations of

Whether or not Matarazzo was typical of the immigrant group, it is apparent that his generation dominated Paulista industry until the early 1930's. Crespi, Siciliano, Pinotti Gamba, Scarpa, Jafet, and the rest had all arrived or started off in manufacturing in the decade bracketing 1900. Not until they retired did entrepreneurship take on a new style and techniques. Matarazzo, therefore, will reappear in this study, not only as the most successful and loquacious of the immigrant industrialists, but also as its doyen, shrewdest and oldest in experience.

the origin of entrepreneurship. *Empresário e emprêsa na biografia do Conde Matarazzo.*

CHAPTER V

The Merger of Emerging Elites

The industrialists of São Paulo emerged, during the thirty years following the establishment of the Republic, as a large and distinct economic group, nearly as important as the plantation and mercantile elites from which they evolved. Can it be said that they had come to constitute a self-conscious industrial bourgeoisie? The question is of interest, because the extent of the manufacturers' cohesiveness and self-awareness would predetermine their willingness to force a showdown in the political arena. A further transformation of society depended upon changes in tariff and fiscal policies, in the redistribution of government income, and perhaps even in the attitude of the government toward land concentration and the status of rural labor.

The consciousness of the plantation elite was manifest. Although the planters' fortunes may have been recent, their lineage was not. The empire had ennobled some and bestowed orders and honorifics on many more. The virtuous Republic had transformed them into citizens, but citizens who dwelt on genealogy. Paulista society, said one of them in 1920, "is not a *parvenu* civilization, it feels within it the great impulse to accomplish of the past." Their economic program, evident in the legislation that had transformed transport, labor, and landholding, was epitomized in the phrase constantly repeated: Brazil is an essentially agricultural country. Nor were the planters unaware of the potential threat from the industrialists. Coffee yielded excellent profits in most years, but it was a form of capitalism that was impossible to expand indefinitely. To double one's fortune, one would have to double one's groves. To the planters, then, the wealth of a Matarazzo appeared frighteningly large and capable of unlimited ramification. Occasionally they spoke of the industrialists as an "aristocracy of money," an "industrial plutocracy," or even a "bunch of sharks." When the planters considered how frequently the new manufacturer was an immigrant, they complained of foreigners who came over in third class and "impoverished old families of the rural aristocracy, genuinely Brazilian."[1]

These phrases describe a situation that the plantation elite had itself created. Paradoxically, they had presided over an economic expansion that necessarily called forth new factors of production and new men to manipulate them. A European visitor to São Paulo in 1930 described a society "not at all comparable to that, profoundly differentiated, of old peoples." He found a class system indeed, but "not in the slightest closed, they do not at all resemble castes. . . . The one great principle of the social hierarchy is money, which freely changes hands." In the process, some of the plantation families might find themselves the losers. Of nine cotton mills founded by planters before 1900, all but two had been sold to importers by 1917. In the meantime six new mills had been built with coffee money; nevertheless, these alienations of manufacturing interests heightened fears of being overtaken by the foreigners.[2]

There were, furthermore, some more generalized complaints against the industrialists. One of these was rural wage levels. It was believed by the planters that the factory represented a drain upon plantation labor and that, were there no alternatives in the city, their work force would be satisfied with lower wages. A second complaint, and this was a secular argument, was that the greater part of Brazilian industry

[1] Antônio Carneiro Leão, *S. Paulo em 1920*, pp. 28–29; quotes in Humberto Bastos, *O pensamento industrial no Brasil*, pp. 157, 186; *O Estado de São Paulo* (September 22, 1919).

[2] Louis Mouralis, *Un séjour aux États-Unis du Brésil*, pp. 88–90.

was "artificial," that is, it required imported raw materials. The origin of this complaint appears to lie in the tendency of the tariff schedule to attach a higher rate to a finished product without simultaneously adding to the duties on the ingredients or parts of which the product was composed. As a result firms would be organized that did nothing more than combine or assemble the final product. Thus match factories merely dipped the already-fashioned sticks in phosphorous and arrayed them in boxes, while perfume factories diluted the imported essences and poured the solution in bottles. Even these rudimentary operations, it would be expected, reduced slightly the total costs of imports and provided a few more jobs for Brazilians. Nevertheless, to Brazilians, especially to planters, these operations had a fraudulent air and they were resented.

The real object of the planters' anger, however, was not these modest workshops, which tended to "nationalize" progressively as tariffs were continually scaled upward, but the factories that employed foreign raw materials when there was a domestic, planter-produced alternative available in São Paulo. Thus the workshops that made coffee hullers with imported pig iron did not suffer reprisals because they did not send to Minas Gerais for domestic iron, but the factories that weaved woolens and silks or made bagging from imported jute were objects of unremitting hostility, because they reduced the consumption of Paulista cotton.

It did not happen that the industrialists were obliged to limit themselves invariably to the transformation of local materials. It has been seen that even the planters invested in a number of activities that employed imported raw materials, such as iron and steel, since these companies produced machines and castings that would have been more expensive to procure abroad. Finally, the industrialists were producing goods that were consumed mainly by the lower classes; those operations involved no deprivation for the landholding elite and did not arouse their enmity.

The planters, it may be surmised, were at least potentially ready to block the path of the industrialists if an occasion was offered them. The industrialists, on the other hand, were much less ready to push their gains too far or to press for political advantages at the expense of the planters. Perhaps the principle reason for this reluctance lay in the difficulty in establishing a separate identity. Most of the planters who turned to manufacturing continued to own estates, and not infrequently the immigrant entrepreneur would buy land, in some cases to obtain raw materials and in others to speculate or to enhance his self-esteem. Some factories and even a few plantations were partnerships of planters and immigrants. Furthermore, it was difficult for the industrialists to conceive of the development of the Paulista economy in terms different from those embraced by the planter and the importer, at least until the 1930's. Self-evidently coffee had created his market; to do it any harm would be nearly suicidal. Indeed, he was always ready to offer suggestions for its aggrandizement.[3]

The contrast with the antebellum economic conflicts of the United States is quite striking. As Roberto Simonsen has pointed out, it is explained in part by mere proximity: in Brazil the loci of the most rapidly growing agricultural and industrial areas were not distinct but identical. The possibility existed, therefore, that these two interests would merge at many points. Another difference renders inapplicable an analogy with the United States. The cotton, sugar, hides, vegetable oils and cereals that the manufacturers transformed were not the principal Paulista exports. In fact they were products that were unsaleable abroad in normal times. Thus the planters who grew these crops on land unsuited to coffee looked favorably on the industrialists for providing them with a secondary market. For their part, the industrialists encouraged this diversification. Cotton mill owners, for example, distributed free seeds and saw cotton production triple between 1905 and 1913.[4]

The most significant political test in the emergence of an industrial bourgeoisie, it might be expected, would be their demand to employ the tariff as an instrument of protection. Here, too, the Brazilian experience is unlike that of the United States and of many other countries, because the planters were as unwilling as the industrialists to reduce the rates of the tariff schedule. The motives of the industrialists

---

[3] JCSP lists agricultural as well as industrial and commercial corporations.

[4] Roberto Simonsen, *Ensaios sociais, políticos e econômicos*, p. 175; Isaltino Costa, "As origens da cultura do algodão em São Paulo," pp. 8–9.

are obvious; the attitude of the planters seems eccentric. Their acquies-
cence was, in fact, *faute de mieux*. The central government of the
Republic spent more money than had the Empire; the tariff continued
to be, however, the only significant scource of revenue that the planters
would grant. The available alternatives would obviously be more pain-
ful to them: a tax on land or a tax on incomes or profit. Therefore the
federal government, whose expenses had grown from 434,000 contos
($87,000,000) to 1,227,000 contos ($257,000,000) between 1900
and 1920, relied on customs duties to provide about 70 per cent of its
income. Though such a tariff would necessarily be protective in effect,
its intent was merely fiscal. Joaquim Murtinho, Minister of Finance
under President Campos Salles, abandoned the policy of tariff reduction, begun in 1897, when he saw that it led inevitably to an increase
in the flow of imports, hence to a decline in the value of the milreis,
which was precisely the equivalent in its effect on imports to an increase in tariffs.[5]

There was another reason that a high tariff was considered inevitable.
The republican government, to a much greater extent than its imperial
predecessor, was unsuccessful in procuring sufficient revenues to cover
its growing expenditures. Periodically its debt was funded by means
of foreign loans. Because the milreis was not convertible into gold, the
European bankers would not accept it in repayment. The only way the
federal government could lay its hands on gold was by taxing imports.
A gold quota was therefore fixed on the normal duties, and it grew
from year to year. It was initiated in 1891 at 2 per cent of the ad
valorem duties; in 1898 it was raised to 10 per cent, in 1900, to 25 per
cent. By 1922 the quota amounted to 60 per cent.[6]

Even though the quantity of imports that Brazil could afford at any
given time was predetermined by the state of the coffee trade and the
fiscal requirements of the federal government, the structure of the
tariff could and did reflect the economic interests of both planters and

[5] Nícia Vilela Luz, *A luta pela industrialização do Brasil*, pp. 111–116;
Afonso de Toledo Bandeira de Mello, *Politique commerciale du Brésil*, pp.
71–73.

[6] Mello, *Politique* . . ., p. 79.

industrialists. After the general revision of the tariff in 1900, which affected both classification and the system of collection, there was no new schedule published until 1934. During all this time new rates were decided individually for each product. This system, or lack of one, afforded a maximum opportunity for lobbying to be carried on by individual firms. It was therefore possible for manufacturers to find adequate protection without exposing themselves on a broad front to the wrath of agricultural interests. Only in 1928, when a group of industrialists organized openly and lobbied for a more general revision of the tariff, did they encounter resistance. The more clandestine forms of pressure employed until the late 1920's rarely appear in documents, but the following case was dealt with in a routine manner by the consular official who investigated it: on the complaint of a Pittsburgh sanitary ware manufacturer, who had heard that the tariff on bathtubs was to be raised from 300 to 500 per cent ad valorem, the American chargé in Rio replied that the cause was the recent establishment of a factory there to make bathtubs. "They possess much political influence, having the support, so I am credibly informed, of Senator Pinheiro Machado, the political 'boss' of Brazil, and of many prominent deputies."[7]

Planters, on the other hand, represented their interests as a group—the more easily since they were concerned with a narrower range of issues. Raw cotton was unfailingly among the most costly products to import because of high tariffs, and fertilizers were never produced in quantity in Brazil until very recently because the planters insisted on very low tariffs.

The particularism of the industrialists' claims to government favors led to a dependency upon the existing political structure. The industrialists were represented in the Paulista Republican Party by politicians sympathetic to their interests, such as Alfredo Pujol and Carlos de Campos—indeed more directly by industrialists such as Arthur Diederichsen and Lacerda Franco—but they were not heavily influential within "the situation" except on the narrowest of issues. In effect they had aligned themselves not with the reformist middle class but with

[7] U.S. National Archives, Department of State [hereafter NA-DS], Rives to Secretary of State, December 2, 1911, 632.113 San/3.

the landowners, and invariably they provided unquestioning political support. Industrialism, with its potential for social transformation, was thwarted in effect by a regressive and opportunistic alliance with the class least likely to favor that transformation.

Circumstantial factors in the early industrialization of São Paulo mitigated the conflicts between factory owners and planters and persuaded the former to accept the dominance of the latter in political as well as economic matters. The social relationships between the plantation elite and the newly enriched immigrants tended to allay still further antagonisms that were at least potentially present.

It might seem that the planters, with their fears of an industrial plutocracy and resentment over displacement by steerage immigrants, would be impelled to restore the newly rich to an inferior position in the social order. On the other hand the immigrants, one might also hypothesize, would feel themselves discriminated against and would in turn use economic power to gain social position, thereby further antagonizing the plantation elite and intensifying the economic conflict.

The evidence suggests, however, that these potential sources of mutual social hostility did not become active. Most striking of all is the degree of intermarriage between immigrant and plantation families. For the first generation this phenomenon was fairly rare, since some of the immigrants arrived already married and others were, it appears, betrothed. However, Siciliano and Noschese, both of whom arrived as children, and the Simonsens, who were born in Brazil, married Brazilian women. The second generation very commonly married into Paulista families. All of the children of John Kenworthy, Guilherme Georgi, and Pedro Morganti married Brazilians. Rodolfo Crespi's daughter married a Da Silva Prado, and the Weiszflogs, Siciliano, Matarazzo, Byington, Pereira Ignácio, Scarpa, Oetterer, and others all acquired connections among the plantation elite in the same manner. The mutual advantages of these alliances were in some cases highly visible: John Kenworthy, for example, managed textile mills for the Pires de Campos family; then one of his daughters married into it. The son-in-law then entered Kenworthy's own factory either by way of a dowry or as a representative of Campos funds. Rodolfo Crespi interested himself in at least one of the Prado plantations through his son-in-law Fábio da Silva Prado. Another case is that of Alberto Lion, an importer of machinery and agricultural goods, who was able to prosper partly through contacts made through the family of his Brazilian wife which secured him government contracts. Finally, the alliance of his daughter with a Brazilian brought about a total "nationalization" of the business in the 1930's.[8]

The immigrant industrialist who became most successfully connected with plantation interests was, perhaps, Alexandre Siciliano. A native of San Nicolà Arcella, a town on the Bay of Salerno, he came to São Paulo in 1869 at the age of nine. An uncle and an older brother preceded him and settled at Piracicaba, where they opened a general store; there the young Alexandre went to work. In 1881 he married Laura Augusta de Mello Coelho, the daughter of a rich and influential planter. Shortly afterward he and his brother Francesco formed a partnership with João Conrado Engelberg to produce Engelberg's coffee-processing machine.

After the sale of the patents in the United States, Siciliano moved to the capital and took part in the founding of three companies whose total capitalization was 10,000 contos ($4,750,000): a new bank, an importing house, and a machine shop and foundry. Siciliano became president of the last. The capital was obtained perhaps partly from profits earned in Piracicaba and in the patent sale. Nevertheless, it seems most likely that the larger part was contributed by the planters who had originally funded him and who were now his relatives. Siciliano's new shop, the Companhia Mechanica e Importadora, was constructed on a large scale, the largest that São Paulo had yet seen. It included a foundry, a machinery section, a sawmill and carpentry shop, and a brick- and tileyard. He was able to produce railway coach bodies, hullers, and other agricultural machinery and was equipped

8 Genealogical information from *Quem é quem no Brasil*, 1948 to 1963; *Personalidades no Brasil*; Hugo Schlesinger, *Enciclopédia da indústria brasileira*; Ronald Hilton, *Who's Who in Latin America*, pt. IV, *Brazil*; Afrânio Coutinho, *Brasil e os brasileiros de hoje*; "Lion SA Keeps Pace With São Paulo's Industrial Growth," *Brazilian Business* (August 1961), pp. 26–27; *Commercial Encyclopedia, Third Sectional Issue, South America*, p. 583.

to undertake all kinds of civil engineering construction. The new business prospered. Siciliano's codirectors were four of the largest and most influential planters in the state, and still others appear to have been associated with him. He obtained contracts for public buildings and built bridges for the planter-owned railroads and structures for the Prado-organized packing plant at Barretos. The company operated a vast importing business in mechanical equipment and construction materials, including locomotives, automobiles, generators, steel rails, and cement.[9]

Siciliano gradually began to buy out his planter associates until finally he was sole owner. At the same time he managed to expand the business considerably. He added nail- and screw-making machinery and equipment for metal plating and bought out another shop in Jundiaí. Siciliano also acquired interests in a variety of other manufacturing companies, most probably because he had supplied them with equipment or had built new structures for them. He eventually came to control a metal enameling factory, the Dumont Sugar Central, the Brasital textile mills, and a jute mill.[10]

So closely did Siciliano come to identify his interests with those of the planters that he provided them the germ of the idea for the coffee valorization scheme. In 1903 he wrote a book that advocated a state-supported loan for the purpose of buying up a part of the crop in bad years and then gradually marketing it in good years. This appears to have been the first discussion of such a plan in São Paulo, and he was widely credited with being its originator when it was put into effect four years later.[11]

In those days of family ownership of the firm the alliance of economic interests through intermarriage was a significant form of capital accumulation, in spite of the incomplete control exercised over the

[9] Antonio Piccarolo and Lino Finocchi, *O desenvolvimento industrial*, p. 218; Lino Finocchi, *In memoria* [Count Alexandre Siciliano]; Monte Domecq', p. 648; Roberto Capri, *O Estado de São Paulo e seus municípios*, pp. 141–152; *Memorial historico da industria de 1933*, p. 84.

[10] *Memorial historico*; Finocchi, *In memoria*; JCSP, files.

[11] *Valorização do café, bases de contracto entre um syndicato e o governo federal apresentadas à Sociedade Paulista de Agricultura.*

daughter's choice of mate. Once the selection of partners is no longer the absolute right of the father and once the dowry is no longer bestowed, as appeared to be the case in São Paulo, the effects of the marriage alliance became somewhat risky. It nevertheless remained all-important, at least as long as the family refused to entrust management to outsiders. The paterfamilias-businessman still retained, however, a few elements of choice. The decision to allow the son-in-law to control his daughter's inheritance was still his, as was the decision to allow the son-in-law to participate in the company's management. Even when the entrepreneur had sons of his own, the selection of his succession was likely to be calculating rather than consanguineous. It may also be that the shift from arranged to "romantic" marriages was not altogether laden with risk from the father's point of view. If Freud is right, the daughter may well have been motivated to select a mate whose personality resembled that of her aggressive and domineering father, and she may have been as fully concerned as her parents over the maintenance of her status. At least the frequency with which sons-in-law acquired control of Paulista firms all through the first half of this century leads one to believe some such principles were operative.[12]

The willingness of the plantation elite to accept immigrant sons-in-law was partly the result of rational calculation, no doubt. It may also have been caused by a more generalized attitude of optimism and self-assurance more common than feelings of resentment. A Paulista of an old family, writing in 1920, admitted that much had been accomplished by the immigrants who had come to the state in such a flood, but he insisted that the "initiative" had been Brazilian and that "the force and prestige of the Brazilians are perfectly in control." The worth of the Paulistas had been proved, in his opinion, by their readiness not to exclude, but to absorb, the newcomers.[13]

The fact of widespread intermarriage did not signify complete absence of tensions between immigrant entrepreneurs and plantation elite.

---

[12] The theoretical question was posed by Daniel Bell, "The Break-up of Family Capitalism," *Partisan Review* (Spring 1957), pp. 317–320.

[13] Antônio Carneiro Leão, *S. Paulo em 1920*, p. 29.

The planters could not resist the desire to snub. For example, as late as 1918 certain immigrants were not allowed in the more prestigious social clubs, The Jockey, The Automobile, and The São Paulo, and even today the names of immigrants are not often to be found on their boards of directors. An acid portrayal of Paulista society in the 1940's suggests that the immigrants and the planters, still socially distinct, coexisted in a repellent form of symbiosis, the immigrants dependent on the "quatrocentões" for status alliances, the planters upon the immigrants for money. And yet these petty cruelties were insignificant compared to the social malaise that infected the unreconciled elites of Boston and other cities of the northern United States, where Irish, Italian, Jews, and others struggled harder to acquire social status than they did to get rich.[14]

Even the discrimination against what appears to be the one exceptional immigrant group in São Paulo, the Syrians and Lebanese, seems, by comparison with the American experience, unimportant. The case of this group is quite unusual among Paulista immigrants, for the Syrian and Lebanese entrepreneurial families almost invariably married within their community and not infrequently married within the extended family group, including first cousins. Furthermore, they appear to be the only group that has accused Brazilian society in general of prejudice.

Clark Knowlton, through interviews gleaned in the early 1950's, relates frequent assertions by members of this group that other Brazilians were discriminating against them and accepts these reports as true, although he provides no further corroboration. In the absence of such proof it might be hypothesized that the reports were to a degree subjective, reflecting inner states of mind rather than verifiable fact. Knowlton's study itself provides some basis for this interpretation. It records many admissions by Syrian and Lebanese businessmen of sharp practices, illegalities, and conspiracies to destroy competitors which necessarily accompany the sort of marginal business typically Syrian or Lebanese in São Paulo and which might have to be justified

[14] Aureliano Leite, *Subsídios para a história da civilização paulista*, p. 288; Joel Silveira, *Grã-finos em São Paulo e outras notícias do Brasil.*

by projective mechanisms. Knowlton reports parallel subjective statements still more difficult to demonstrate objectively—for example, the assertion that other immigrant groups remained as unassimilated as the Syrian and Lebanese and the exaggerated self-estimate of Syrian and Lebanese importance in trade and industry.[15]

This evidence—partially negative, it is true—against the existence of significant social tensions between the industrial and agricultural sectors of the elite might be explained in sheerly economic terms. Common interests prevented the creation of social distinctions, and the rapid growth of the economy as a whole, at least until 1928—by which time most of the external immigration was over—suppressed any hard questions about the sharing of social gains. But it should also be noted that the immigrants to Brazil were fairly easily assimilable. The great majority were of the same religion. The languages they spoke were similar to Portuguese. Furthermore, they were bearers of a culture the Brazilians, especially the Brazilian elite, were eager to imitate.

Few of the immigrants to North America, by contrast, could satisfy the natives that they were by education, experience, or inherent ability superior to the native population, but many Europeans could impress the Brazilians that this was so, even when it was not. The Europeans, at least until 1914, were secure in their enjoyment of a vast African and Asian colonial empire, and they demonstrated what seemed to outsiders an innate capacity for technical and financial betterment. It was easy for the Europeans and North Americans to ascribe the relative backwardness of Latin Americans to race. This was true not only of Anglo-Saxons, like the businessman Percival Farquahar, who "preferred men of German or other recent European background as they were more literate and dependable" to work on his railroad, or the English textile expert, A. S. Pearse, who believed Europeans to be dominant in trade because of the Brazilians' "want of continued application and cool commercial intelligence. . . . The many lotteries that exist seem to have created a speculative instinct." Even the Italians,

[15] "Spacial and Social Mobility of the Syrians and Lebanese in the City of São Paulo, Brazil" (unpublished Ph.D. dissertation, Vanderbilt University, 1955), pp. 223–233.

whose imperial pretensions were almost wholly ineffectual, whose economic backwardness required the emigration of millions of its peasants, and who were obliged to accept a decidedly inferior position in the United States, were in Brazil entitled to condescend to the natives. To the socialist Ferrucio Mosconi the lower classes were "degenerate," devoting themselves only to drink and women and refusing to work, while the upper classes were slothful, backward, and untrained, for "here they all dedicate themselves to the study of law, unless they decide to dedicate themselves to women." The Italian consul in São Paulo thought it quite reasonable that the Negro was generally consigned to day labor on the plantations, since he was "indolent, if not servile, and dedicated to *pinga* [cane brand]." The mulatto in his opinion was more intelligent "and even handsome," but not equal to the Italian in farming ability.[16]

It was not surprising that the Brazilian elite partially accepted the European beliefs. Dependent as it was on Europe for capital, machinery, markets, luxury articles, and literature, the elite appears to have looked to Europe for cues to acceptable social behavior as well. The Brazilian upper classes learned to feel shame for the "fearfully mongrel aspect" of their population, to identify their interests not with their fellow countrymen but with their fellow whites from Europe, and to look to European immigration, to the "bleaching" of the population, as the cure for the economic backwardness of the country. Hence the ready hospitality of the Brazilians, the partnerships, and the marriage alliances.

Besides the perception of social distance that the ideology of imperialistic Europe imposed on the Paulista elite, there was evidently a real distance created by the conditions of the plantation and the factory. Both the planter and the factory owner were proprietors and therefore remote in outlook and interests from those whom they employed, more remote than either had been from their workers in the days of subsistence farms and craftshops. The differences in outlook

---

[16] Charles Gauld. *The Last Titan*, p. 217; Arno S. Pearse, *Brazilian Cotton*, p. 20; Ferrucio Mosconi, "Le classi sociali al Brasile e loro funzioni," *La Riforma Sociale* (1897), p. 593; Eugenio Bonardelli, *Lo stato di S. Paolo del Brasile e l'emigrazione italiana*, p. 43.

between plantation and factory owners and between native Brazilian aristocracy and immigrant *nouveau riche* were not sufficiently great to prevent the formation of a generalized bourgeois identity that embraced all of them as employers, property owners, and as members of a regional elite. The consequences for the promotion of industrialization were not necessarily favorable.

PART TWO

•

INDUSTRIAL GROWTH: CIRCUMSTANCE AND STRUCTURE

1914–1930

CHAPTER VI

The Effects of World War

The manufacturing plant of São Paulo grew rapidly during the first thirty years of the Republic. The seventeen cotton mills of 1900 became forty-one by 1915 and employed four times as many workers. Some of the new plants were equipped to weave woolens as well as cotton and jute, or could make prints, and there were also a few knitting mills, mainly for producing hosiery. Other flour mills were constructed and challenged Matarazzo. The ceramic, woodworking, hatmaking, and shoemaking businesses all expanded. The value of Paulista industrial output was estimated at 110,000 contos in 1905, 189,000 in 1910, and 274,000 in 1915 ($34,000,000, $56,000,000 and $67,000,000, respectively).[1]

There was very little difficulty in obtaining bank credit in the years following the valorization. Bankers worried about inactive cash drawers, and the discount rate declined. The textile factories at least were no longer competing with foreign goods, which they undersold by as

---

[1] Paulo R. Pestana, "As industrias manufactureiras de São Paulo," *Revista da Associação Commercial de São Paulo* (March 1923), pp. 147–148; *Boletim da Directoria de Industria* (March 1917), pp. 117–125, 215.

much as half, but with each other, justifying fully their installation and widening the demand for their cloth year by year.[2]

What was the cause, or causes, of this very rapid advance in industrialization? First of all it can be seen that the market of São Paulo was broadening geographically and was becoming independent of Rio de Janeiro. The latter city had acted as entrepôt for São Paulo, but was ceasing to play this role. Goods unloaded at Rio were burdened with a 2 per cent federal port improvements tax, but not at the Santos docks, because these were privately owned. Meanwhile service on the Central Railroad that connected the two cities fell into decline as the Paraíba Valley lost its significance as a coffee-growing area. Probably for these reasons several Rio importers decided to open branches in São Paulo, and a few transferred all their business there. The railway lines that were constructed to bring the Paulista coffee to market all converged on the city of São Paulo, making a single market of the entire state. Furthermore, these lines pushed out to the state boundaries and brought the Paraná north, southern Mato Grosso, the Minas "Triangle," and the area served by the Sul Mineira Railway all into that market as well.[3]

Another favoring circumstance was government fiscal policy, which, although not consistently designed to favor industry before World War I, quite generally overlooked the potential revenue in domestic manufacturers. It has been mentioned in another connection that between 1900 and 1920 the federal government raised about 70 per cent of its income from import tariffs, designed usually to extract a maximum return, and most of the rest was raised from excise taxes. Some part of this burden fell on domestic products as well as on imports, because manufacturers had to buy machinery and some of their raw materials abroad, and because the excise taxes, being recessive, fell heavily on everyday items, which were domestically produced for the most part. However, these taxes were not imposed directly on industry and could be mitigated: it seems to have been fairly easy, for example,

[2] Stanley Stein. *The Brazilian Cotton Manufacture*, p. 105.

[3] *Retrospecto Commercial* (1895), p. 1, and (1897), p. 61; *Commercial Encyclopedia, Third Sectional Issue, South America*, p. 383; *Commercial Encyclopedia, Fourth Sectional Issue, South America*, p. 370.

to obtain tariff exemptions for machinery. State taxation in São Paulo was still more favorable. The 1891 constitution granted states the right to levy export duties. All the states did so, but São Paulo was fortunate in being able to tap the vast coffee trade; it was able to raise almost all its revenue thereby. Indeed, from 1893 to 1904 there was no other state tax.[4]

Various other government measures had a marginal effect on domestic production. The structure of tariffs, as has already been noted, tended to favor the importation of semifinished goods, such as matches and perfumes, for final transformation. This was not a consistent policy, however, and often seemed to be a matter of caprice. Newsprint, for example, was accorded a very low rate in order to buy the political support of journalists, but at the same time paper production was discouraged by levying higher rates on pulp. Another seeming concession to industry was the often-mentioned Law of Similars, a measure first promulgated in 1890, then rewritten in 1911, which prohibited tariff exemption for imports that would compete with similar goods already produced within the country. Actually, it is evident in the preambles to these laws that they were written as rather desperate attempts to stem the tide of exemptions that increased yearly and that their intent was primarily fiscal, not protective. Neither law was adequately enforced.[5]

It is evident that the continued growth of Paulista industry was a result of the growth of the coffee trade. The coffee business provided the demand, the prospects of the coffee business stimulated investment, much of it from the coffee sector, and the coffee business created the necessary economic overhead and paid the taxes. During the years when coffee sold well, industry appears to have been most profitable and expanded more rapidly. During bad years in the coffee trade, as in 1892, 1895, and 1898 and again from 1902 to 1906, local industry was moribund. The Paulista manufacturing plant seems to have grown

[4] São Paulo (state), Departamento Estadual de Estatística, *Dados gerais do Estado: 1890–1938*.

[5] *Revista de Commercio e Industria* (June 1916), pp. 153–154; Decrees 947A, November 4, 1890, 8592, March 8, 1911; Centro Industrial do Brasil, *Relatorio* (1912), pp. 9, 28–29, 38–40.

fastest from 1907 to 1913, in that brief period between the government coffee purchase scheme of 1906 and the outbreak of the Second
Balkan War. The first event ended the long-term world decline in
coffee prices, brought renewed credit to expand coffee plantings, and
appreciated the milreis by 25 per cent. The value of coffee shipments
through Santos averaged more than $145,000,000 in 1911, 1912, and
1913, almost double the value of the preceding three years and triple
the value of the poor years of 1902 to 1904. As a consequence the
terms of trade improved by 30 per cent in the last prewar years, and
the entrepreneurs of São Paulo re-equipped and expanded their plants.
Imports of machinery and iron and steel products more than doubled
from 1909 to 1913, increasing from 70,000 to 195,000 metric tons,
sure evidence that the manufacturing capacity of the state was expanding.[6]

The Second Balkan War marked the end of this euphoria because it
caused an outflow from Brazil of European capital and because this
outflow paid for an enormously increased quantity of competing imports. For the first time in 27 years the country experienced a net
import balance, so large that it could only have been paid for with
200,000 contos ($63,000,000) in capital transfers.

Although the role of coffee exports in stimulating industry is generally acknowledged by those who have analyzed São Paulo's early
development, strangely enough it is usually asserted that the development of industry there was not the result of the growth of the coffee
trade, but of its gradual breakdown. It is assumed that the demand
created by coffee would have been totally supplied by imports, had
not coffee become increasingly unable to pay for them. Werner Baer,
summarizing the hypotheses of several Brazilian economic historians,
asserts that the industrial surges that took place in the early decades of

---

[6] Comissão Mista Brasil-Estados Unidos para Desenvolvimento Econômico,
Relatório geral, I, 95, for terms of trade; São Paulo (state) Secretaria de
Agricultura, Indústria e Commercio, *Estatística do commercio do porto de
Santos com os paizes estrangeiros* (1911–1912, 1913–1914). Surplus of capital
funds noted in Banco de Commercio e Industria, *Relatorio* (1911), quoted in
O Estado de São Paulo, Supplemento Comercial e Industrial (March 1949),
p. 16.

the twentieth century were caused principally by shocks from the external sector. The "shocks," he explains, were wars or trade depressions, which either interrupted foreign supplies physically or reduced the amount of exchange available to buy foreign goods.[7]

In the case of a decline in foreign exchange, it seems indeed true that one result was a higher tariff and other pressures on the value of the milreis. It has been pointed out that a major cause of tariff increases was the tendency of the federal government to pay off its debts by funding them abroad. The foreign loans had to be redeemed in gold, and the only way to acquire it was by placing a surcharge on the tariff. But this tendency of the government to pre-empt foreign exchange and of the milreis to decline in value might also be looked upon as a shock not merely to the importing sector but to the economy as a whole. During such downturns in the coffee trade São Paulo also experienced a shrinkage in demand. The lowering of rural wages was often accompanied by an outflow of immigrants (along with their remittances) and of capital. Furthermore, during those times manufacturers found raw materials, fuels, machines, and spare parts more costly to import. On balance can it truly be claimed that the decline of the coffee trade was good for business?

Indeed, such a position is not consistently maintained. Baer also mentions, as contributory to prewar manufacturing development, the Caixa de Conversão. In 1906 this federal agency was created to buy foreign exchange at a constant rate of fifteen pence to the milreis. In 1910 the milreis was increased in value to sixteen pence. Both because the agency stabilized seasonal exchange rates and because it made foreign exchange cheaper, it must have facilitated the inflow of imports. And yet Baer, following Dorival Teixeira Vieira, states that industry profited because it enabled manufacturers to acquire machinery, instruments, and raw materials more cheaply.[8]

There is less ambiguity in the position adopted by most historians concerning the other sort of shock mentioned by Baer: the outbreak of

[7] *Industrialization and Economic Development in Brazil*, p. 15.

[8] *Ibid.*, p. 16; Law 1575, December 6, 1906; Dorival Teixeira Vieira, "The Industrialization of Brazil," in T. Lynn Smith, ed., *Brazil, Portrait of Half a Continent*, p. 249–250.

TABLE VI-1. Commercial Balance of Brazil, 1904–1918

	Exports (thousands of contos)	Imports (thousands of contos)	Net (thousands of contos)	Net (thousands of pounds)
1904–1908	3,827	2,678	+1,149	+70,739
1909–1913	5,058	4,056	+1,002	+68,733
1914–1918	5,262	3,779	+1,583	+79,400

SOURCE: *O Brasil em números*, p. 84. Trade balance in pounds sterling derived from exchange rates listed *ibid.*, p. 146.

war in the industrialized world. In such a case the flow of manufactured goods would be considerably reduced, while exports, it may be presumed, would remain high and therefore so would demand. War in the advanced countries would consequently present an opportunity readily seized upon by local manufacturers. Roberto Simonsen expounded this view in a brief survey on Brazilian industry published in 1939. Although he traced the beginning of Brazilian industry to an earlier period, he stated that the war accelerated development, provided "an added impulse," and "called forth great diversification in the manufacture of new products." Later writers have accepted these views. Caio Prado further defined the mechanism by pointing to a decline in the exchange rate as well as to a decline in imports. Baer, Teixeira Vieira, Fernando Henrique Cardoso, and Nícia Vilela Luz, relying mainly on proofs furnished by Simonsen, have all concurred in his thesis.[9]

Indeed, the balance in favor of exports did increase during the war, as compared with the five previous years, but not spectacularly (see Table VI-1). The gain in sterling, a more revealing indicator than milreis, amounted to 15.5 per cent. The government, furthermore,

[9] Roberto Simonsen, *Brazil's Industrial Evolution*, pp. 25, 30, 36; Caio Prado, *Historia econômica do Brasil*, p. 267; Fernando Henrique Cardoso, "A estrutura da indústria de São Paulo," *Educação e Ciências Sociais* (February 1960), p. 39; Nícia Vilela Luz, *A luta pela industrialização do Brasil*, p. 145.

TABLE VI-2. **Brazil's Terms of Trade, 1905–1919**

	Quantum of Imports	Capacity to Import	Terms of Trade
1905–1909	100	100	100
1910–1914	136	111	130
1915–1919	60	60	60

SOURCE: Adapted from Comissão Mista Brasil–Estados Unidos para Desenvolvimento Econômico, *Relatório geral*, I, 95.

relaxed its hold somewhat on foreign exchange during the war because it was able to fund its loans just before the outbreak, thereby reducing the yearly charges of amortization and interest; and after 1914 it was unable to contract any new loans. Annual costs of amortization and interest, nearly £64,000 between 1909 and 1913, fell to an average £47,000 during the war. The Brazilian economy, therefore, generated about $135,000,000 more in effective demand during the war years than it had from 1909 to 1913.

More striking than the increasing gap in the values of exports and imports was the reversal suffered in the terms of trade. Although sugar, hides, cocoa, and rubber all became more costly for the allies, coffee declined and the prices of Brazil's principal imports—wheat and wheat flour, petroleum and kerosene, coal, salt codfish, and iron sheets and bars—all increased enormously (see Table VI-2). Transportation from 1909 to 1913 represented 14.7 per cent of the delivered value; between 1914 and 1918 it represented 21.3 per cent.[10]

As the war became more widespread and total, the terms of trade continued to deteriorate and the quantities of goods imported continued to decline. Until the United States entered the war, Brazil's overseas trade did not greatly suffer. The United States bought the major part of Brazil's exports and provided many of the manufactured goods previously obtained from Europe. Trade with the European neutral countries also increased, partly because German exporters were

[10] *O Brasil em números*, pp. 87–93.

TABLE VI-3. **Imports via the Port of Santos, 1909–1918**
(thousands of metric tons)

	1909–1913	1914–1918	Decline (%)
Food products	1,008	943	6
Paper and paper products	48	45	6
Chemicals and pharmaceuticals	58	33	43
Cotton textiles	13	5	62
Iron and steel	98	33	66
Iron and steel products	536	148	70
Machinery	136	37	73

SOURCE: São Paulo (state), *Anuario estatistico de São Paulo*, 1909 to 1919.

setting up fronts in Sweden and Denmark. The year 1917 marked the beginning of real crisis. In March the British banned all imports of coffee for lack of shipping facilities and began to restrict the amount of cargo space Brazilian exports might occupy in its freighters, lest any goods find their way to the Central Powers. The entrance into the war of the United States in April reduced Brazil's trading possibilities sharply. Finally Brazil revoked its neutrality in June and declared war in October.[11]

It is evident from the foregoing statistics that during the war, as Baer has asserted, supplies from overseas were interrupted. Whether this represented a "great opportunity for Brazilian infant industries" is another matter. First of all, it is necessary to mention another aspect of the disruption of trade: the importation of capital goods and of raw materials was far more sharply reduced than the importation of consumer goods, consisting mostly of foodstuffs. This can be observed through trade statistics of the port of Santos (see Table VI-3).

The percentage of decline in imports correlates very closely with the degree to which the import category contained capital goods. Although cotton textiles appears to be an exception, imports in this category

[11] Percy A. Martin, *Latin America and the war*, pp. 39, 54, 66–67.

TABLE VI-4. Industrial Production of São Paulo

	Number of Firms	Capital (contos)	Value of Production (contos)	Number of Workers
1907	326	127,702	118,087	24,186
1920	4,154	537,817	986,110	83,998

Sources: Centro Industrial do Brasil, Commissão d'Expansão Economica do Brasil, *O Brasil*, III; Census, 1920, V, 1ª, 139.

obviously represented only a trifling proportion of the market for textiles in São Paulo. The challenge to industry posed by World War I, therefore, seems to have consisted mainly in the maintenance of equipment and production rather than in the expansion of domestic outlets.

Since the exclusion of imports from São Paulo hardly affected the market for the sort of goods Paulista manufacturers were producing, how can it be supposed that these manufacturers benefited thereby? The assertion that industrialization nevertheless did proceed very rapidly is derived principally from three sets of statistics: the industrial censuses of 1907 and 1920, tax receipts on certain excised products, and various surveys made at the request of federal and state governmental agencies during the war to gauge the ability of domestic producers to lessen shortages of supply.[12]

The census reports do indeed show a very rapid increase in production (see Table VI-4). The interval between the two censuses, however, also includes six prewar and two postwar years. How can it be known for certain that the greatest increase occurred during the war? Tax returns and wartime surveys seem, at first glance, to support such a belief. Simonsen, employing this data, produced a table displaying industrial production as a series of index numbers (reproduced as Table VI-5), and other writers have optimistically evaluated increases in production during the war years by employing portions of

[12] Luz, *A luta*, p. 145.

the same data. Nícia Vilela Luz, for example, cites the increase in production of cotton goods, hats, and shoes, all to be found in excise revenue records.

All of these statistical series, however, have grave defects and when corrected tend to show a considerably slower rate of industrial growth. The census of 1907, it must be noted first of all, was not a genuine census but a survey undertaken by a private organization. In its introduction to the published data, the Centro Industrial goes to considerable lengths to demonstrate its incompleteness and, on the basis of comparisons with tax data, suggests that the total "value produced" should be increased by 25 per cent for Rio de Janeiro. Perhaps it should have been increased still more, since the amount collected by the fisc could not possibly represent the total value either. The data collected at long distance from Rio were still less complete. São Paulo's larger firms in sugar refining, nails, copper and tin plating, railroad equipment, and enamelware were entirely absent from the list, although they had appeared in earlier surveys. Other branches of industry were quite inadequately canvassed, and larger towns like Ribeirão Prêto were represented

TABLE VI-5. **Index Numbers of Cost of Living and of Industrial Production**

	Cost of Living	Industrial Production (São Paulo)	
		Nominal	Weighted
1914	100	100	100
1915	108.5	129	119
1916	116.5	169	145
1917	128.3	264	206
1918	144.1	262	181
1919	148.8	335	226
1920	163.8	336	206

SOURCES: Roberto Simonsen, *Brazil's Industrial Evolution*, p. 37. The cost of living index was produced by the Ministério da Fazenda; an analysis may be found in P. Walle, *Au pays de l'or rouge*, p. 75, and *Retrospecto Commercial* (1919), p. 83.

by a handful of firms. The census of 1920 reported 727 firms in São Paulo founded before 1905 and still existing in 1920.[13]

Finally, the survey is biased in favor of larger firms, and this has led to further confusion in interpreting the impact of the war. The average number of workers per firm in São Paulo, as recorded in all census since 1920, has varied between nineteen and twenty-one. In the 1907 survey the average is seventy-nine. Most writers have ignored the incompleteness of the survey and assumed that small and medium-sized businesses in São Paulo must have begun during World War I. Taking into consideration both the disclaimers of the survey organizers and the many omissions listed above, this appears to be an inadmissable conclusion. If an adjustment is made only for the last-mentioned bias, the size of the Paulista industrial plant will be seen to have been considerably larger in 1907, and the concept of the *surtos industriáis*, or industrial surges, will thereby be appreciably diluted.[14]

Assuming that the average size of the uncounted businesses was five workers, the true figures for the Paulista survey would have been about 1,500 establishments and 30,000 workers. Assuming further that the productivity of the smaller firms was as high as that of the larger firms (as it appears to be in the 1920 census), this would increase the "value produced" by one-third, to 155,000 contos.

The calculations made by Simonsen for the war years also require considerable correction (see Table VI-6). Three principal objections may be raised. First, the use of 1914 as a base year exaggerates the real rate of growth. Business was quite slow during the first months of the war; there was a moratorium in effect until January 1915; and 1914 was therefore a year of recession. The use of 1913 or of 1910 to 1913 would have produced a substantially different result. Second, the absence of data on value added by manufacturing may lead to a distorted estimate of industrial growth. The data on exports and imports show clearly that the raw materials, fuels, and machinery needed by industry rose to about four times their prewar prices. Even local cotton, diverted

[13] Centro Industrial do Brasil, *O Brasil*, III, 372–375; Census, 1920, V, 1ª, 160–161.

[14] Paulo R. Pestana, "As nossas industrias durante a guerra," *Revista de Commercio e Industria* (November 1918), pp. 387–388.

TABLE VI-6. **Trade Balance: Rio de Janeiro and São Paulo Compared, 1912–1913** (contos)

	Exports	Imports	Net
Port of Rio (1912)	158,919	371,295	−213,376
Port of Santos (1912)	530,135	248,698	281,447
Port of Rio (1913)	119,508	392,329	−272,821
Port of Santos (1913)	490,279	273,103	271,176

SOURCE: *Retrospecto Commercial*, 1914, plate 27.

by overseas demand and in short supply for local mills, increased from about 900 milreis per ton in 1914–1915 to 3,700 per ton in 1918. Furthermore, excise and stamp taxes more than doubled during the war years. It cannot be assumed that value added by manufacturing increased from 1914 to 1919 at the same rate as sales; the costs of manufacturers were obviously rising faster than the cost of living.[15]

Third, Simonsen's use of cost-of-living data to deflate values is improper, because the index he employed was inaccurate and unrelated to the increase in the prices of manufactured goods. Especially misleading is the avoidance, in the index, of the use of imported products. The enormous consumption of imported wheat and wheat flour, salt codfish, and kerosene is quite definitely underrepresented. Furthermore, it is entirely possible that the index was deliberately unrepresentative, even fraudulent. The inflationary policy of the government, the shortages caused by the war, the attempts at fixing price ceilings, and lagging wage levels all gave rise to considerable social unrest. The fact that the Ministry of the Treasury thought it worth while to compile such an index was evidence of its concern over a situation probably considerably more inflationary than the index reveals. Second, since industry was more dependent on imports than was the average consumer, and because imports increased more steeply in price than domestic goods, it follows that a cost-of-living index compiled for

[15] Paulo R. Pestana, "As industrias manufactureiras . . .," pp. 147–148.

consumers underrates the degree of inflation in the prices of manufactured products. A comparison of production and "value" is possible
in the case of cotton textiles. Between 1914 and 1917 production rose
from 70,000,000 to 160,000,000 meters (one of the few great advances during the war), while the value of production rose from
35,000 to 184,000 contos. The apparent increase in value of 525 per
cent must in this case be deflated by a factor of about 230, not 128.3
as Simsonsen shows for 1917.[16]

Even if full weight is given to these possible adjustments in the
available statistical series, it still would not be proper to conclude that
there was no advance at all in industrial production during the war
years. Almost no new electrical capacity was installed and only a very
few new mills were built; therefore whatever increases occurred were
achieved mainly by running existing machinery longer hours or in
handicraft production. Yet even this sort of increase would appear
anomalous if the thesis of this chapter—that industry expanded because
the export trade grew—is correct. After all, the coffee trade declined
drastically from 1915 to 1918, both because of the war and because of
a severe frost that occurred in 1918.[17]

If each instance of increased industrial activity is examined, however, it can be seen that there is no paradox. Domestic manufacturing
did not gird itself to supply a ravenous internal market; instead, almost all the new capacity and most of the increased production occurred in sectors of industry which were diverting their output to
exportation. The composition of São Paulo's exports changed as the
Allies reduced their intake of nonessentials such as coffee but increased
their purchases of meat, cereals, beans, sugar, and other basic sources
of calories and protein. There was, as we have seen, no decline in the
value of Brazil's exports during the war as compared with the five
preceding years. Most of the new exports were agricultural; indeed,
quite a few of them were subtracted from the supply available to the

[16] Paul Walle, *Au pays de l'or rouge*, p. 234; Roberto Simonsen, *A margem
da profissão*, p. 73; *A Gazeta* (May 1917).

[17] *Anuario estatistico de São Paulo* (1917, 1918); E. Lloyd Rolfe, *Brazil's
Trade and Industry* Report on in 1918, p. 53.

city masses and were not at all the result of increased production. Some of these agricultural commodities, however, required a certain amount of processing prior to shipment, hence the installation of new plants for beef canning and refrigerating and for sugar grinding and refining, which constituted almost all the new capital invested in food processing. Meat packing especially intrigued the planters because it offered a means of valorizing lands beyond or behind the coffee frontier. The first ton of frozen meat was exported by a plant at Barretos in 1914, and by 1918 there were three more plants that shipped a total of 32,000 tons. The early promise of the packing business was not fulfilled, however. In the postwar period only the plants in Rio Grande do Sul managed to compete with the far better organized trade of Argentina.

Another product that came to be exported was cotton textiles. The markets of Argentina and South Africa were quite dependent on Europe for cloth, and São Paulo supplied them as long as the war lasted. A comparison of export and production figures suggests, however, that a considerable part of the overseas sales, like those in cereals and beans, was achieved by diverting domestic supplies. Tax receipts (once more underestimating true values) for 1916 and 1917 show only 97,800 and 183,800 contos worth of cotton textiles produced in São Paulo. Indeed, by the middle of 1918 the government was threatening to restrict exports of cotton cloth.

There was one other sort of new market exploited by Paulista industry during the war, in a sense internal but for São Paulo really another external market: that of Rio de Janeiro and its hinterland. The city of Rio, like the capital of São Paulo, was the distribution center for a vast area of the interior. It included Rio state and the bulk of Minas Gerais, then the most populous state of the federation. But the Rio market was dependent on imports to a much greater extent than São Paulo. Rio imported more than it exported and required federal taxes and foreign loans to cover the difference. When war came Rio was more exposed than São Paulo to the shortages of transport and the interruption of trade (see Table VI-6). Furthermore, the industrial park of Rio seems not to have had as much excess capacity at the start of the war as São Paulo. Consequently, in lines like textiles it could not expand very much. The diffusion of Paulista goods into this wider market can be observed in statistics of shipments via the Central railroad and via coastal steamers from Santos (see Table VI-7). The value of freight sent along these two principal routes grew from an average 79,000 contos ($25,000,000) in 1911–1913 to an average 296,000 ($74,000,000) in 1916–1918. For the latter years shipments abroad were only 30 per cent greater than those to other states. The greater part of this new trade consisted of foodstuffs, but manufactured goods were important, with textiles amounting to 35 per cent of the total. It can be said, then, that during the years before 1960 São Paulo was a market at the disposal of Rio, that between 1906 and 1914 São Paulo became independent, and that after 1914 São Paulo began to invade the market of the capital. It might be argued that this progressive development owed less to the circumstances of war than to the prewar installation of new machinery and the increasing size and affluence of the Paulista market.

Another kind of industrial development, indubitably the result of the war, must be mentioned. It is likely that one of the areas of diversification that Simonsen had in mind was metalworking. Scrap metal could be reworked, and foundries required only the simplest of equipment to go into business. Therefore numerous metalworking shops

TABLE VI-7. Exports of São Paulo, 1911–1918 (contos)

	Foreign	Cabotage	Railroads
1911	480,900	20,365	48,615
1912	530,135	20,915	59,878
1913	490,281	26,866	59,822
1914	352,949	24,498	30,922
1915	465,213	48,263	102,797
1916	489,632	59,582	131,177
1917	422,334	69,989	327,563
1918	371,446	84,596	218,083

SOURCE: *Anuario estatístico de São Paulo* (1911 to 1918). Railroad shipments are not available before 1911.

were opened which made parts and entire machines of cast iron for agriculture and other uses. A great deal of their work, however, was the repairing of already existing equipment. Naturally, most of the shops went out of business as soon as the war ended, for the success of the postwar coffee trade made it easy to buy new machines abroad. These small enterprises ought not to be regarded as a further development of industry, however. Repair shops would seem to fall outside Paul Mantoux's definition: "To us handwork in small workshops, by workmen whose individual skill makes up for the deficiencies of their primitive tools, is the exact opposite of the factory system . . ." "The essential characteristic," he says, is "the internal organization and the technical equipment." At any rate, had the war lasted still longer the shops would surely have disappeared totally as the machinery became impossible to repair further.[18]

Nevertheless, not all the companies that originated during the war were engaged merely in repairing machinery, nor did they all disappear at war's end. The Companhia Industrial Martins Barros announced in advertisements in late 1918 that all its repair sections had been enlarged and that they worked "incessantly," but it also reported that at the next industrial exhibition it would show cotton gins and presses of its own manufacture. The English immigrant F. D. Pirie opened a repair shop for elevators early in the war and later went into partnership with Carlos Villares. Sometime after the war they began to make elevators and other kinds of machinery on a large scale.

If all or most of the revisionist arguments presented above are valid, then World War I was not in itself particularly stimulating to Paulista industry. Such a conclusion would give rise to the further question: why has everyone up to now maintained the opposite opinion? In regard to contemporary witnesses who reported to posterity a very rapid increase in industrialization, it might be assumed that they experienced, in the midst of war, a heightened dependence on local resources and felt obliged to survey, exploit, and control them to a far greater extent than in peacetime. The manufacturer ceased to be mar-

---

[18] *Retrospecto Commercial* (1918), pp. 260–261; Paul Mantoux, *The Industrial Revolution in the Eighteenth Century*, p. 29.

ginal and no longer had to decoy the consumer with stolen labels. Domestic production was patriotic. Newspapers, government documents, and trade associations reported with considerable pride the "response" to the challenge of warfare, which in some cases merely represented manufacturers who were reporting their activities for the first time or were fraudulently seeking a subsidy. The first manufacturers' expositions in São Paulo took place during the war, in September 1917 and September 1918. The Commodity Exchange dates from 1917, and the Stock Market was formed in the same year. The first overseas exhibition of Brazilian industrial products took place in Buenos Aires in 1917, sponsored by the government. In other words, industry during the crisis of war is more *visible* than in peacetime.[19]

As for the tendency of later observers to accept the contemporary accounts at face value, it may be suggested that a theory that associates growth with the breakdown of trade is agreeable to nationalistic sentiments because it implies that foreign sources of supply are unreliable and that domestic production is capable of meeting any challenge. Furthermore, such a theory is useful to urban Brazilian intellectuals and bureaucrats because it demonstrates to recalcitrant economic elites the inevitability of industrialization. The writings of Celso Furtado, for example, are laden with this message. Foreigners, on the other hand, find it agreeable to assume that the industrialization of a dependent area like Brazil was the product of circumstance, a temporary phenomenon that could be reversed by peace among the industrial nations and the encouragement of free trade.[20]

Even though total war in the industrialized world did not provoke further industrialization in São Paulo, at least two changes in economic structure did occur which affected local industry strikingly: Paulista entrepreneurs had received credit both from the Central Powers and from the Allies before the war. The difficulties faced by German interests, first in maintaining contact with overseas associates and then in

---

[19] *Jornal do Commercio (São Paulo)* (September 15, 1918); "Villares Four-Part Industrial Empire," *Brazilian Business* (December 1957), pp. 32–36.

[20] One observer who reported differently, however, was Stanley Stein, *The Brazilian Cotton Manufacture*, p. 103: half of all Brazilian cotton machinery in 1950 was pre-1914!

rebuilding their commercial empire after Germany's defeat, meant that
local manufacturers would have to seek alternate sources of finance
among the Allies. Second, the extreme scarcity of certain raw materials
and fuels caused those who had access to them to gain entry into the
industrial sector, which rearranged the pattern of ownership to a considerable degree.

The Brazilian government took action relatively early in the war
against German banks, but much of the coffee trade and much of
industry was so dependent upon their lines of credit that for more than
a year the government limited its reprisals to a prohibition on trading
with the enemy. Finally, betweeen July and November 1918 they were
liquidated. Meanwhile the British and American consulates drew up
Enemy Trading Lists, and the Center of Commerce and Industry of
São Paulo found expelled members thereon. Brazilian firms financed
by the Germans were so important to the local economy and German
money was so crucial to many Brazilian firms that the local consulates
were frequently faced with a dilemma. The Companhia Antarctica
Paulista was owned by the Zerenner-Bülow importing house, which
was financed by the Brasilianische Bank für Deutschland. It brewed
almost all of São Paulo's beer, produced soft drinks and ice, and held
a mortgage on the local glass bottle factory. Mindful of the popular
demonstrations over the cost of living, the consulate urged the Secretary of State not to withhold raw materials from Antarctica lest the city
masses turn against the United States. In the case of the Companhia
Brasileira de Metallurgia, the local vice-consul reported that the two
partners, Arens and Sensaud, had turned over almost all their stock
to the trading firm of Theodor Wille, who had given them in return
a fifteen-year sales contract. The partners, both Brazilians, were unable
to find anyone willing to buy Wille's shares. The consuls also found
many who were willing to inform on competitors for the sake of some
advantage. Lion e Companhia was the object of false rumors concerning its nationality which were circulated by another importer eager to
make off, successful as it turned out, with Lion's agency for a certain
brand of gunpowder.[21]

[21] NA-DS, "Firms of Enemy Nationality in São Paulo, Brazil," enclosure
in Charles Hoover to Secretary of State, July 13, 1917, 763.72112/4379;

It was, of course, a matter of legitimate concern to the Allied governments to block the movement of funds and trade goods to the Central Powers, but they were not immune from the same passions that enflamed would-be dealers in gunpowder, and there was present, therefore, an undercurrent of rivalry, an eye to the postwar world in which the Americans and British, especially, hoped to dominate in trade. By November 1916 the municipality of São Paulo had turned to New York for a loan, an event regarded by the local consul as an opening wedge, and indeed it was followed by further loans in the 1920's. July 1918 marked the first time in twenty-six years that a scheduled American merchant vessel entered the harbor of Rio de Janeiro, and in 1919 the first branch of an American bank was opened. The new meat-packing plants were built with British capital, and the activities of the ill-starred Percival Farquhar, financed by French, British, and American bankers, gained momentum during the war. The American ambassador, Edwin V. Morgan, wrote the Secretary of State in December 1917, half apprehensively, half pugnaciously, that the Allies were engaged in a clandestine commercial war among themselves and that the British and French were determined to regain ground lost to the United States while it was neutral.[22]

In some cases entrepreneurs in São Paulo threatened with the exposure of their German connections responded very resourcefully. Ernesto Diederichsen, connected with the Theodor Wille firm, seems to have employed some Italo-Brazilians to front for him temporarily in his Argos Industrial textile bill, changing the name to "Manufatura Italiana de Tecidos." Another interesting defense was that of Bromberg, Hacker e Companhia, a trading firm which had installed machinery in many Paulista textile mills and vegetable oil plants, thereby acquiring majority interests. Under a directorate led by some of the

Monthly Journal of the British Chamber of Commerce (January 1918), pp. 21–29; *Revista de Commercio e Industria* (January 1918), p. 28; NA-DS, Hoover to Secretary, October 7, 1918, 763.72112A/3916; Robert Keiser to Secretary, February 20, 1918, 763.72112A/748.

[22] RRIAB, Charles Hoover to Secretary of State, November 25, 1916, 832.51/140; NA-DS, Edwin V. Morgan to Secretary, December 12, 1917, 632.119/403.

leading politicians of the conservative wing of the state's Republican Party, including Carlos de Campos and Altino Arantes, a single corporation was formed to contain these plants. Although the new company, Companhia de Industrias Textis, was clearly a makeshift, its political connections served it well; it remained off the black list until the end of August 1918. Diederichsen also had connections. The Rodrigues Alves family, according to an exposé published pseudonymously, fronted for him in his electric company at Rio Claro. Other German immigrants simply migrated to Montevideo or Buenos Aires or waited out the war with a reduced staff.[23]

Examples of the changes in industrial ownership wrought by the shortages of certain raw materials are the sudden fortunes of Antônio Pereira Ignácio and Nicolau Scarpa. Windfall profits in cotton textiles were available only to those manufacturers who could lay hands on a supply of cotton. For the small mills out in the countryside, many of which owned their own fields, this was not a problem. But the large mills in the cities were prey to the cotton ginners, who suddenly attained a very strategic position.

Two who knew best how to coin advantage from these circumstances were Pereira Ignácio and Scarpa, both cotton traders and owners of gins in the Sorocaba region. Antônio Pereira Ignácio was born in the town of Baltar in Portugal, the son of a shoemaker. He emigrated with his father to Sorocaba in 1884, when he was ten years old. He worked at his father's trade for a while, then spent four years in São Paulo and Rio working in importing houses. From 1892 to 1899 he opened general stores in São Manuel do Paraíso and Botucatu, in the Tietê region northwest of Sorocaba. At first he dealt in hides; then he began to accept cotton in payment for his dry goods and cereals. In 1899 he closed the stores and opened cotton gins in Tatuí and Conchas, also in the Tietê cotton region. Within four years Pereira Ignácio had prospered sufficiently to persuade his backer in the gin mill operation, João Reynaldo de Faria, a Rio textile importer, to finance a trip to the

---

[23] JCSP, index; Ivan Subiroff, *A obligarchia paulista*, pp. 13–24, 41–54; Monte Domecq' et Cie., pp. 532–551; NA-DS, Charles Hoover to Secretary of State, August 29, 1918, 763.72112A/3094; Otto Bürger, *Brasilien*, p. 262.

United States to learn the cotton business. He spent two years there, mostly working in cotton mills and cottonseed plants in North Carolina. He returned with purchases paid for by Faria: equipment for a cottonseed oil press, two new gins, seeds, and rice-milling machinery.[24]

The cotton ginning and cottonseed oil business was successful enough to add fourteen more ginning agencies, to buy into a telephone company, and to purchase the Rodovalho cement plant. He also bought a small electric generating station that supplied power for a cotton mill owned by John Kenworthy. Associated with Kenworthy in this mill was Nicolau Scarpa, an immigrant from Salerno who, like Pereira Ignácio, had gone into trade in the Tietê region and begun to deal in cotton. He, too, prospered in the trade. By 1912 his share in the Kenworthy factory had increased to 46 per cent. He set up cotton gins and a soap factory and bought shares in Pereira Ignácio's telephone company.[25]

When war came, Scarpa and Pereira Ignácio found that their ginning capacity defined, in good part, the limits of the cotton supply for mills in Sorocaba and the capital. Furthermore, several of the planters who had been operating cotton mills inefficiently could not depend on coffee to cover the losses and were vulnerable to offers to buy them out. Scarpa and Pereira Ignácio associated with another cotton broker, P. G. Meirelles, and acquired the three mills in the capital owned by the successors of Anhaia and Diogo de Barros. Scarpa bought into and finally took over a planter-owned mill in Sorocaba.[26]

Finally, the partners approached the directors of the Banco União in Sorocaba to ask for a lease on the bank's most important property, the Votorantim mill. The bank was the same one founded by Lacerda Franco in 1890. Originally a bank of emission, it never regained its equilibrium when the right was reclaimed by the federal government.

[24] Monte Domecq' et Cie., pp. 180–186; Empreza Editora, pp. 286–287; *Twentieth Century Impressions of Brazil*, pp. 406, 732; Alfredo Cusano, *Italia d'oltre mare*, pp. 288–290.

[25] JCSP, index.

[26] *Boletim da Directoria de Industria e Commercio* (July 1912), pp. 310–311; *A Gazeta* (May 11, 1917). Charges of conspiracy were aired in the press concerning the sale, *O Estado de São Paulo* (July 22–25, 1917); *Jornal de Commercio (São Paulo)* (August 3, 1917).

In 1917 it was failing. Votorantim was the second mill of São Paulo; only Crespi's, in the capital, was larger. The mill, capitalized at 40,000 contos ($10,000,000), had 55,000 spindles and more than twice the printing capacity of all the other plants in the state combined. Yet it was in great difficulties in the spring of 1917. Workers at the plant were on strike because they had not been paid for three months. The directors of the bank accepted the proposals of the partners for a rental of 1,140 contos ($285,000) a year. This sum was not enough to bail out the bank, and in the following August it went into receivership. In the liquidation of its assets, Scarpa and Pereira Ignácio bought the factory at auction for only 5,000 contos.

The partnership between Scarpa and Pereira Ignácio did not last long. It was said that Scarpa, thinking that his associate had no more reserves he could draw upon, offered to sell him out or buy him out. Pereira immediately said he would buy and obtained the cash from Faria in Rio de Janeiro. Scarpa accepted one of the smaller mills and 2,000 contos for his share and also bought Pereira Ignácio's cottonseed oil plant. Thus in one year the firm of Pereira Ignácio had acquired about 17 per cent of the cotton textile capacity of the state and had 122,000 contos ($30,500,000) in working capital.[27]

In summary, World War I increased considerably the demand for domestic manufactured goods but made it almost impossible to enlarge the productive plant to meet that demand. The fortunes that were made during the war grew out of new lines of exports, twenty-four-hour-a-day production, or out of mergers and reorganizations. New plants and new lines of manufacture were not significant. It might be asked if the industrialization of São Paulo would not have proceeded faster had there been no war.

[27] Aluísio de Almeida, "Biografias sorocabanas," *Revista do Arquivo Municipal* (October 1952), p. 36; Pestana, "As industrias manufactureiras . . .," p. 148.

CHAPTER VII

Growth and the Structure of Industry

From 1900 to 1920 the industrial plant of São Paulo expanded quite rapidly. Even if the assertions concerning the salutary effects of war are discounted, the resurgence of trade during the two years after the war is undeniable and imparted to the census of 1920 a very favorable aspect of development. A rough estimate of this growth may be extracted from data already presented in the preceding chapters, if a few guesses may be permitted to fill out the lacunae (see Table VII-1). The yearly rate of growth would seem to be about 8 per cent. Some of the guesses inserted in this table may be inaccurate; however, they have been framed so that the more likely revisions would result in a greater, rather than a lesser, rate of growth.

The succeeding score of years witnessed a slower rate of industrial development, perhaps no more than half that of 1900 to 1920. The industrial censuses of 1920 and 1940 bracket the later period and provide indicators that are more certain. The raw data seem to demonstrate a very rapid rate of growth in the interwar years, but when corrections are made for population increase and the declining value of the milreis, most of the apparent gain melts away (see Table VII-

TABLE VII-1. Industrial Production per Capita, São Paulo

	(a) Value Produced (contos)	(b) Population (millions)	(c) (a)/(b) (milreis)	(d) Cost-of- Living Index	(e) (c)/(d) (milreis)
1900	(50,000)	2.28	22	(100)	22
1905	110,000	...	...	...	...
1907	(155,000)	(3.30)	47	(100)	47
1910	186,000	...	...	...	...
1915	274,000	...	...	...	...
1920	986,000	4.59	214	(250)	85

SOURCES: (a) See Table VI-4. (b) Census data. Figures in parentheses are author's estimates. (a) 1900: a comparison of the number of plants listed by Bandeira in 1901 (170) with the number probably existing in 1907 suggests that industrial plants had more than tripled in the interval; (b) 1907: an estimate from *Anuario estatístico de São Paulo, 1906 to 1921*; (d) cost-of-living data in Table VI-5, adjusted for probable tendency to minimize real rate of inflation.

TABLE VII-2. Industrial Production per Capita, São Paulo

	(a) Industrial Pro- duction, Value Added (contos)	(b) Population (millions)	(c) (a)/(b) (milreis)	(d) Cost-of- Living Index	(e) (c)/(d) (milreis)
1920	440,366	4.59	96	100	96
1940	2,988,920	7.18	416	200	208

SOURCES: (a) and (b) Censuses of 1920 and 1940. (d) Henry W. Spiegel, *The Brazilian Economy, Chronic Inflation and Sporadic Industrialization*, pp. 97–98. Roberto Simonsen's index compares closely with Spiegel. Note that value added in production, not value produced, has been employed in this table.

2). A per capita output somewhat more than doubled in twenty years is the equivalent of a yearly increase of about 4 per cent. It is probable that the rate of growth fluctuated within this twenty-year period, but no adequate estimates can be drawn for São Paulo out of the widely varying estimates made by Simonsen or other observers. The statistical material published by the state Department of Statistics between 1928 and 1938, by the Department's own admission, was only a partial listing of existing firms.[1]

Those who have regarded World War I as a stimulus to industrialization have, with consistent logic from their point of view, maintained that during the world depression of the 1930's Brazil experienced a period of rapid industrial growth. The same argument is advanced: the reduction in the value of imports stimulated domestic substitutes. If this theory were correct, the curve of manufacturing production would bear an inverse relationship to the curve of imports. Although the manufacturing curve for São Paulo cannot be plotted as neatly as the flow of imports, it seems fairly safe to say that this relationship was positive. The years that witnessed setbacks in imports—1921, 1926, 1930, 1932, and 1938—were also the worst years for manufacturers, while the years of the greatest increase in importation—1923–1925, 1928, 1935, 1936, and 1939—were also very good years for industry. It is likely that for the whole period from 1920 to 1940 manufacturing output progressed fairly steadily with negative rates of growth only in 1926 and in 1930 and 1931. It is true that industry continued to prosper during much of the depression decade, but not because of a crisis in the import trade. In fact, during the 1930's Brazil's capacity to export was considerably greater than it had been during the previous decade because export volume rose faster than prices fell.[2]

[1] Varying estimates given in Roberto Simonsen, *A evolução industrial do Brasil,* Appendix; *Ensaios sociais, políticos e econômicos,* p. 176; Centro das Industrias do Estado de São Paulo, *Relatório* (1929), p. 3; São Paulo (state), Secretaria da Agricultura, Industria e Commercio, Directoria de Estatistica, Industria e Commercio, *Estatistica Industrial do Estado de São Paulo* (1930), p. 4.

[2] Comissão Mista, I, 95–97; Celso Furtado, *Diagnosis of the Brazilian Crisis,* p. 101.

No very pronounced transformation in the structure of Paulista industry is to be observed during these two decades. Although very greatly increased production can be pointed out for a few sectors in the 1930's, especially cotton textiles, cement, and pig iron, it must be noted that cotton textiles were no longer an innovation and that most of the capacity for all three had already been installed by 1929. Baer, although he supports Furtado's thesis, has compared the structure of the work force in 1920 and 1940 and discovered that industrial occupations rose only slightly—from 13 to 14 per cent of the total—in the interval. Apparently taken aback, he surmised that productivity had risen much faster, adducing a priori as causes the fuller employment of depression-created idle capacity and the greater efficiency of newly installed plants. However, the same censuses, if corrected for the decline in the milreis, seem to show that productivity increased by a mere 4 per cent in twenty years (see Table VII-3). Other sources, including Simonsen,

TABLE VII-3. **Productivity per Worker, São Paulo**

	(a) Value Added (contos)	(b) Work Force	(c) (a)/(b) (milreis)	(d) Cost-of- Living Index	(e) (c)/(d)
1920	440,366	83,998	5,240	100	5,240
1940	2,988,920	272,865	10,950	200	5,475

SOURCES: (a) and (b) Censuses of 1920 and 1940. (d) See Table VII-2, column (d).

have pointed out that real wages remained at the same level between 1920 and 1940, which would lend support to the conclusion to be derived from the census. It should also be noted that mechanization proceeded very slowly during this period. The average Paulista worker used only 1.2 horsepower in 1920 and only 1.6 horsepower in 1940.[3]

[3] Werner Baer, *Industrialization*, pp. 18, 20–24. Carlos Paláez has written a criticism, extremely well argued and supported, of the theory that the trade

One indicator seems to contradict this pattern of slow development in the interwar years. The number of workers in manufacturing seems to have grown faster from 1920 to 1940 than the general population or industrial production per capita, and indeed the rate seems to be fastest during the depth of the depression. A report on economic conditions by the governor of São Paulo alleged an increase from 1932 to 1935 almost as great as that of the preceding twelve years. However, it is likely that this seemingly disproportionate increase in the size of the work force is due in large measure to the effective enforcement, during the early part of the Vargas regime, of a labor law which required all workers to register with the government and to carry identity cards. Two kinds of evidence support this hypothesis. First, the governor accompanied his report with statistics that show an unaccountable rise in the number of workers per firm, up to 27.5 in 1935, although he paradoxically asserts that the increase in the work force is due to the multiplication of craft shops. Second, it appears that the employers wholeheartedly supported registration of the workers, because they had long advocated it as a means of identifying union organizers. If this hypothesis is true, then it follows that the work force in the 1920's was really somewhat larger than revealed in census data, and it would then follow that productivity did increase slightly between 1920 and 1940. This is a more plausible eventuality than the complete stagnation observed in the census data.[4]

Even though it can be demonstrated that the growth of industry was slow in São Paulo between the wars, thereby largely invalidating the attempts of Furtado and Baer to explain why Paulista industry grew rapidly, their reasoning might still be employed to explain how it managed to get along as well as it did. Why, in view of the decline of world trade and the painfully slow development of European and American markets, was there no industrial depression in Brazil? Wasn't industrial growth hampered by the poor demand from the agricultural sector? Svennilson's study of the European economy between the wars suggests that there are no anomalies to be explained,

---

depression caused growth: "A balança comercial, a grande depressão, e a industrialização, *Revista Brasileira de Economia* (March 1968), pp. 15–47.

[4] Armando Salles Oliveira, *Jornada democrática*, p. 53.

because Brazil's relatively slight indisposition during the depression of the 1930's closely parallels the experience of those European nations whose economies were only partially industrialized and who participated in international trade mainly as agricultural exporters. These countries, in contrast to their heavily industrialized neighbors, did not experience a very severe recession and managed to resume higher levels of production at an earlier date.[5]

Diversification did not cease in São Paulo in spite of the limited amount of growth. It will be useful to indicate where new investments were made during the period in order to see how the structure of industry was changing. The most important addition to overhead was a new hydroelectric station built by the São Paulo Traction, Light and Power Company at Cubatão, near Santos. Several small rivers were backed up and then sent plunging down the coastal palisade to generators that developed 200,000 horsepower. A secular transportation problem had become in a newer age of technology a very great asset. Little improvement, on the other hand, was brought to transportation; railroad building was very slow until the late 1930's, and there were only 3,189 kilometers of improved road in São Paulo as late as 1933, almost none of it paved.

Besides the new plants producing pig iron and cement, the Paulistas began to manufacture electrical hardware, electric motors, textile machinery, sugar-processing equipment, automobile parts, accessories, and tools, agricultural implements, gas appliances, timekeeping and weighing devices, and rayon textiles. Existing sectors of industry continued to grow, even the meat-packing plants, which began to serve the domestic market.

The capital for these new factories came partly from the same sources as before. Although foreign capital continued to flow into the country during most of the years from 1920 to 1940, it did not represent as large a share of venture capital for industry as it had during the two previous decades. British investments in Brazil worth about £110,000,000 in 1923 expanded significantly only in matches and

[5] Ingvar Svennilson, *Growth and Stagnation in the European Economy*, p. 214.

tobacco and seem to have remained almost stationary from 1929 onward. American manufacturing investment was worth $45,000,000 in
1933. American producers of vehicles and machinery, notably Ford
and General Motors, began the assembly of their products from imported parts principally because knocked-down equipment was cheaper
to transport and because marketing decisions like color and body style
were easier to accommodate locally. Anderson Clayton and Corn Products Refining Company began to process food products. Some investment was made by Europeans in pharmaceuticals and rubber products
and by Canadians, in cement.[6]

All these investments were direct; no new cases of indirect investment were found for these years, although a few instances of the
recession of portfolio investments can be traced. Various companies—
for example, Votorantim and the Companhia Nacional de Estamparia
—managed to pay off large mortgages contracted in London before the
war. The Clark shoe manufacturing company, incorporated in 1903
in Edinburgh, had invested £25,000 in Brazil. Twenty years later the
company liquidated holdings in Rio and São Paulo worth £200,000,
apparently in favor of a group of English immigrants. The Brasital
(Dell'Acqua) Textile Company, Rawlinson-Müller, the City of São
Paulo Improvements and Freehold Land Company, the Barretos packing plant, and numerous others all became more Brazilian in ownership
as the interest of foreign backers waned and local entrepreneurs
bought them out. Two of the major new plants constructed during the
1920's with foreign money, the Perús cement plant and Votorantim's
rayon plant, were wholly renationalized by Brazilian partners before
World War II. It would seem that by the late 1940's a fairly consistent
pattern could be observed: foreign capital tended to recede from those
sectors of industry which had become technologically stabilized. Of
course, from 1929 to 1947 this tendency was superimposed over a

[6] *Wileman's Review* (June 23, 1923); Great Britain, Department of Overseas Trade, *Economic Conditions in Brazil* (1944), p. 14; Dudley Maynard
Phelps, *Migration of Industry to South America*, pp. 20–21, "Anderson Clayton Celebrates 25 Years in Brazil," *Brazilian Business* (January 1960), pp.
24–25.

more general pattern of capital flight to Europe; therefore it may not be a recurrent phenomenon.[7]

Domestic capital, as before, was contributed by both planters and importers. It has been suggested that the planters, disillusioned by the 1930 decline in coffee prices, transferred much of their capital to industry. The planting of new trees was much reduced between 1933 and 1942. It is likely that some planters, just as before, were able to recognize the profit potential inherent in the enlarging markets and were able to employ their political influence to advantage in obtaining the necessary government support, but it should be noted that the shift from coffee was not sudden. Production was steady through 1940. Furthermore, other opportunities besides coffee or industrial investment were open to planters. During most of the interwar period a great expansion occurred in the production of cotton for export, and production for the internal market of cattle, rice, sugar, citrus, beans, and corn paralleled the vegetative growth of the population. Other planters seem to have invested in urban real estate and construction, insurance, or trade. Commercial banking continued to be almost entirely the province of the plantation elite. By subdividing some of their older estates or by opening new subdivisions on the "pioneer fringe," while at the same time retaining control of facilities for credit, marketing, and transportation, still other planters probably made as great a profit as before, even though they had alienated some of their land holdings. Nevertheless, the emergence of several large enterprises in railroad equipment and heavy machinery was due to transfers from agriculture. Smaller investments were made in textiles, ceramics, and iron and steel in the 1920's and in textiles, metal fabrication, and iron in the 1930's.[8]

Importers were less involved in the development of industry in the 1920's and 1930's, although the pattern of distribution remained much the same as before. Even the largest manufacturers continued to market

[7] JCSP, files.

[8] *Boletim do Ministério das Relações Exteriores* (June 1943), p. 369, shows coffee trees, 1920 to 1944. Geraldo Banas, *Nos bastidores do setor bancário; Boletim da Directoria de Industria e Commercio* (January–February 1927), p. 7; JCSP, files. See also Paláez, "A balança comercial . . .," pp. 43–47.

their goods through importers, who then sold to wholesalers. This arrangement certainly added to the costs of distribution, but was necessary because the importers were still advancing short-term credit to the manufacturers. In textiles only a few mills managed to break free of the importers by the 1940's. Stanley Stein mentions Lundgren, a northern manufacturer who developed his own retail chain, and a couple of the smaller mills. There is some evidence that Matarazzo had not made any move in this direction by the mid-1930's, but that Votorantim had broken with Afonso Vizeu, the Rio importer. At least three of the larger mercantile companies transferred capital into fabrication during the 1930's: Lion, Dias Martins, and Theodor Wille.[9]

It is likely that the investments of planters and importers were less important to the growth of industry during this period than reinvestment by industrialists. The modest cotton mills constructed by planters in the interior, for example, did not cause any significant redistribution of markets, because the mills of the capital were increasing their capacity still more rapidly. The phenomenon of integration, already noted, continued, and the established industrialists entered more aggressively into new fields of production. Jafet, Votorantim, and Siciliano started to produce iron and steel; Matarazzo and Votorantim both built rayon factories; Villares expanded from elevators into basic metals and machine tools. Matarazzo also began sugar grinding and cottonseed oil pressing. It appears that a number of the larger industrialists transferred some of their profits out of industry. Sizable investments were made by the Jafets, Klabins, Cicero Prado, and Pereira Ignácio in new subdivisions of São Paulo: Votorantim, for example, owned 1,400,000 square meters in Brooklyn Paulista.[10]

From this description it can be seen that no rapid accumulation of industrial capital occurred in the interwar period. It seems probable

---

[9] Henri van Deursen, "L'Émancipation industrielle du Brésil," *Revue Economique Internationale* (August 1934), pp. 287–288, 320; Stanley Stein, *The Brazilian Cotton Manufacture*, p. 120; Fernand Maurette, *Alguns aspectos sociais do desenvolvimento actual e futuro da economia brasileira*, p. 35; Raul Carvalho Bastos, *Homens e fatos do meu tempo*, p. 325.

[10] JCSP; *O Estado de São Paulo* (January 13, 1929; June 28, 1921) for real estate advertising.

that the stagnation of the coffee trade restrained new investment by planters and importers and indirectly held back the industrialists by cutting off their credit from importers and foreign bankers. The relative decline in foreign investment was obviously related to the breakdown of world trade patterns. In the long run the most significant additions to the Paulista industrial plant may have been the small shops that began to appear in technically advanced sectors of industry, such as electrical equipment, machine tools, plastics, and automobile parts. From the point of view of accumulated capital these firms would not have appeared to be important before 1940, but from the point of view of the eventual transformation of the structure of industry they were indeed important. A list was made of all the firms in São Paulo in one of these lines of production, machinery, which were founded between 1920 and 1940 and which employed more than one hundred workers by 1961 (see Table VII-4). Transfers of capital from other sectors were substantial in fewer than half of the total of thirty-seven firms. The rest seem to have financed themselves out of profits.

TABLE VII-4. **Firms with More Than 100 Workers,**
          Producing Machinery, São Paulo, 1961–1963,
          and Founded between 1920 and 1940

Firm	Date Founded	Capital Sources
Ribeiro	1920	
Industria Brasileira de Artefatos de Ferro	1920	
Dedini-Ometto	1920	Transfer-planter (in part)
Andrighetti	1922	
Lorenzetti	1923	
Fichet–Schwartz Haumont	1923	Foreign direct
Pugliese, Irmãos	1923	
Philips	1924	
Masiero	1924	
Nardini	1924	

TABLE VII-4 (*Continued*)

Firm	Date Founded	Capital Sources
Itaúna	1925	Transfer-planter
Tecelagem São Paulo	1925	
Martins Ferreira	1925	
Zaccaria	1925	
Fiel	1926	Transfer-importing
International Harvester	1926	Foreign direct
Fundição Brasil	1927	
SOMA	1929	Transfer-planter
Brasil–Motores Elétricos	1930	
Tupy, Artefatos de Aço	1933	Foreign direct
Hora	1933	
Anel	1935	
Forest	1935	
Piratininga	1935	Transfer-planter
Ferro-Enamel	1935	Foreign direct
Zauli	1936	
Honneger	1936	
Pignatari	1936	Transfer-industry
Barra Mansa	1937	Transfer-industry
Nossa Senhora de Aparecida	1937	Transfer-planter
Hero	1938	Transfer-importing
Cardobrasil	1938	Transfer-planter
Pontal, Material Rodante	1938	Transfer-importing
Romi	1938	
Villares	1939	Transfer-industry
Walita	1939	
Arno	1940	Transfer-importing (in part)
Arbame	1940	Foreign direct

SOURCES: *Anuário Banas: A indústria de material elétrico e eletrónico, 1961*; *Anuário Banas: A indústria brasileira de máquinas, 1962*; *Anuário Banas: máquinas e ferramentas, 1963*; São Paulo (state), *Estatística Industrial do Estado de S. Paulo, 1930*, pp. 79–83. Ownership information from JCSP.

The origins of this new group of entrepreneurs are in most cases obscure; however, if a generalization can be extended from a few cases, it appears that they were generally town-bred members of the lower fringes of the middle class, most often first or second generation immigrants who had obtained technical training of sorts. Américo Emílio Romi was born in the interior town of São José do Rio Pardo, the son of a machinist and trader who took his family back to Italy before World War I. The young Romi worked for Brown-Boveri in Milan and returned to São Paulo in 1924. He operated repair shops, worked for Chevrolet and Alfa-Romeo dealers, and finally opened an agricultural implement factory in 1933. During the war he began to produce lathes. Paulo Andrighetti, a graduate of a technical high school in São Paulo, began a repair shop in 1922 and made salt milling machinery on the side. After becoming expert in the repair of textile machinery, he began to produce it himself in the 1930's. Mario Dedini emigrated to Brazil from Lendinaria, near Padua, and became a mechanic for a sugar-grinding mill. By 1915 he was managing the Santa Bárbara mill. In 1920 he left this job to open a machine repair shop in the nearby town of Piracicaba. In 1930 he employed about forty workers; by 1942 he was employing between seventy-five and one hundred. Increasingly he specialized in the repair and finally in the production of sugar mill equipment.[11]

Two striking characteristics of Paulista industry must be pointed out which possibly explain its slow growth in the 1920's and 1930's: the absence of any tendency toward concentration and the organization of cartels and other price- and production-controlling associations. A comparison of the censuses of 1920 and 1940 may understate the degree of concentration (see Table VII-5), because the earlier census does not clearly define the term "establishment," and it may be that the term "firm" in the later census does not define the real status of ownership. The largest companies owned establishments in varied

---

[11] *Visão* (August 11, 1961), pp. 20–23; "Maquinas para tecelagem," *Revista Paulista de Indústria* (September 1955), pp. 8–21; Lawrence W. Witt, "Brazilian Business Families," *American Universities Field Staff Reports*, East Coast South America Series (November 21, 1952); *Quem é quem no Brasil* (1963).

TABLE VII-5. Size of Firms, São Paulo

	(a) Number	(b) Work Force	(c) (b)/(a)	(d) Value Added (contos)	(e) (d)/(a) (contos)	(f) (d)/(a) (1920 contos)
1920 (establish- ments)	4,154	83,998	21	440,366	106	106
1940 (establish- ments)	14,225	272,865	19	2,988,920	209	105
1940 (firms)	11,588	272,865	24	2,988,920	258	129

SOURCES: (a) to (e) Censuses of 1920 and 1940. (f) see Table VII-2, column (d).

areas of production, and even the smaller entrepreneurs—according to the apparently well-informed author of a pamphlet advising Jewish refugee businessmen on relocation in Brazil—commonly owned four or five shops unconnected except for a central sales office. It should also be noticed that industry in most of the rest of Brazil suffered a remarkable decline in concentration during this period. The number of workers per establishment in Rio de Janeiro (Guanabara state) and in the state of Rio de Janeiro, taken together, declined from thirty-eight to twenty-six and in Brazil as a whole, from twenty-two to sixteen.[12]

Even if a full measure of caution is granted to these strictures, the apparent lack of concentration in Paulista industry has been remarkable and therefore the subject of some speculation. Two sorts of explanations are offered: those that account for the ability of small firms to survive and those that account for the inability of larger and medium-sized firms to fuse.

The first kind of explanation includes high transportation costs, tax

[12] Herbert Frankenstein, *Brasilien als Aufnahmeland der jüdischen Auswanderung aus Deutschland*, p. 13.

evasion and other sorts of illegalities by the smaller units, and monopolistic price-setting policies on the part of the larger firms. Transportation costs may partly explain the survival of the smaller firms in the interior, indeed of primitive crafts: observers found homespun cotton cloth being produced in Minas Gerais in the 1920's. But they cannot account for the very common coexistence of large and small shops in the cities. O. Pupo Nogueira, who in his position as secretary of the textile manufacturers' association represented the larger producers, claimed that the smallest units survived because they used inferior materials and evaded taxes and labor regulations. However, shoddy workmanship would surely have obliged them to sell for lower, and presumably unprofitable, prices. Illegalities seem to have been no more a forte of the craft shops than the factories; even though the latter were more easily observed, they could also more readily employ lawyers, accountants, and politicians to screen their operations. The price policies of the largest manufacturers, therefore, would seem to be a more valid explanation for the burgeoning underbrush of craft shops. A recent analysis of the problems of economic development in Latin America refers to a "tacit dividing-up of the market." However, it cannot be assumed that the factories really possessed greater margins for profit than the craft shops. As in Europe, the largest firms in São Paulo between the wars seemed to be not very much more productive than the smallest. In 1940 corporations produced 50 per cent more per worker than individually owned firms (see Table VII-6), not an impressive difference, considering the greater outlays for administration, distribution, and the amortization of equipment which would have to be made by the larger plants.[13]

The lack of any tendency toward fusion on the part of larger and medium-sized firms is possibly related, it has also been suggested, to

---

[13] Simonsen, *A Evolução industrial*, p. 28; Preston E. James, "Industrial Development in São Paulo State, Brazil," *Economic Geography* (July 1935), pp. 258–266; Arno S. Pearse, *Brazilian Cotton*, p. 25; O. Pupo Nogueira, "Em Torno de uma estatistica industrial," *Observador Economico e Financeiro* (January 1937), p. 20; van Deursen, "L'Émancipation industrielle . . .," p. 284; United Nations, Economic Commission for Latin America, *Problemas y perspectivas del desarrollo industrial latinoamericano*, pp. 14–15.

TABLE VII-6. Productivity of Industrial Firms, São Paulo, 1940

	(a) Number	(b) Work Force	(c) (b)/(a)	(d) Value Added (contos)	(e) (d)/(b) (milreis)
Individual Firms	7,721	52,808	6	447,355	8,460
Corporations	1,255	170,526	135	2,076,126	12,760

SOURCE: Census, 1940. "Corporations" include a few cooperatives.

the perpetuation of family ownership. Even though the corporate form was often adopted, it masked in almost every case a family-owned company. Few of these companies sold even minority interests to the public. The few private sales registered in the stock markets of São Paulo and Rio usually marked transfers within the family circle. Management of the company was entrusted to relatives, preferably sons or sons-in-law; the infrequent outsider in the company management possessed more of the status of family retainer than of employee. If it can be shown that these limitations upon outside sources of capital and upon the introduction of professional managerial assistance were consciously placed upon the firms by the entrepreneurs themselves, this would be evidence that there is a causal connection between attitudes toward ownership and the size of firms.

A monograph by Fernando Henrique Cardoso that employs sociological data gathered since the early 1960's tends to demonstrate that in Brazil these limitations are, in recent times at least, self-imposed. The industrialists he surveyed were "too busy" to think of absorbing other firms and were too proud of the family name to allow their own firm to be merged with others. Their planning methods were largely intuitive. Their enterprises were frequently driven to the wall because their managerial assistants were recruited more for loyalty than competence, while the second generation was frequently incapable of assuming responsibility. Some historical evidence confirms this pessimistic report. The Klabins, it is said, turned over control of the Nitro-Química rayon plant to Votorantim because they lacked enough managerial talent within the family. Family bickering sometimes disrupted the growth of industrial firms. The sons of Pereira Ignácio, feeling cheated out of their rightful control of the firm by José Ermírio de Moraes, who was Pereira Ignácio's son-in-law, decided finally to sell their interests to a third party. The sale was apparently malicious; they passed over a higher bid in order to present Moraes with a personal enemy for a new partner.[14]

It is necessary to recognize, however, that the identification of firm and family patrimony is a universal characteristic of early capitalism; there is no reason to expect the entrepreneur to allow his company to slip from his personal control unless something or someone forces it upon him. In the United States the process of amalgamation was much earlier and more pervasive, probably because of the existence of an enormous market, as Alfred Chandler explains, which at first drove most entrepreneurs to seek refuge in cartelization, then encouraged a brilliant few to create genuine consolidations along functional lines, with a greater degree of specialization than capitalism had ever seen before. In Europe the process was much slower, and in Brazil it is yet to be completed, also for reasons of market size. Until the 1950's the Brazilian national market existed only in a limited sense, partly because interior transport was costly, and because, until the late 1930's, the several states were dependent on interstate tariffs for part of their income.[15]

Therefore, it was possible for a firm to remain in the personal control of a single entrepreneur and his relatives and yet be large enough to maintain an oligopolistic position in the Paulista market. Furthermore, family control was not necessarily unenterprising. Manufacturers often made considerable efforts to train their sons to inherit the business. Matarazzo, Morganti, Moraes, the Klabins, the Jafets, and others insisted on technical or business training for their sons. The intrafamily squabbles were sometimes a symptom that the more competent,

---

[14] *Empresário industrial e desenvolvimento econômico*, pp. 97–108, 115–118; *A Provincial do Pará* (February 10, 1967); R. C. Bastos, *Homens e fatos*, p. 129.

[15] Ross Robertson, *History of the American Economy*, pp. 332–358; Alfred Chandler, "The Beginnings of 'Big Business' in American Industry," *Business History Review* (Spring 1959), pp. 1–31.

or perhaps the more ruthless, of the heirs was taking charge. It is conceivable, nevertheless, that the ideology which justified family capitalism retarded the perception of new opportunities later on. The direct consequences of the patrimonialistic ideology of the entrepreneurs will be considered in another chapter.

Although amalgamation did not occur in Paulista industry, it would be mistaken to assume that there were no attempts at combination. On the contrary, cartels were formed in most of the lines of production that were at all mechanized, and a few firms achieved monopolies in certain kinds of goods. There were, by the mid-1920's, trade associations that probably engaged in price fixing in metallurgy, shoes, leather and hides, lumber, and drugs. There were quite certainly cartels at one time or another in flour milling, paper, hats, jute sacking, and beer. In matches, plate glass, cottonseed oil, sewing thread, beer, meat packing, cement, pig iron, and rayon no more than three firms owned 80 per cent or more of productive capacity. Sugar refining was a logical field for amalgamation, since a refinery could process the output of several grinding mills. The largest refiners, therefore, were partnerships composed of various mill owners.[16]

Only in cotton textiles, of all the major lines of production, was there no cartel established. Probably this circumstance is related to the large number of mills in operation and the too wide variation in their efficiency. Although the Center for Spinning and Weaving Manufacturers of São Paulo (hereafter cited as CIFTSP, after its Portuguese initials) was founded in 1919 partly to "take precautions against possible harmful competition," these "precautions" were apparently never taken. It was suggested to the membership in 1926, 1928, and

[16] Dirceu Lino de Mattos, "O parque industrial paulistano," in Associação dos Geógrafos Brasileiros, Secção Regional de São Paulo, *A cidade de São Paulo*, III, 50–55; "Brazil's Milling Industry," *Brazilian Business* (October 1951), p. 39; Horácio Lafer, "Brazil's Paper Industry," *The Commercial*, Published by the *Manchester Guardian* (June 27, 1929), p. 24; *Twentieth Century Impressions of Brazil*, p. 676; *O Estado de São Paulo* (September 22, 1919); Geraldo Banas, *Relatório industrial: indústria de bebidas*, p. 38; Comissão Americana de Técnicos em Óleos Vegetais, *O Brasil e os óleos vegetais*; Aguinaldo Costa, "Monópolio da indústria e do comercio de vidro," *Revista Brasiliense* (November–December 1955), p. 132.

in 1930 that either production be limited or prices be artificially maintained; in 1926 the motion failed because of the opposition of Matarazzo, who resigned the presidency of the Center in protest. Possibly he believed his plant was more efficient than most of the others; it does not appear that he was opposed to restraint of trade in principle.[17]

Another sort of combination began to be practiced as early as the 1920's among Paulista industrialists: the pooling of capital resources among several families, or the endowment of more distant relatives in order to branch into new lines of production. Thus the paper and pulp and other interests of the Klabins and the Lafers are by now intertwined. Giulio Pignatari, involved in special steels, was a son-in-law of Matarazzo, and another Matarazzo, who appears to have been related, put together a paper combine during World War I. The Klabins were interested along with Pereira Ignácio in the Nitro-Química plant. The Monteiro Carvalho and Souza Aranha interests became merged in engineering and automobile parts companies and in turn merged with Vidigal in a commercial bank.

The sugar mill equipment maker, Mario Dedini, who had only one son, was fortunate enough to have his daughter marry a member of the Ometto family. The Ometto fortune was evidently larger than Dedini's but meshed precisely with his. The former owned a great deal of sugar land in the Piracicaba region and six or seven sugar mills. Dedini's son began to manage the technical end of the business while the Ometto son ran the commercial operations. Another son-in-law operated Dedini's agricultural holdings. The two families, with a certain amount of coordination, began to expand their holdings in sugar. By the late 1940's they were the third- or fourth-largest interest in sugar grinding in São Paulo, with sixteen or seventeen mills, and had equipped the machinery company so that it was capable of building a mill from the ground up. Dedini and the Omettos were willing to finance other entrepreneurs who could supply them or use their by-products; thus they acquired controlling interests in firms that made

[17]CIFTSP, Atas das sessões extraordinarias (October 1, 1919; July 16, 17, 1926); CIFTSP, *A crise textil*, p. 39; CIFTSP, *Circulares* (May 8, 1930).

machine parts, insecticides, fertilizer, transformers, and ceramics, and they also operated an International Harvester agency.[18]

The largest of the family partnerships or clientele combinations, displaying a certain stability and diversification in real estate, trade, and banking, came to be called "groups." They brought together considerable quantities of capital, plant, and political power without the necessity of "going public" or consolidating.

One other continuing characteristic of Paulista industry must be noticed before proceeding to an account of the changing circumstances of the 1920's: to a large degree it remained marginal and somewhat disreputable. The public held the industrialists in disesteem for matters that were not wholly their fault, such as poor quality and high prices, but they also observed many instances of manifest greed and opportunism. Entrepreneurs unfamiliar with cost accounting were even less likely to recognize the value of public relations, so that considerable documentation can be found for a "robber baron" approach to Paulista capitalism. A good deal of this material was produced by aggrieved business partners or journalists who were thwarted blackmailers. Industrialists found themselves on various occasions accused in print of usury, cheating at cards, engaging in businesses reserved by law for nationals, milking government concessions to introduce contraband, bilking shareholders of dividends, and cadging formulas from government analytical laboratories. It is quite likely that entrepreneurs also copied patented products, engaged in dumping, and pirated labels.[19]

Alfredo Montenegro, shadowy frontman for the German-financed Companhia Industrias Textis already mentioned, was once publicly defamed as a bigamist by his codirectors. In return he claimed that

[18] Lawrence F. Witt, "Brazilian Business Families"; *Quem é quem no Brasil* (1963).

[19] A. d'Arti, *L'État de São Paulo*, pp. 132–135, 154, 157–159; *O Estado de São Paulo* (February 1, 1929); RRIAB, July 13, 1914, 832.54H83; October 11, 1919, 832.543/9; *Boletim Official da Associação Commercial* (August 1928), pp. 455–459; Great Britain, Department of Overseas Trade, *Economic Conditions in Brazil* (1937), p. 86.

they had grown rich by diverting the company's income to other business interests they owned. One of the directors, a woman, he alleged to be an ex-prostitute. Montenegro sued for libel and was vindicated; he proved that he had never legally married his first "wife"![20]

Another of the public scandals was more revealing of the ways in which windfall profits might be achieved on the frontiers of capitalism. A Rio importer of dyestuffs named Max Naegeli had discovered an intriguing flaw in Brazilian patent law: a search of existing patents was not a prerequisite for the registration of a new claim. Naegeli mused upon this point and decided to patent the basic formulas for aniline dyes. He laid his plans carefully; he noted that the law stipulated that complaints of prior registration had to be filed within one year. Naegeli obtained his patent in 1913 and laid low until dye shipments were resumed in 1920; then he began to embargo them. Immediately an outcry arose from the Centro Industrial in Rio and, of course, from foreign manufacturers. It is not clear what Naegeli hoped to gain from this maneuvre. The United States consul in Rio de Janeiro reported in 1919 that another importer there had registered more than a hundred American patents, including Evinrude, Dodge, and Eveready. His purpose was to cause the competing products to be temporarily impounded so that mounting warehouse charges would make it unprofitable to have them released. Naegeli probably intended to do the same. Nevertheless within four months the courts had denied the validity of his patents, and anilines began to be freely imported again.[21]

Naegeli had filched yet another product of European inventiveness, however, and this one he employed more tellingly. In 1919 he had obtained a patent on the process for making rayon. This action was challenged by Courtaulds, Limited, in a suit that took seven and a half years to settle. This time Naegeli won on the technicality that Courtaulds was not an interested party. According to Brazilian law, in such a situation only a customer, not a manufacturer, could sue. Naegeli, therefore, was free to market a very valuable property. He leased it to Matarazzo, who built a rayon plant and enjoyed a very

[20] *O Estado de São Paulo* (November 6, 8, 29, 1921).

[21] NA-DS, Memorandum, U.S. Embassy to Brazilian Foreign Office, September 17, 1920; RRIAB, March 3, 1920 to April 2, 1921, 832.542N12/1–16.

successful monopoly until 1934. Because the patent was to expire in that year, Naegeli petitioned for an extension equal to the seven and a half years he had fought Courtaulds' suit. The government was unwilling to countenance Matarazzo's monopoly any longer, however, and not only did it deny the extension, it also granted a license to Votorantim to import a second rayon plant. Naegeli asked Matarazzo for an accounting; he was supposed to have been paid 5 per cent of the profits. Matarazzo, according to the *Diario de São Paulo,* informed him that he had not made any profit! Matarazzo also tried to counter the threat from Votorantim. As soon as the new plant opened he lowered prices for the synthetic from forty-five milreis to ten milreis a kilo. The government stopped him by threatening to invoke an anti-trust law.[22]

Some of these revelations appeared in what was probably the most thorough piece of yellow journalism São Paulo ever witnessed. In September 1945 Assis Chateaubriand, owner of a chain of newspapers called the Diarios Associados, started in his editorial column to attack Francisco Matarazzo, Jr., by then the heir to his father's fortune. In retaliation the younger Matarazzo bought interests in two São Paulo newspapers and lowered their prices in the hope of driving Assis' local affiliate out of business. Assis then began to vilify Matarazzo in earnest. Besides recalling the circumstances of the rayon affair and detailing the *nouveau riche* pretensions attending the impending marriage of Matarazzo's daughter, he also accused him of selling goods above ceiling prices, of illegally transferring foreign exchange, of prejudicing the interests of other shareholders in subsidiary corporations, and of bilking his coheirs out of part of their share of his father's fortune. Although there is some speculation concerning Assis' original motive for airing these matters in public, the facts of the rayon scandal are verifiable from other sources, and the ill feeling among the heirs of the elder Matarazzo was strong enough to generate civil suits over the management of IRFM.[23]

[22] *Boletim do Ministerio de Trabalho, Industria e Commercio* (October 1936), pp. 113–126; *Diario de São Paulo* (September 22, 28, 1945).

[23] *Ibid.,* (September 19–28, October 5); São Paulo (state), Tribunal de Justiça, *Outros balanços do Conde Francisco Matarazzo Junior.*

Although there was evidently a large measure of truth in the popular tales of dishonesty and unfair dealings by the industrialists, there was much exaggeration as well. The belief, for example, that counterfeiting in secret basements was the origin of a fortune attached to the name of several industrialists. This kind of story is clearly evidence of a failure to develop a capitalistic ideology. The masses who worked in the factories and the middle class who consumed the products of industrialism were not convinced that riches on such a scale could be honestly gained. In their naïve conception, so much money could be acquired only in some sort of pact with the devil. The legitimacy of industrial capitalism was at stake, however, even in the recounting of illegalities that really took place. One senses in the yellow journalism of the era not a desire to punish an individual who had trespassed against an accepted set of rules, but rather a desire to show that the system itself was unjust.

The entrepreneurs of São Paulo were never able to impose upon the channels of communications a more favorable view of their activities, perhaps because they were not capable of such a degree of organization, but more likely because they were not capable of the necessary degree of self-deception. Unlike many an American businessman, who believed his riches were the outward sign of virtue and a trust from God, the Paulista manufacturers probably agreed with Matarazzo who believed neither in self-effacement nor popularity. He displayed his first lard-rendering kettle in his vast headquarters building as a demonstration that he had succeeded where others had failed and told the newspapermen, "Ah, no, I don't believe in social equality. Look at the children. They argue with violence to get possession of a toy. It's instinct that guides them, and instinct will never die."[24]

The industrial growth of São Paulo slowed down in the 1920's and 1930's, probably because the coffee trade did not stimulate local manufacturing as effectively as it had for the previous thirty years. The rural market did not grow as fast and new infusions of capital were scarce. It is also possible that certain structural characteristics of industry—the dispersion of effort in small shops, family control, cartels,

---

[24] Matarazzo, *Scelta di discorsi e interviste*, p. 151.

and price-fixing—are partly to blame. At any rate, they are all, along with a tendency to operate outside social and legal norms, significant factors of "conjuncture," aspects of the environment in which the entrepreneur acted. They must be taken into account in order to understand the industrialists' perception of the opportunities open to them as they tried to aggrandize their position in the market and in society during the interwar years.

CHAPTER VIII

Conflicts among the Elites: The Beginning
of Self-Consciousness

The industrialists of São Paulo did not perceive the trend of slower development in the postwar economy until the early 1930's. Instead they attributed their setbacks to a series of fortuitous events. In 1921 they complained of the sharp decline in export income; in 1924, of the looting and destruction during the army rebellion; in 1925, of the shortage of electric power caused by drought; in 1926, of the deflationary policy of the federal government; and from 1927 to 1929, of the competition of foreign imports. The industrialists recognized, of course, that the serious decline in sales they suffered in the first years of the 1930's was caused primarily by the world trade depression. Later on there were many references to "oversupply," that is, to a temporary glut on the market.

The tone of public statements by industrialists was therefore optimistic about the long run. Matarazzo, in a newspaper interview in 1928, was inspired to predict the "colossal possibilities" of Brazil's future "that promise everything to the labor of man." Brazil was going to have, "in a time not far distant, ample and rapid means of transport, developed auxiliary industries, improved agriculture, a population multiplied. . . . All this will contribute to the cheapening of living costs, to the reduction of all the costs of production in general, then our industries will be able to produce as cheaply as in the countries more technically advanced." He pointed to the United States, which had exported only foodstuffs to Brazil before the war. "Today the United States not only has achieved its emancipation from European imports, but besides producing what it requires for internal consumption, it exports everything it used to import. . . . To have thought of such a thing thirty years ago would have seemed utopian. . . . We have the faith that the same will be achieved in Brazil, a privileged land, whose inexhaustible wealth makes possible the exploitation of almost every industry." When faced by the immediate crisis, the entrepreneur was stoic. The Commercial Association of São Paulo heard Egydio Pinotti Gamba, a miller and sugar refiner, discuss the alternatives for stopping the deflation of 1926 and raised no dissent when he discarded them all in favor of inaction until the inevitable "fatal cycle" ran its course.[1]

Owner of a construction company and a brickyard, Roberto Simonsen, who was more perceptive than the others, nevertheless expressed no feeling of disappointment until 1934. In one of his speeches in that year he referred to the "creation of wealth," which "seems to follow, among us, a rhythm inferior to the growth of population. A grave fact." Basing his calculation only on the value of exports, he concluded, "If, in the forty years of the Republic, we have achieved a material progress in absolute terms, in relative terms it has been minimal." But this sort of thought was not characteristic of Simonsen, either; generally he spoke of evolution, of growth, and saw opportunities instead of obstacles. On the open-sided trolley cars of the city tramlines, the Light company began to paint the legend "The Greatest Industrial Center of Latin America," and the Paulistas were immensely pleased.[2]

Although the industrialists were not inclined to betray discourage-

---

[1] *Brasil Economico* (August 1, 1928), pp. 15–17; *Boletim Official da Associação Commercial* (May–June 1926), pp. 234–235.

[2] *Ordem econômica, padrão de vida, e algumas realidades brasileiras*, pp. 24–25.

ment and were unconscious of long-term trends in the rate of development, the difficulties they were beginning to experience in the more
hazardous environment of the 1920's found expression in an increased level of conflict in their relations with other sectors of the
economy. As it became more difficult to make a profit, it became
necessary to analyze one's expenses more critically, and this led inevitably to a more critical view of the efficiency of the others. As a
result the manufacturers began to think in terms of their group interests
in opposition to the interests of others—the planters, the importers,
the middle class. This in turn led to the beginnings of cohesiveness
and of self-consciousness. This chapter will examine some of the economic and political struggles in which the industrialists participated
during the 1920's that led, finally, to the organization of their own
trade association and to the elaboration of an explicit ideology of
industrialism. It will also attempt to show why these early manifestations of solidarity were necessarily limited in their significance.

It is rather surprising to find that the industrialists were less inclined
to a confrontation with planters than with the government or the import merchants. It is possible to discern in retrospect a number of
grievances that the Paulista manufacturers might have harbored against
the landowners. There is, for example, their insistence that "machines,
tools, and instruments destined for agricultural purposes and their
respective parts and accessories, . . . as well as tractors, and vehicles for
mechanical agriculture and road transport, and natural and chemical
fertilizers . . . shall be exempt for taxes of consumption and exportation, paying only a service charge of 2 per cent." This prohibition,
included in a tariff law of 1922, excluded the manufacturers from a
market that consumed more than 10,000 contos ($1,200,000) worth
of fertilizers in 1925 and 1926 and possessed, according to the 1920
census, 118,000 contos ($25,000,000) in stocks of farm machinery, an
amount greater than the total value of textile machinery in the state.[3]

The industrialists realized that in the broadest sense their prosperity
was dependent on the agricultural sector. They must have been dis-
comfited by signs of the incapacity of the planters to increase their
efficiency. The productivity of the rural sector failed to increase signifi-

[3] Law 4625, December 31, 1922; RRIAB, December 15, 1927, 832.659/3.

cantly in the interwar period; evidence can be found in the unchanging value of farm machinery stocks from 1920 to 1940, in spite of a 35 per cent increase in cultivated surface. It was reported that production of the sugar industry declined during most of the 1920's, not because of failing demand but because of various new cane diseases that the planters were not defending themselves against. Only three of the mills had analytical laboratories. A delegation of English cotton experts in 1921 found only one plantation where scientific plant selection had been attempted; it belonged to the textile mill of Rawlinson, Müller e Cia. The more imaginative of the industrialists might well have mused how much this stagnation cost them in restricted rural markets and in higher food prices for their work force.[4]

Nevertheless, the manufacturers chose not to challenge the planters' definition of the agricultural problem. According to them the difficulty consisted not in their inability to lower the costs of production, or in their unwillingness to allow marginal producers to be removed from the market, but in the general decline of world commodity prices. In 1921 valorization was again attempted in the midst of a sudden slump in coffee sales. The planters, faced with prices only one-quarter those of 1919, persuaded the federal government to buy almost one-third of the crop. Luckily, by 1925 these stocks had been sold off because of smaller harvests in the intervening years. But the federal government, under a Mineiro president, Arthur Bernardes, had grown weary of supporting the coffee planters, and the next valorization had therefore to be carried out under the direction of the semiprivate Coffee Institute, financed by foreign loans and the state-owned Banco do Estado de São Paulo. The buying-up of stocks became a continuous operation that encouraged further plantings of new trees. In 1928 a heavy crop compelled the purchase of 16,000,000 bags, a burden that had to be backed with nearly $100,000,000 from bankers in London and New York. The revolutionary government found it necessary to reassume federal responsibility for the coffee problem in 1930. Stocks in the hands of state governments were bought up and destroyed. By 1937 more than 70 per cent was burned or dumped at sea. To a degree this drastic

[4] Census, 1920, III, 3ª; 1940, XVII, vol. 3; Arno S. Pearse, *Brazilian Cotton*, p. 80.

program was born out of desperation and was pump-priming on an unprecedented scale, as Celso Furtado has pointed out. But it was also a profoundly political response. The revolutionary government could not abandon the planters and survive; indeed the most provocative of the last acts of the overthrown regime was its refusal to refund the valorization.[5]

Seemingly the industrialists also had the financial resources necessary to influence the redistribution of income by the government, but the planters possessed more than money. It was they who earned foreign exchange, without which the government could not pay off its numerous and onerous foreign loans. Furthermore the planters, through their thorough control of the rural electorate, were in actual possession of the government. The industrialists, therefore, prudently chose to support the planters and the conservative wing of the Paulista Republican Party in return for intermittent favors. This policy was modestly successful. The manufacturers campaigned for all of the official candidates for governor, from 1916 to the end of the old Republic, and received appropriate rewards. Altino Arantes obligingly expelled labor "agitators," Carlos de Campos fronted for Bromberg-Hacker's factories and was involved in Pereira Ignácio's absorption of Votorantim, and both Washington Luis and Júlio Prestes favored manufacturers' interests against the importers. But the potential political consequences of industrialism, in these circumstances, were largely dissipated.[6]

The manufacturers risked a confrontation with the planters only on one issue. It was narrow enough to evade the question of political legitimacy, yet critical enough from the point of view of profits: the inability of the Paulista plantations to supply the textile mills with enough cotton. Before World War I the textile industry had provided the impetus for an expansion of commercial cotton farming in São Paulo. Local production exceeded imports from abroad and from other states by 1913, and in 1919 a sizable quantity was exported. Although

[5] Celso Furtado, *Economic Growth of Brazil*, p. 211; U.S. Tariff Commission, *Economic Controls and Commercial Policy in Brazil*, pp. 21–24.

[6] Francesco Matarazzo, *Scelta di discorsi e interviste*, p. 64; *O Estado de São Paulo* (June 5, 1928); Dunshee d'Abranches, *Governos e Congressos*, II, 239–240; Victor Nunes Leal, *Coronelismo, enxada e voto*, pp. 188–189.

it was demonstrated in that year that a bumper crop of Paulista cotton could sweep away outside competition, the planters appeared to regard cotton as a speculation. They planted it in 1918 because a frost had ruined their coffee groves. They received good prices and managed to double their exports in the year following. But the price of coffee rose faster than the price of cotton during the early 1920's, and when the price fell after 1926 it did not fall as far.

New coffee trees continued to be planted, therefore, and the planters indulged in cotton as a sideline, invariably planting more after a season of high prices and less after a season of low prices, so that the price and the supply suffered extreme variations and inevitably discouraged steady investment or improvement in quality. The largest crop of cotton, almost 27,000 metric tons, was grown in 1925; more than 9,000 tons of it were exported, and in order to fill the demand of Paulista mills, which consumed nearly as much cotton as the planters produced in that year, it was necessary to import more than 7,000 tons from the northern states. From 1926 until 1932 cotton production within the state constantly declined, and consequently the manufacturers became more and more dependent on outside suppliers. It may be that this pattern reflected a nearly full utilization of available resources in São Paulo's agricultural sector and a decision, more or less deliberate, by the planters to leave the production of the less profitable commodity to outsiders.[7]

The impersonal workings of comparative advantage very greatly annoyed the cotton manufacturers, who felt that they were being forced to pay more for their raw materials. The northern states taxed their cotton exports just as São Paulo taxed its coffee, and shipping charges increased the cost still more. The manufacturers began to decry speculation and to complain that the cotton of São Paulo was ungraded, short stapled, and inferior in quality. Jorge Street asserted in the newspapers that Paulista cotton was piled high in the exporters' warehouses simply because it was in normal times unexportable.[8]

[7] *Revista do Algodão* (February 1935), pp. 22, 27; N. S. Pearse, *Cotton Progress in Brazil*, pp. 8–9, 146–149.

[8] *Brasil Economico* (November 1, 1928), p. 5; CIFTSP, *A crise textil*, pp. 8–11.

There was a time when the manufacturers themselves had been speculators: the Brazilian Industrial Center at Rio de Janeiro had petitioned the federal government in November 1918 to end the wartime prohibition on raw cotton exports. This request would seem to be inimical to the mill owners' need for cheap raw materials, but the Center was reasoning, in this case, that the stocks of finished textiles that they were speculating with would lose their value if cotton supplies were to increase. Nevertheless, by 1923 the manufacturers had come to see the necessity of a steady and cheap supply of cotton. A great deal of attention was paid to the problem by the CIFTSP. It published pamphlets urging the government to assist the planters by providing free seeds and insecticides, minimum prices on a par with Liverpool, and preferential rates on the railroads. The CIFTSP itself attempted to encourage more rational production by publishing the *Boletim Algodoeira*, which provided information on techniques of cotton growing and lobbied for standardization in grading, inspection during ginning and pressing, and standard contracts in marketing. It also published data on acreage and stocks in an effort to reduce speculation.[9]

All this officious meliorism was possibly appreciated by the planters; but there was a combative side as well to the manufacturers' activities. What must the planters have thought of Rodolfo Crespi's public speech in 1926, recorded by the journalist A. M. Bittencourt: "Since one of the most direct causes of the crisis that threatens us is the high cost of raw materials, merely raising the tariff doesn't resolve the industrial problem. It would be indispensable at the same time that tariffs are raised, and as a complementary measure, to open our customs to the competition of foreign raw materials . . . to bring prices to a more reasonable level." This demand, along with a proposal by the CIFTSP in 1928 that exports of raw cotton be restricted by the government, was a direct challenge to the planters which would have provoked radical changes in the economy if cotton had been a more

_____

[9] *Retrospecto Commercial* (1918), pp. 257–258; *Boletim Algodoeira* (1921–1923); CIFTSP, *A vida das industrias textis do Estado de São Paulo durante um decennio 1912–1921*; *A crise textil*, pp. 33–41.

central concern of the planters, or if the manufacturers had been better prepared in the 1920's to provoke them further.[10]

As it happened, the denouement was peaceful. The decline in cotton production took place while textile sales ebbed, and the revivified textile business was accompanied by the very great expansion of cotton planting for export. Since several of the mill owners had either begun as ginners or had later acquired gins and presses, it was possible not only to divert some of the cotton to their mills, but also to assume the lucrative role of exporter. By 1935 Pereira Ignácio was the third-largest shipper of cotton in the state, and José Ermirio de Moraes, his son-in-law, was president of the Commodity Exchange of São Paulo. Six other manufacturers, among them Matarazzo and Jafet, were listed as exporters of cotton, and twenty-three more mills possessed their own ginneries. Once again the resilience of the export trade and the peculiar articulation of the agricultural and industrial sectors had allayed the need for a confrontation.[11]

A more consequential antagonism arose between the industrialists and the importers. In the beginning, as we have seen, the industry of São Paulo was heavily in debt to the importers for machinery, capital, and markets. They had originated as mere adjunctive maintenance shops and parts suppliers for the more strategic and lucrative business of importing. As they grew, the importers sensed no potential threat because they marketed indifferently what the domestic or the foreign manufacturers had for sale. The proportion of locally produced goods in the São Paulo market increased between 1910 and 1928 from about half to perhaps three-quarters of the total. The importer Jaime Loureiro of the importing house of Martins Costa told the president of the Commercial Association in 1927 that local products accounted for 85 per cent of sales in the city, a slight exaggeration due perhaps to Loureiro's desire to demonstrate his firm's lack of prejudice against a "sound" tariff.[12]

[10] A. M. Bittencourt, *Os postulados da revolução*, pp. 167, 176–177; *A crise textil*, p. 41.

[11] *Revista do Algodão* (February 1935), pp. 22, 27; N. S. Pearse, *Cotton Progress*, pp. 179–183.

[12] Associação Commercial de São Paulo, Atas (February 10, 1928), p. 9.

In spite of the increase in the sale of domestic products, the import business was not absolutely declining. The Paulista consumed on the average about twenty-eight dollars worth of imports per year in the last half of the 1920's compared with eighteen dollars per capita in the five prosperous years before World War I. Furthermore, the importers still occupied several strategic positions. They continued to manage the influential trade associations, such as the Commercial Association of São Paulo, which possessed a mixed membership. Some evidence of the translation of this sort of prestige into political power can be found in the composition of the federal Superior Council of Commerce and Industry, created by presidential decree in 1923, which was supposed to advise the government on economic matters and to propose projects of its own. Besides a majority of federal bureaucrats with financial and trade responsibilities, the Council was to contain eight "representatives of commerce" but only four of industry. The importers could also count on the support of the urban middle class, which was the chief victim of the inflation brought on by high tariffs and cheap money. Although it was small in numbers and incapable of influencing the direction of politics in the normal course of events, the 1920's were no longer normal, and the middle class was becoming, if not revolutionary, at least radically dissatisfied.

The manufacturers on the other hand had gained something more than tolerance from the planters by refraining from a frontal attack upon their privileges. They were usually ready to collaborate when the common enemy was the middle class and the importers. The most profitable employment of this alliance was the deliberately inflationary policy extracted from the federal government from 1920 to 1923. During World War I and for five years thereafter the planters had been able to pay off their indebtedness painlessly because of the government's heavy reliance on the emission of paper money. The industrialists were pleased with this policy, on the whole, because inflation increased the price of imports and widened their profit margins. The Paulista Republican Party, ever responsive to the demands of the planters, relentlessly pursued a policy of emissions and easy credit in the federal congress. In 1923, while Paulistas controlled both the Ministry of Finance and the Bank of Brazil, the emissions of paper money reached their highest point. Between 1920 and 1923 the amount of currency in circulation, the cost of living, and the price of foreign exchange all doubled.

President Arthur Bernardes, who was not a Paulista, became seriously alarmed. He was subjected to strong criticism from the articulate, reformist middle class, including younger army officers, who looked upon the planters not simply as antagonists but as betrayers of the republican ideal, since their control of the government was perpetuated only through electoral fraud and manipulation. At this moment Bernardes also had to endure the presence of a delegation from London who made clear to him the impossibility of securing further loans under the circumstances and then humiliated him with suggestions on how to balance the federal budget. The manifesto of the army rebels in São Paulo, whose unsuccessful coup broke out in July 1924, complained about inflation as though it were as great a crime as electoral fraud.[13]

With all these pressures Bernardes was obliged to reverse his financial policy. He removed the Paulista, Cincinato Braga, from the Bank of Brazil and began withdrawing paper money from circulation. By May 1926 he had burned 316,000 contos ($50,000,000), and the dollar had fallen from over 10 milreis to less than 7. The planters were spared the consequences of this ruthless deflation through the flotation of an extraordinary loan by São Paulo's Coffee Institute, but the manufacturers remained wholly vulnerable.

They did not give political expression to their dismay, however, for several reasons. Many agreed with Roberto Simonsen, who expressed several times the belief that a stable currency was Brazil's most pressing economic problem. Pinotti Gamba, quoted earlier in this chapter, displayed equanimity before the greatly accelerated rate of bankruptcies, perhaps partly because most of them were the misfortune of smaller firms. Of the larger manufacturers, only two disappeared during this prolonged crisis. One was the Companhia Puglisi, with liabilities worth 100,000 contos ($15,000,000). Giuseppe and Nicolá Puglisi, who had

[13] Georges LaFond, "Les raisons économiques de l'agitation politique au Brésil," *La Vie des Peuples* (1924), pp. 539–553; RRIAB, November 26, 1924, 832.501D/2.

been involved in the founding of the Banco Francês e Italiano, owned a flour mill and a hat factory and held important interests in the Hotel Esplanade, a ribbon factory, the Refinadora Paulista, and a warehousing company. Crespi, Morganti, Ugliengo, and others absorbed their holdings. The Puglisis were accompanied into bankruptcy by John Moore and Co., an importer and a principal creditor. The other failure was the Companhia Industria de Papeis e Cartonagens, a fusion of several small paper makers, which was worth 42,000 contos ($5,200,000). It had received credit from the Banco Francês e Italiano and was also in debt to Siciliano, the Royal Bank of Canada, and Francisco Matarazzo.[14]

The industrialists petitioned Bernardes to order the Bank of Brazil to ease commercial discounting and to make loans on the stocks in factory warehouses. But assistance was not granted until the inauguration of another Paulista, Washington Luis, into the presidency. He immediately acted upon the manufacturers' alternative proposal, "an exchange stabilization, at a reasonable rate." He reinstituted the conversion mechanism of the Bank of Brazil, thereby assuring a steady exchange rate, but set it at a level considerably lower than Bernardes had attained. In this fashion the planters and manufacturers were given back their cheap money at the same time that the fear of further inflation was dispelled for the importers and the middle class.[15]

A second test of the relative strength of the importers and the industrialists began to appear as the controversy over the exchange was dissipated. The industrialists began in 1926 and 1927 to propose a general increase in the tariff. Since 1900 no general schedule had been written; instead rates were increased individually, after lobbying by an association or even by a single firm. Sometimes the revision was revoked in the same manner by importers whose business suffered the consequences. The case of the Companhia Agro-Fabril is instructive. It had persuaded the Minister of Agriculture, in July 1926, to increase the tariff on sewing thread, its principal product, by showing him

---

[14] Roberto Simonsen, *As crises no Brasil*, p. 39; *À margem da profissão*, pp. 144, 151, 177; RRIAB, June 27, 1926, 832.50/27; June 8, 1926, 832.50/24.

[15] Centro Industrial do Brasil, *Annaes, 1926–1928*, p. 52; *Boletim Official da Associação Commercial* (May–June 1926), pp. 202, 221.

documents purportedly stolen from the agency of Machine Cottons, Ltd., revealing a conspiracy to eliminate domestic manufacturers by dumping and offering rebates to merchants. The case was lent circumstantial force by the fact that three spinning mills had recently failed and Machine Cottons had bought one of them. But Agro-Fabril's coup was short-lived. Importers all over Brazil protested that the company was already selling cheaper than the foreigners, among whom there had always existed intense competition. Furthermore, they alleged, only colored thread was being imported, and Agro-Fabril's assortment was limited and inferior technically. The Commercial Association of Rio Grande do Sul regretted profoundly the harm done to "thousands of women, widows, children, and orphans who gain their subsistence in the hand labor of dress making." According to the *Boletim* of the Commercial Association of São Paulo, the documents were forgeries. The government at first insisted on the truth of Agro-Fabril's charges, but finally yielded to these representations, or perhaps to others, in August 1927: the tariff increase was revoked.[16]

Agro-Fabril was a small firm, without allies, confronted by a foreign company that had behaved ruthlessly in the past, and its action had cost too many competitors too much money all at once. A full-scale effort directed against a more significant class of imports, such as cotton and woolen goods, might be more successful, but a great deal of money would have to be spent for propaganda and lobbying and some sort of organization would have to be created to mobilize support from industrialists as a group. It is likely that this line of reasoning evolved as a conscious strategy among the industrialists as protectionist sentiment grew among them.

The Commercial Association of São Paulo was at the time the principal spokesman for business in the state. It had been founded in 1894 by both merchants and manufacturers and had absorbed a similar organization, called the Center of Commerce and Industry of São Paulo, in 1917. After this fusion the Commercial Association seems to have been controlled by the merchants and importers, and the con-

---

[16] *Ibid.* (August–December 1926), pp. 407–411; continuing references through September 1927, pp. 360, 368.

cerns of commerce came to dominate its agenda. Evidently much of
this business was noncontroversial; the industrialists also favored the
self-regulation of commerce, the avoidance of as many taxes as possible, and the promotion of transportation and storage facilities. Both
the industrialists and the importers, for example, disliked the sales tax,
which burdened them equally and continually increased in scope during
the 1920's. Nevertheless, the industrialists would sooner or later want
to use the prestige of the organization to promote their exclusive
ends.[17]

In January 1928 the membership was surprised to discover that a
slate of dissidents had been nominated to oppose the candidates indicated by the outgoing directorate. The dissident slate was composed
entirely of manufacturers and was led by Jorge Street. The official
slate contained only merchants. Furthermore, the two lists were politically polarized: the dissidents were supported by the machinery of the
Paulista Republican Party and possessed the endorsement of the governor, while the official slate was led by Horácio Rodrigues, a member
of the newly organized, mildly reformist Democratic Party. On no
other occasion was the emerging political realignment in São Paulo so
clearly delineated. The industrialists were not the vanguard of political
reformism and the ambitious middle class; instead they identified with
"the situation" and all that it implied. Rodrigues was able to win sympathy for his candidacy by pointing out that Street had advocated opposition to the law on paid vacations, one of the few progressive acts
of the federal government during the 1920's, while *A Platéa,* a pro-
Street newspaper, sought to demonstrate the illegitimacy of Rodrigues'
candidacy by drawing a connection between his advocacy of the secret
ballot in the Association election and the demand of the Democratic
Party for the secret ballot in political elections. The latter was indeed
a plank of the reformist middle class; they hoped by means of it to
free the rural laborer from political fealty to the planters. On the

[17] Associação Commercial de São Paulo, Atas (February 12, 1926); *Relatorios das directorias de 1924 e 1925;* "Há sessenta anos faz-se ouvir nos acontecimentos de maior relevância para a vida do estado e do país," in *Ensaios
paulistas,* pp. 458–472; Centro de Commercio e Industria de São Paulo, "Relatorio de 1917," *Revista de Commercio e Industria* (January 1918), p. 28.

other hand it is grotesque that a propagandist for the manufacturers could imagine that he had scored a point by alluding to their opposition to it.[18]

The rift in the Association was patched up by the joint appointment of a new nominating committee which selected an entirely new slate of candidates. The election that followed was the most heavily attended in the history of the Association. The conciliation candidates, led by Antonio Carlos de Assumpção, an importer and exporter with industrial interests, were duly elected and the members of the two original slates were given seats in the advisory council. Assumpção's inaugural speech attempted to reconcile every wounded interest. The defense of coffee prices, he asserted, was a legitimate principle of commercial policy, comparable to the British attempts to fix the price of rubber or to the American control of oil prices. "Commerce and industry can and should, many times, meet with hands joined, uniting and complementing their efforts." Protectionism need not be inimical to the interests of the merchants; they would have more national products to sell. It was reported to him that 95 per cent of the goods locally sold were already domestic products.[19]

The industrialists, however, were not willing to accept this ambiguous position, and decided, only a few months later, to found a separate trade association, which they named the Center of Industries of the State of São Paulo. Matarazzo was its first president and Roberto Simonsen its first vice-president. In his inaugural address Matarazzo publicly expressed, for perhaps the first time in São Paulo, the essence of that possibly insincere identification with the common good that seems so indispensable to the expropriation of political power: "It is obvious that there is an absolute correlation between the ends that industrialists have in view and the true interests of the nation. The increase in the nation's capacity to consume will represent the opening of a formidable market for Brazilian industrialists; consumption and production, rising in harmony, will increase wealth, will bring

---

[18] *O Estado de São Paulo* (January 5, 10, 13, 17, 1928).

[19] *Ibid.* (January 22, 29, 1928); Associação Commercial de São Paulo, Atas (February 10, 1928); Stanley Stein, *The Brazilian Cotton Manufacture*, p. 119n.

greatness to the country, well-being and tranquility to the population
. . ."

Nevertheless, the creation of the Center gave rise to recrimination
in the press, which claimed that it was the first step in the campaign
for a protective tariff. It does indeed appear that the subsequent drive
to increase the tariffs on cotton and woolen textiles was more than
coincidental. Stanley Stein has described the propaganda and lobbying
activities of the CIFTSP and its counterpart in Rio de Janeiro beginning in August 1928 to have the clauses "readjusted." The textile
manufacturers, who had enjoyed a few exceedingly prosperous years
after the war, had seen their sales decline in 1924 and thereafter remain
fixed at something over 500,000,000 meters. This they attributed not
to their entrepreneurial insufficiencies but to increased competition
from abroad. Imports of foreign cotton textile, most of it dyed or
printed, surpassed eight thousand tons in 1928, more than 13 per cent
of total consumption. According to the manufacturers, the British
were desperately seeking an alternative to their vanishing Indian markets. They hoped that they could regain their former prominence in
the Brazilian trade by ruining domestic manufacturers with dumping
and illegal undervaluation in customs. Furthermore, they claimed, the
higher price levels of the postwar decade had not been accompanied
by revisions in the ad valorem schedules. Effective protection was consequently only half that intended in the 1900 tariff.[20]

The *Jornal do Commercio*, the *Estado de São Paulo*, and other
newspapers that represented the merchants and the reformist middle
class attacked the mill owners savagely. In Rio de Janeiro A. M. Bittencourt, who wrote for the *Diario Carioca*, claimed that "the industrialists . . . instead of employing their time and intelligence to the
solution of problems that inevitably arise every day in industry, . . .
have wasted their precious energy in surrounding the government, the
press, and the people with captious, tendentious, and false arguments,
. . . in order to free themselves of 'lemons' that their incapacity has
generated." Bittencourt owned an importing house and later supported
the Liberal Alliance. The press criticism was of little weight, however,

[20] *Ibid.*, pp. 123–128; 192–193; Jorge Street, *Carta aberta*.

compared to the political influence of the industrialists. The chairmen of the banking committees both in the Senate and the Chamber of Deputies were responsive to their wishes. One of the Senate Committee's members, Lacerda Franco, was himself a shareholder in Paulista cotton mills. There were also rumors of an immense lobbying fund. The cotton clauses were therefore revised in January 1929.[21]

Perhaps other campaigns would have followed this successful attack by the textile manufacturers, but the onset of depression drained the tariff struggle of its significance. Imported cloth almost completely disappeared from the market in the three years following the revision, principally because the Brazilian economy could on longer afford to buy it. It is interesting to see, nevertheless, the sophisticated efforts of a few of the representatives of industry in the late 1920's to enlist allies in the foreseeable struggle against the importers. The strategy of Roberto Simonsen and Alexandre Siciliano, Jr., son of the immigrant industrialist who had conceived the valorization scheme, was to appeal to the nationalism of the middle class and to the cupidity of the planters.

The appointment of Roberto Simonsen to the post of Vice-President of the Center of Industries marked the beginning of a career as spokesman of the manufacturers that lasted through the late 1940's. Simonsen belonged to a family that had been in Brazil for three generations and had married into the plantation elite. The family's interests including exporting, banking, and coffee, but Roberto, who had obtained a degree at the Polytechnic School in construction engineering, devoted himself mainly to industry. His construction company in Santos was the first in Brazil to engage in general contracting. His first big deal was presented to him by Pandiá Calógeras, a fellow Paulista and then Minister of War. He was to build army barracks in thirty-six cities across the country. Simonsen completed the work in record time and at a low cost by standardizing plans and materials. Simonsen then organized or participated in a meat-packing plant, a brick and tile company, a rubber products factory, and a copperworking shop. His polit-

---

[21] Bittencourt, *Os postulados*, pp. 170, 173–175; Stein, *Brazilian Cotton Manufacture*, p. 128.

ical contacts within the Paulista Republican Party were excellent, and he soon began to use them to represent the industrialists within the party.[22]

Simonsen's early speeches and essays go far beyond the propaganda produced by Jorge Street. He thought more deeply concerning the relationship of industry to the state and to agriculture and gradually absorbed European and American theories of political economy. He remained, however, thoroughly the product of the plantation society in his understanding, or lack of understanding, concerning the power of industry to transform society. His Listian economic attitudes did not proceed from a desire to increase social mobility or to employ human resources more fully. For him the workers were "good and simple souls" who needed to be bought off with better wages in order to avoid the introduction into Brazil of the class struggle. He agreed with Ortega y Gassett's estimate of mass man and preferred to see society controlled by an educated elite.[23]

It is likely that these attitudes, so confidently expressed, were also those of his audience. At the inauguration of the Center of Industries Simonsen did not dwell on the social consequences of industrialization; instead he told his listeners that industrialization would make the country economically independent. Those who "combat the implantation or diffusion of industries in the country," he asserted, "are consciously or unconsciously acting in behalf of foreign nations interested in the conquest of our markets, working to return us to the position of a colony of foreign producers." Furthermore, he said, domestic manufactures resolve the government's exchange crisis; if it were not for them, Brazilians would have to buy much more abroad. Then he set about answering the objections that he sensed in the larger public. To the complaints of the middle class that domestic industry raised the cost of living and "contributed nothing to the enrichment of Brazil," he insisted that this was because the tariffs were irrational—they increased the cost of raw materials as well as finished goods. Besides, he ended lamely, at most the extra cost couldn't amount to more than 6 per cent, because domestic manufacturing produced only a small

---

[22] Heitor Ferreira Lima, *Mauá e Roberto Simonsen*, pp. 43–61.
[23] Simonsen, *À margem da profissão*, pp. 18–20; *Rumo à verdade*, pp. 33–40.

part of domestic consumption. As for enrichment, "wherever in the world it is installed," industry raises wealth and salaries. To the charge that Brazilian industry was monopolistic, enriching a half-dozen men at the expense of millions of others, he replied with individualistic fervor that what six Brazilians could do, anyone could do.[24]

His answers to the complaints constantly raised by the planters were similarly oblique and unsatisfactory. Is Brazilian industry "artificial"? Then so is British industry, because it imports an even higher proportion of its raw materials. As for the charge that domestic manufacturing raises the cost of agricultural labor by drawing workers to the city, Simonsen objected, quite inaccurately, that industry could hardly exercise much of an influence, since it employed only 1 per cent [sic] of the work force. This last reply is especially significant; it is obvious that industry does indeed increase the wages of labor, and an aggressive and fervent promoter of industrialization would almost certainly claim this effect as his principal goal. But Simonsen could not. It would derail the alliance he sought to achieve: Paulista industrialization would have to be contained within the existing structure: its potentially revolutionary effects would have to be diverted.

The arguments of Alexandre Siciliano, Jr., were more original. He developed them at length in a pamphlet published in 1931 designed to convince the planters of the need for a protective tariff. First of all, he insisted, the Brazilian tariff was not yet genuinely protectionist. A tariff capable of stimulating manufactures would have to include variable rates to encourage reciprocity, specialized nomenclature to accompany industrial evolution, and stability ("a protectionist tariff . . . is a promise, a formal moral obligation of the government"). In return he offered the planters an incentive: the government would earn so much money taxing the importation of products that compete with similar domestic goods that it could afford to bargain for the reduction of tariffs on noncompetitive imports. Of course, the basis for bargaining would be reciprocity; the foreigners would have to admit Brazilian agricultural products on more generous terms.[25]

[24] Simonsen, *À margem de profissão*, pp. 168–173.
[25] Alexandre Siciliano, Jr., *Agricultura, comercio e industria no Brasil*, pp. 4–10, 44.

Then Siciliano described benefits to be reaped by agriculture from further industrialization. The income of the masses would be increased, because industrial workers are on the average eleven times as productive as rural workers, and this enlarged income would be spent on more agricultural produce. He reminded the planters that just nine farm products accounted for more than 90 per cent of Brazil's exports; all the rest had to be sold in the internal market. Protective tariffs would secure the jobs of all these consuming masses, especially against the swarming Indians and Africans whom their colonial masters kept in a state of disguised slavery. Agricultural countries are the economic colonies of the industrialized countries. Siciliano wrote, and then he pointed to Soviet Russia, which had been obliged to industrialize "in five years" in the face of external threats. It is remarkable how frequently the conservative Brazilian elite referred to the Soviets. As much as they feared them, they were impressed by their achievements. The revolution itself had frightened them briefly, but the image that endured was that of a central government directing an orderly and rapid economic development. Siciliano drew still another lesson from the European experience. Industrialization was necessary for self-sufficiency as well as for independence, because the Europeans, who needed their high tariffs to pay for their interminable wars, would involve Brazil in their quarrels once again unless steps were taken to insulate Brazil economically.[26]

Finally, Siciliano attempted to dissuade the planters from two of their favorite theories, "artificial industries" and free trade. Every country, he argued, seeks to carry out the processing of agricultural raw materials in its own territory in order to protect national firms and to maintain distribution in local hands. Thus, just as Brazilian firms convert imported jute sacking into bags, the Americans roast imported coffee and refine imported sugar. As for free trade, it is a theory adaptable only to countries that are on the offensive economically. It was appropriate to England because it was the world's industrial leader, but, for countries not yet ready to penetrate foreign markets, defense is a more reasonable stance. In spite of Siciliano's manifest nationalism,

[26] *Ibid.*, pp. 19–20.

he rather hoped that one of the results of a protective tariff and other favors for industry would be an increased flow of European capital to Brazil. But he imagined an ideal sort of investment—portfolio money, not branch operations—and an almost total reinvestment of profits by the capitalists, whom he pictured in fear of "the tax system of some European countries that today practice a disguised state socialism."[27]

Although a few of the manufacturers were capable of articulating a reasoned defense of group interests, and although many more by adhering to the Center of Industrialists displayed a certain sense of class solidarity, it cannot be said that the cohesiveness of the manufacturers went much further. Too much antagonism was provoked by the rigors of competition or by the process of production, which made some of them the suppliers or customers of others. In some cases the fabricating plants opposed the implantation of basic manufacturing as bitterly as the importers opposed the fabricating plants. The textile manufacturers, for example, fought against tariff protection not only for cotton but also for dyestuffs and machinery. The few small firms producing carbon black and anilines never enjoyed protectionist rates, and loom manufacturers like Nardini were in the 1930's faced with demands by the textile manufacturers that domestic production be halted. The paper manufacturers, who had obtained a prohibition on the importation of paper-making equipment, complained to the government when they discovered that Klabin planned to set up cellulose production, which they assumed would be attached to additional paper-making capacity. They also insisted that domestic manufacture of paper machinery be limited to replacement of existing plants, since the industry was in "a state of over-production." The printers, on the other hand, presented the government with a memorial denying the paper makers' allegations and demanding that new machinery be installed.[28]

The Paulista representatives in the federal congress, in order to protect the state's iron and steel fabricators, who merely melted down

[27] *Ibid.*, pp. 26–33.

[28] *Ibid.*, p. 10; "Côres e corantes," *Revista Paulista de Industria* (January 1955), pp. 5–18; *Boletim do Ministerio de Trabalho, Industria e Commercio* (April 1937), pp. 136–142.

scrap, consistently opposed the creation of an ore-transforming industry in Minas Gerais. In turn the construction companies demanded that the Commercial Association combat attempts by the fabricators to raise the tariff on steel imports. Matarazzo, who had built an aluminum-rolling mill to produce appropriate thicknesses and shapes for the production of aluminumware, decided to monopolize the supply of sheet aluminum to other firms by petitioning the government for lower tariffs on bars and plates and higher tariffs on sheets and foil. He claimed that he had sufficient machinery to supply the market and that he couldn't compete at the current rates because the foreign suppliers were organized in a trust. The domestic producers of aluminumware protested to the Commercial Association that Matarazzo was overstating his capacity by 100 per cent and that he was already making considerable profits. Furthermore, with the advantage of integration he would be able to drive the independents out of business. In reply Matarazzo alleged that the other producers were themselves connected with the foreign trust and that this was the real reason for their opposition. Protection for an aluminum-rolling mill, he insisted, would provide the government with a new source of domestic revenue and would encourage future exploitation of domestic ores.[29]

Cases such as these suggest that the prior implantation of consumer goods industries may have retarded the development of more basic industry, because each consuming unit, whether the ultimate consumer or an intermediary, would tend to oppose an increase in the costs of his purchases.

One is struck by the absence, in all the polemical literature of the industrialists between the wars, of any exhortations in behalf of new industries. They called in very general terms for further investments in areas that would reduce their costs, such as cotton production and transportation, but their concern for the protection of industry embraced only existing lines of production. During this period it was not the "entrepreneurs" but engineers, journalists, and bureaucrats who spoke in favor of the immediate creation of steel, petroleum, and chemical industries.

[29] *Boletim Official da Associação Commercial* (August-December 1926), p. 378; (October 1927), pp. 459–460; *O Estado de São Paulo* (October 5, 1927).

PART THREE

●

THE INDUSTRIALISTS CONFRONT SOCIETY
AND THE STATE
1920–1945

CHAPTER IX

The Industrialists and "The Social Question"

The conflict between manufacturers and workers is significant to the study of entrepreneurship because the employers, in their treatment of labor, reveal a great deal about what they think of society and of their role within it. The task of keeping men, and women and children, at wearying and even dangerous work for long hours at meager pay requires more rationalization than the defense of protective tariffs or easy credit. The workers and their unions were not merely economic rivals for claims upon profits; they were also witnesses and critics of the factory system and of capitalism.

The conditions of labor in São Paula were difficult to justify. In 1920 the average Paulista industrial worker earned about four milreis (sixty cents) a day, for which he worked ten hours or more, six days a week. Women formed about one-third of the work force, and there were many children; perhaps half of all workers were under eighteen and almost 8 per cent were under fourteen. Since four milreis barely sufficed to buy a half kilo each of rice, macaroni, lard, sugar, and coffee, it is not surprising that whole families went to work, even though women and children were paid less for equivalent tasks. A budget for a family of seven published by a government agency in Rio de Janeiro in 1919 allotted four times as much just for food as the average worker earned in São Paulo. The industrial worker was not much better paid than rural day laborers, who got about 3$700 a day, and he was perhaps less well paid than the coffee *colonos*, although he had to buy more of his necessities than either. Working conditions were very hard; many of the structures housing the machinery were not designed for the purpose, were poorly lit and ventilated, and without sanitary facilities. The machinery was crowded together and brandished unshielded gears and belts. Accidents were frequent because the weary workers, sometimes put to overtime at no increase in salary or to work on Sundays, were docked for tardiness and errors if they were adults, or were beaten if they were children. In 1917 a visitor to a plant in Moóca, in the suburbs of the capital, listened to the complaints of twelve- and thirteen-year-old workers on the night shift that they were frequently struck, and they showed him bruises and wounds in proof. The occasional photograph of the changing of the shifts at one factory or another shows a horde of gaunt and ragged specters swarming out of doors preceded by barefoot and rachitic waifs, their faces all listlessly turned to the camera, or to the ground.[1]

The manufacturers contended, however, that the workers were not ill paid—on the contrary, "scarcity and extremely high wages are the realities, in spite of theoretical or opportunistic fictions of labor surplus and low pay," in the words of Eduardo Jafet. The workers were unproductive, he explained, because they were poorly trained and lacked a professional attitude; furthermore, transportation, taxes, machinery, and working capital were expensive and influenced the remuneration of labor. Labor's share was indeed low: in 1920 it amounted to less than 11 per cent of value added through manufacture. A survey printed by the International Labor Office in 1937 agreed that low wages in part explained the success of Paulista industry and that they were comparable with Japanese, rather than European, scales. Simonsen advanced a cultural explanation for the discrepancy. "In

[1] Census, 1920, V, 1ª, 2ª; *Retrospecto Commercial* (1919), p. 83; Paul Walle, *Au pays de l'or rouge*, pp. 74–75; *Boletim do Departamento Estadual de Trabalho* (1911), pp. 41–68; (1919), pp. 202–203; (1920), p. 15; Azis Simão, *Sindicato e estado*, pp. 65–76.

the more advanced industries, we note, with sorrow, that the national element is not, in general, sufficiently prepared, in training or in diet, to render the output in the productive role offered by other human elements coming from countries where the individual has reached a high stage of progress." Matarazzo evidently agreed with his analysis; his trips to Italy in 1922 and 1924 were undertaken partly to stimulate further migration.[2]

It is common enough in the early stages of industrialization for workers to prefer leisure to additional wages at a point just beyond the threshold of subsistence and for entrepreneurs to promote immigration to reduce the consequent "scarcity of labor." Stanley Stein, for example, found a "repugnance for unbroken supervised toil" at an earlier date in the textile mills of Rio de Janeiro. It is unlikely, however, that by the 1920's or 1930's there were in São Paulo very many workers who had grown up in a subsistence economy or who were not desperate for additional wages to maintain themselves or their families. Indeed, it was a common practice of the workers, according to the survey of the International Labor Office, to take jobs illegally in another mill during their vacations. Furthermore, the supply of workers was constantly rising. More immigrants flowed into São Paulo from Europe during the 1920's than had come in the previous fifteen years, and when migration was discouraged in the 1930's they were replaced by an even greater tide from the agricultural sector and from outside the state. If workers did not want to stay in the factories, therefore, it may be that any job was preferable to industrial work. The possibility that the entrepreneurs had given almost no thought to the more efficient utilization of their "scarce" labor supply emerges also from responses to a survey made in 1934 of American companies operating in Brazil. Brazilian workers were considered by their foreign managers to be as productive as the American worker, considering the equipment they had at their disposal. It appeared, however, that the

[2] Eduardo Jafet, "Fortalecimento dos mercados internos," thesis presented to the Congresso Brasileiro de Industria, pp. 1–6; Census, 1920, V, 1ª; Fernand Maurette, *Alguns aspectos*, pp. 36–37, 53; Roberto Simonsen, *Ensaios sociais, políticos e econômicos*, p. 165; Francesco Matarazzo, *Scelta di discorsi e interviste*, p. 82.

foreigners hired selectively and paid wages higher than the going rate in order to avoid discontent among the workers and in order to demand higher standards of performance.[3]

To a certain extent the Paulista entrepreneurs supplemented the low pay of the workers with various benefits. There are witnesses to the existence of nurseries and kindergartens, company stores, churches, restaurants, company housing, and medical aid. Visitors to the Votorantim mill, for example, reported the presence of all these services and still others: a cinema, a swimming pool, tennis courts, a football field, sewer systems, piped water, and electricity. Votorantim was an unusual case because it was a very large factory several miles distant from the nearest town of Sorocaba. Nevertheless, it might be assumed that a spirit of paternalism moved Pereira Ignácio to provide these services so bountifully that the epithet "father of the poor" fell "spontaneously from the sincere lips of the workers." It does not appear from these accounts, however, that the management was running these services below cost. The factory's wage bill seems to have been considerably less than the state average for the textile industry; therefore even the nursery and recreation facilities, it might be argued, were deducted from the workers' earnings. Furthermore, only a few of these services were free. Housing cost nine to twelve milreis out of an average wage of eighty-eight milreis a month, electricity another two milreis per bulb, and medical services were deducted at a rate of 2 per cent of the monthly wage. The school was staffed by the state—only the building was provided by the mill—and the company store was leased. It may be assumed that the storekeeper was not expected to run his business at a loss, since the management inspected his prices from time to time merely to make certain that they did not *exceed* those of the city. Workers who wanted to visit Sorocaba traveled on the company railroad and seem to have paid as much as one milreis each way, to judge by the gross revenues quoted to observers. Possibly the high fare was designed to discourage too frequent contact with the outside. One can hardly imagine the gaunt inhabitants of the weaving sheds on the tennis

[3] Stanley Stein, *The Brazilian Cotton Manufacture*, p. 55; Maurette, *Alguns aspectos*, p. 53; Dudley Maynard Phelps, *Migration of Industry*, pp. 234, 245–250, 273.

courts or the diving board after a ten-hour shift in front of the relent-less machines; these were evidently perquisites of the staff.[4]

Inquiries by the state Department of Labor in 1911 and 1919, furthermore, showed that the provisions of benefits for the workers were not at all generalized; in the cities they were almost nonexistent. About half of the thirty factories questioned in each of the surveys pro-vided medical assistance, but almost all charged for the service. Those few mills that provided housing charged as much as forty-four milreis a month for it, almost half the wage of the average worker. Statements by the manufacturers tend to demonstrate that these extra services were not primarily designed as worker incentives. Some of them were surely considered necessary arrangements to maintain the work process, analogous to the lubrication of machinery or the replacement of worn parts. Nurseries and kindergartens, for example, reflected a desire to extract larger quantities of work at the least possible cost. Mothers could not be expected to put in a full day's work if they had to tend children who were not yet old enough for factory work. In the same spirit the Ipiranga mill operated a restaurant at cost that provided, according to the management, "all the calories that each worker needs daily, all under the supervision of a doctor specializing in the matter of the diet of workers." During the lunch hour a radio apparatus played music.

This behaviorism, which treated the workers as an extension of the machinery, might be regarded as more progressive than the attitude of paternalism represented by the phrase "father of the poor," because, at least, it portended a fuller and more rational exploitation of the workers' potentialities. The tendencies toward paternalism are supposed to be very strong in the early stages of industrialization, since neither the worker nor the entrepreneur has cast off the reciprocal longing for security and veneration that is peculiar to traditional society. Never-

---

[4] *Twentieth Century Impressions of Brazil*, p. 373; Stein, *Brazilian Cotton Manufacture*, pp. 57, 58; *Jornal do Commercio (São Paulo)* (August 19, 1917); Alfredo Cusano, *Il Brasile, gl'italiani e la guerra*, pp. 297–299; "As industrias paulistas," *Revista do Algodão* (July 1935), pp. 301–311; Monte Domecq' et Cie., pp. 269–278; *Boletim do Departamento Estadual do Trabalho* (1919), pp. 202–203.

theless, paternalism was regarded by contemporaries in São Paulo as the more advanced of the two roles, in spite of the clear implication that the worker would have to remain morally and politically a child before the *patrão*. Jorge Street, for example, who managed the Maria Zélia mill in the capital, was considered an industrialist with an exceptionally well developed social conscience. He provided numerous benefits for his workers, as he told a visiting English delegation, not as charity but in place of higher wages, "which would be frittered away on useless things." He also insisted that all of the workers in his model village observed a nine o'clock curfew and abstain from hard liquor. In the kindergarten the children learned cleanliness and weaving designs; others were not docked for time taken from the machines to nurse their infants.[5]

But paternalism is, itself, a form of rational labor exploitation the moment it becomes self-conscious. Street was not distributing charity; in his own words it was in place of higher wages. As soon as the entrepreneur is able to make this calculation he is exploiting a vulnerability of the workers, that is, their continued unselfconscious attitude of dependence. As long as this vulnerability persists, the "paternalism" of the employer is a more rational method of manipulation than impersonal regulations. But when the workers themselves no longer believe in the benevolence of the employers, two distinct mutations seem to appear. Either the forms of the paternalistic relationship endure, masking an exchange of services which is calculated on both sides, as Juárez Brandão Lopes describes as having occurred in a factory town in southern Minas Gerais, or the workers themselves will unmask the pretended beneficence of the employers. This was what occurred in all of the larger towns of São Paulo, partly because the European tradition of labor militance was imported with the laborers themselves. The response of the industrialists consisted at first in further paternalism, conditioned upon a return to innocence. The Companhia Nacional de Estamparia in Sorocaba, for example, in-

[5] "Condições do trabalho na industria textil no Estado de São Paulo," *Boletim do Departamento Estadual do Trabalho* (1911), pp. 35–77, and (1919), pp. 202–203; Antônio Jafet, *Vida e obra*, pp. 124–128; Arno S. Pearse, *Brazilian Cotton*, p. 42.

formed the other members of the CIFTSP that its workers were entitled to pensions, family allowances, free funerals, and many other fringe benefits, but only on condition of "good conduct." They would be withdrawn from anyone who took part "directly or indirectly" in a strike. Bruno Belli, who managed the Brasital plant, informed his fellow entrepreneurs that his company stores were operating below cost, because of sharply increasing prices at the moment (November 1924), but once prices fell he intended to make up the loss. Meanwhile the losses were endurable. The reduced prices were excellent retardants of strikes, because the workers realized that when the factory closed, so would the stores, and they would be obliged to pay the exhorbitant prices of the local merchants.[6]

This course of action was limited in its effect, however, partly by the emerging solidarity of the industrialists themselves. They did not hesitate to apply sanctions against one of their number who was playing the paternalistic role too liberally. Both the Companhia Nacional and Belli had felt it necessary to explain their activities in meetings of the CIFTSP. Belli was harshly criticized because he was operating at a loss and was obliged to state exactly how much he was losing—15 contos ($1,650) a month. When Pereira Ignácio decided, in 1924, that the cost of the workers' housing at Votorantim had been amortized, and abolished the rents, compensating those not in company housing at a rate of ten milreis a month, the other factory owners in the Sorocaba area were furious. Faced with strikes from their own workers demanding the same benefits, they demanded through the CIFTSP that Votorantim restore the rents. Jorge Street, who had so successfully projected an image of philanthropic concern, seems to have been edged out of the managerial positions he had held in jute and cotton factories and was made first a director of the Center of Industries and then director of the state Department of Labor.[7]

The "social question" became a politically negotiable issue during

[6] Juárez Rubens Brandão Lopes, "Relações industriais na sociedade tradicional brasileira"; CIFTSP, *Circulares* (April 7, 1924; November 1, 1924; November 5, 1924).

[7] *Ibid.* (October 20, 1924); *O Estado de São Paulo* (September 22, 1919; February 24, 1939); Simão, *Sindicato*, pp. 80–81.

World War I. The sudden surge of inflation and the scarcity of food-stuffs caused great hardship to the workers, whose unions grew rapidly in number and militance, and provoked numerous strikes, including general strikes in 1917 and 1919. The plight of the workers aroused the urban middle class to a certain amount of sympathy, for reasons both humanitarian and self-interested. On one hand, the professionals, bureaucrats, and small merchants who employed labor either on a small and casual scale or not at all could afford to scorn the industrialists for their treatment of their workers and to feel morally impelled to rescue these unfortunates from their clutches. On the other hand, the focus of labor's discontent, inflation, was the same that enraged the middle class. Besides, the sorts of measures that the middle class espoused for the elevation of the factory workers seemed most commonly to involve for their implementation the creation of additional middle-class jobs in the bureaucracy. The *Civilista* campaigns in São Paulo in 1910 and 1918 therefore included rhetorical appeals to the workers.[8]

The ability of the articulate middle class to embarrass the conservative manipulators of the Republican Party and the recognition that the workers and their organizations were at least potentially a power to be bought off led to the passage of a few minor pieces of legislation by the state and federal governments. The state Sanitary Code, which included certain dispositions on the employment of minors, was revised in 1917 after the strike movement. It required minors under eighteen to carry work permits bearing proof of age, parents' consent, and attendance at a school for literacy. The measure did not seriously inconvenience the employers, because no minimum age was specified. One of the members of the CIFTSP asked the directorate how to fill out space "J" (literacy) on the required form if the minor in question was illiterate! In 1919 accident insurance was made mandatory in transportation and construction companies and in factories employing machinery. A deceased worker's family might be paid as much as 3,600 milreis ($400) if he had been earning an average salary, and several

---

[8] *Ibid.*, pp. 78–79, 89–98; Law 3724, January 15, 1919; JCSP; CIFTSP, *Circulares* (November 6, December 4, 1922).

new industrial insurance companies were founded in which the names of Paulista politicians figured prominently.[9]

In his presidential campaign of 1922, Arthur Bernardes made an effort to obtain the support of the labor organizations because he considered them a possible counterweight to the army, who regarded his candidacy with great hostility. Accordingly he created, early in his first year in office, the National Labor Council, which was to advise the government on labor affairs. This measure was followed by the organization of pension funds for railroad workers and the declaration that May Day would be a national holiday. These were modest concessions; prolabor deputies had proposed a labor ministry, not a mere advisory council in which labor representatives would be a small minority. In any case, Bernardes ceased to be well disposed toward labor after the army rebellion in São Paulo demonstrated that the unions were more likely to cooperate with the army than to oppose it.

Only one more labor law was passed during his administration: the Law on Holidays, which conceded a two-week paid vacation to all employees. It seems very unlikely that this measure would have passed, considering the effectiveness of the industrialists' lobby in Rio de Janeiro, if it had not been ambiguously worded, so that it appeared to apply only to salaried employees. Only when its implementation was later set out in an executive decree did manufacturers discover that the government intended paid vacations for hourly workers as well. They were appalled. None in São Paulo had ever conceived of granting vacations to workers; it would therefore universally add about 4 per cent to the wage bill. The records of the trade associations in São Paulo contain memorials sent to the government complaining about the burden they would have to bear. Perhaps the most revealing was that of the study committee of the Commercial Association, which reported that although "it did not fail to consider the high objectives of the law," it also had to consider that "Brazil is a new country, which requires the maximum effort of each of its sons to compete with the cost of production of other nations, and especially with those that enjoy perfected machinery and trained and organized work forces." Further-

[9] Everardo Dias, *História das lutas sociais no Brasil*, pp. 120–124, 136–146, 148.

more, reported the committee, "while in many countries of dense population their governments must legislate to organize and distribute work in such a way as to avoid unemployment, we here in Brazil struggle with the contrary phenomenon: the scarcity of labor."[10]

These public representations, and apparently some private ones between June and August 1926, were reasonably successful. Although the issue was kept alive by the political opposition to the Paulista Republican Party, the Law on Holidays was not enforced effectively until the beginning of the Vargas regime.

The inauguration of Washington Luis brought a renewed effort to draw the unions from their militant posture. A law was quickly passed that prohibited the employment of minors under fourteen and the use of minors on night shifts. The juvenile court judge in the capital of São Paulo began almost immediately to prosecute offenders of this new statute, beginning not with factory owners but with the managers of bars, cabarets, cinemas, dance halls, and whorehouses. Within three months he had turned two thousand minors over to the care of state institutions. *O Estado de São Paulo* provided the middle class with enraptured descriptions of the judge's crusading efforts. The CIFTSP's records do not indicate that a similar campaign was directed against their members, or at least not until the passage in December 1927 of a federal decree implementing the law, the so-called Code of Minors. The CIFTSP then began to lobby for the revocation of the law, and the Center of Industrialists regarded it as a challenge at least as important as the passage of the tariff revision, to judge by the amount of space accorded it in its annual reports for 1928 and 1929. Through interviews with the juvenile court judges, they managed to effect a compromise: minors under twelve would be eliminated from the factories, and those twelve and over would be allowed to continue "to exercise their occupations without restriction." The judges considered this concession to be a temporary measure, to allow the manufacturers some time to reorganize their work force. Evidently, however, the manufacturers regarded their ten- and eleven-year-old workers as essential

[10] Associação Commercial de São Paulo, Atas (April 14, 1926; August 16, 1926); *Boletim Official da Associação Commercial* (May–July 1926), pp. 240–242.

elements of production. The directors of the Center informed their membership that they would employ the period of grace they had been granted to lobby for the total repeal of the measure. Although this goal was not achieved, there seems to have been no further attempt by the courts or police to enforce the Code of Minors before the 1930 revolution.[11]

It can be seen that the government was only an occasional champion of the worker and that its intercession came mainly at election time, subject to review when pressure was applied by the manufacturers. The workers themselves regarded the concern of the government with indifference, because it was not directed to the issue that they considerd most important: legal recognition of union contracts. The government recognized only company unions and frequently closed down independent organizations. Furthermore, the anarchist, syndicalist, socialist, and communist unions were too thoroughly critical of the political system of the old Republic to admit of much cooperation even with the radical elements in the middle class or the army. The strength of the unions, and therefore their capacity for bargaining independently of government intervention, had grown greatly since World War I. Azis Simão records the organization of seventy-one unions in São Paulo by 1914 and of seventy-one more by 1923. The vitality of the labor movement became evident to the employers during strikes, which were frequent in São Paulo—Simão found 119 mentioned in the press before World War I, including two generalized movements in 1906 and 1912. The general strike which took place during July 1917 involved more than a hundred factories in the capital and in eleven cities of the interior. Another general strike in 1919 involved even more plants.[12]

The demands of the workers usually included cost-of-living increases in wages, an eight-hour day and the prohibition of Sunday work, prompt payment, the abolition of the system of fines, and the elimination from the plants of children under twelve. In 1917 and 1919,

[11] Law 5083, December 1, 1926; Decree 17943A, December 12, 1927; *O Estado de São Paulo* (July 31, 1927; October 12, 1927); Centro das Industrias do Estado de São Paulo, *Relatorio* (1929), p. 6.

[12] Simão, *Sindicato*, pp. 131–158, 201–219.

while exporters were growing rich by diverting local food supplies to the Allies, they also complained of prices and demanded government inspection and requisitioning of food. At other times the cause of strikes were layoffs, pay cuts, or violence done to workers.[13]

The reaction of the manufacturers was generally peremptory and heavy-handed. It is possible to piece together, through the CIFTSP's minutes and its mimeographed circulars, the collective actions taken by the employers in São Paulo to defend their profits. The CIFTSP was, itself, a trade association founded largely for the purpose of controlling the workers. In its inaugural sessions, alongside the unabashed intention noted "to take precautions against harmful competition," a desire was also expressed to "study all labor questions, labor legislation, and practical means of resolving strikes." This first meeting convened only a few weeks after a generalized strike movement in which the employers had acceded to the workers' demands for an eight-hour day. It is likely that part of the necessity for cooperation among the factory owners proceeded from a common desire to renege on that promise. Since labor unions were not recognized by law, this would not constitute a breach of contract, and there was no fear of a confrontation with the government. But it was clear that a common front against the predictable wrath of the workers would be a prudent measure.

The second and third meetings were wholly occupied with suggestions for putting down a strike that had broken out in sympathy for the workers at the São Paulo Light Company. Rodolfo Crespi moved that the owners attach to their doors a notice that the factories would remain closed for as many days as the workers struck. This idea was gleefully accepted by everyone save the representative from Matarazzo's IRFM, who said he would have to ask his boss. The next day the Count appeared, amid general deference from the members. Pereira Ignácio moved that the assembly congratulate itself on the presence of "the Prince of Paulista Industry." Matarazza, however, was not disposed to participate in the euphoria of the moment. He rose and moved,

---

[13] CIFTSP, *Atas* (October 1, 1919); *Circulares* (April [no date], 1927); Simão, *Sindicato*, p. 110.

without rhetorical flourishes, that the workers simply be invited back to work, since the Light strike had already been resolved. The members, without exception, reversed their stand of the previous day and voted for Matarazzo's motion.

It is striking how often Matarazzo calmed the unbridled tempers of the other industrialists. During the strike movement of 1919 he had remained indifferent to the question of the eight-hour day, although the other employers, even the "humanitarian" Jorge Street, had opposed it strenuously. Matarazzo reasoned coolly that the shorter workday would reduce output, which would increase prices and offset any losses to the manufacturers. Early in March 1920 he again attempted to exercise a restraining influence when one of the members raised the issue of the collection of union dues on company property. It was precipitately decided that all the factories would lock out workers if the unions did not agree to cease the collections forthwith. This seemed to Matarazzo an extreme measure, since only four of the locals had refused to suspend the collections. The union in his own plant was cooperating, he said; therefore he saw no reason to close his doors. Once again Crespi was betrayed by his impulsiveness: he had shut down his factory already and was determined that all the others join him. Matarazzo suggested a lockout fund, but other members persisted in demanding punitive action. He finally withdrew from the association, on the grounds that the members could not demand obedience from each firm on such an important question. Fortunately for the CIFTSP, the lockout was soon swallowed up in a large strike movement, which turned out to be unsuccessful, and Matarazzo rejoined the association, thereby saving the members from further embarrassment.[14]

Far more effective than the unconsidered actions of the assembly were the cunning machinations of its general secretary, O. Pupo Nogueira. During the 1920's he developed and operated a well-coordinated intelligence network directed against the unions. Nogueira, as general secretary, conscientiously tried to lengthen the association's

[14] CIFTSP, *Atas* (October 24, 25, 1919); Matarazzo, *Scelta di discorsi e interviste*, p. 182; CIFTSP, *Atas* (March 5, April 24, 1920; February 28, 1923).

membership list, to build a store of statistical data on the textile industry, and to represent the association to the press and the government.
But these were minor occupations compared with the business of suppressing the unions. His most inspired idea was a blacklist, which he
originally described as a means of identifying thieves but which, he
quickly realized, would be useful as a means of "purging from the work
force certain undesirable elements that operate within it, at times, as
fermenters of indiscipline." The idea was eagerly accepted by the
owners; names began pouring in to the association, and Nogueira
exulted, "Nothing will impede the factories from now on from purging from their personnel professional agitators. . . . When any of the
members wishes to relieve himself of an agitator, he need do nothing
more than communicate with this Center, and the Center will immediately take steps so that the dangerous element will be removed. . . .
His card will be sent to the associated factories, just as will be done
with thieves." For several months, however, no thieves were listed, and
most of the names turned in were not even of organizers, but of simple
workers who had done nothing more than "demonstrate indiscipline."[15]

Nogueira then turned to the even grander project of compiling
dossiers on *all* workers, so that their reliability could be kept track of
continuously and so that workers on strike might be prevented from
finding employment at other mills. By the end of July 1921 this program was completed in Sorocaba, and Nogueira urged that the identification be completed in the capital; "The epoch we have gone through
requires a total and definitive resolution." Bruno Belli supported the
secretary's efforts. "In effect our factories are open to all the adven-
turers, all the social scum rejected by the old civilizations of Europe,
without our industrialists being able to perform a selection of their
personnel." But with a system of permanent identification, he said,
"the proletarian element of the capital and the interior of the state
will be regimented, cleansed, vivified, purified of the evil elements that
poisoned it." It was clear from the context that Belli was referring to
agitators, but he had not forgotten the original issue of thievery. In

[15] *Circulares* (April 28–June 8, 1921); CIFTSP, *Relatorio* (1925, 1926).

his peroration he patched the two issues together again rather neatly: "Our revered president [Matarazzo], so profound an observer, arrived at the conclusion that, for our workers, imbued with new and disquietingly rash ideas, theft is no longer a crime. Theft, robbery, represents tribute paid forcibly by the employer. Whoever takes from the factories, surreptitiously, any object, takes away a part of the profits. Either we are very much mistaken or this is Communism, *en herbe*."

As projects developed for the standardization of purchase contracts and sales contracts, it came to Nogueira that a "laudable standardization" was also possible in labor contracts. He therefore issued a call for information on wages, noting "a tendency, praiseworthy furthermore, as well one might understand, of the uniformization of wages, for the general good." It is clear that the members appreciated Nogueira's unceasing efforts for the general good. The membership list grew until it numbered fifty-one by the middle of 1925, including all of the largest firms. The members seemed to prefer the general secretary's methods to the chaos of the assembly, for, even as the membership increased, the number of general sessions declined.[16]

More effective than any of his intelligence systems, however, was the "harmonious relationship" which Nogueira had established with the police. It is true that the CIFTSP was not the first employers' association to use the police as strikebreakers. It was recorded during the movement of 1917 that both the Companhia Antarctica Paulista and the Ipiranga textile firm belonging to the Jafets had "conferred" with the secretary of the Força Publica on possible countermeasures. A report from the United States consul in São Paulo to the Secretary of State concerning this movement portrays, perhaps better than any Brazilian observer's comments, the hauteur of the bourgeois and their influence with the police. "About the first of June," he wrote, "a number of agitators, mostly Spaniards, arrived from Argentina, where they were not particularly welcome, and proceeded to organize the laboring classes, which was no particularly difficult task, as they are at

---

[16] *Circulares* (July 5, 1922; November 8, 1922; July 10, 1925); CIFTSP, *Relatorio* (1925, 1926); Atas, 1919 to 1921, shows 37 sessions, 1922 to 1926 records only 13.

all times excitable and liable to 'swarm.' The mob spirit was given free rein for about three days during the anti-German riots which took place about the middle of April, and after that time the unrest seemed to spread, so that the field was ripe for the agitators when they arrived." The protection of the law, it seems, had been partially withdrawn to encourage nationalist sentiments, but then the violence had turned against more important people. At this point the authority of the state was reasserted. The police picked up several hundred "agitators," not always, according to the consul, "in a manner prescribed by the law, however justifiable from a standpoint of expediency." Finally it was decided to deport several of them, who were, it was supposed, in the pay of the Germans, although no proof had appeared—two Italians, a Russian ("probably a Polish Jew"), and six Spaniards.[17]

Nogueira did not have to resort to deportations. Once his blacklist was established, it became very difficult for an organizer to find a job within the factory. As soon as one was identified within a plant, the general secretary simply called the police and had the man jailed. The employers were invited to send Nogueira the names of potential troublemakers, if a strike appeared imminent. "The Center will immediately see to it that the worker pointed out will disappear for some time until the atmosphere of agitation has passed." The police, of course, were also employed against pickets. "For a question of trifling importance, the workers of the Companhia Fabril Paulistana declared themselves on strike in the month of June of last year [1921]. The intervention of the Center being asked for, it made itself felt promptly and the strike was resolved without greater difficulties, in large part owing to the rapid and energetic intervention of the police." Nogueira proudly revealed to his employers "how great a cordiality reigns between the Center and the state police headquarters and the Bureau of Investigations. Partly in virtue of personal relations of the Manager of our guild." Not only did the police esteem him, they even deputized him: "In the case of S[ão] Bernardo, the Manager carried instructions

---

[17] *Jornal do Commercio (São Paulo)* (September 11, 1917); NA–DS, Charles Hoover to Secretary of State, (October 20, 1917), 811.108/307.

to operate in the area according to his judgment, with or without the collaboration of the local police."[18]

It is difficult to estimate the effectiveness of collective repressive efforts by the employers. It appears that the number of strikes declined after 1922, but this may be illusory, since the newspapers were reluctant to print information about strikes during the state of siege that lasted until 1927. If there was, in fact, less labor unrest, it is not likely that it was because the employers had become more paternal in their dealings with workers or more manipulative. Wage levels barely kept pace with the cost of living, and owners like Pereira Ignácio still dealt with "indiscipline" by firing workers *en masse* as late as 1928. It is more likely that worker discontent was becoming more political, as more and more sectors of the elite withdrew from active support of the regime and began to seek new kinds of followings. The conflict between factory owners and labor unions was intensifying the crisis of the old Republic.

Nevertheless, the struggle with the workers had impelled the industrialists to define themselves more clearly, to organize themselves, and adopt certain class attitudes. It is interesting, for example, that the enormous efforts expended to put down the workers preceded the battles over deflation and the tariff policy. Had it been a proving ground? Matarazzo, in the midst of the tariff revision, could turn the experience to good account. One of the reasons for the high cost of Brazilian goods, he blandly informed the newspapers in 1928, was the cost of labor, for "Brazil . . . always has led in all the liberal conquests in behalf of the proletariat." Matarazzo, in whose factories inspectors had found half-size machines for the convenience of his child workers, sought to persuade the public to accept higher tariffs as a way of saving the jobs of pampered Brazilian laborers. The encounter with the elite of the plantation must also have been perilous for the self-image of the industrialists; how frequently must the immigrant entrepreneur have heard in private what a blue-blooded governor did not hesitate

[18] RRIAB, no date [after October 9, 1926], 832.504/20 mentions censorship; *Circulares* (April 10, 28, 1928); Dias, *História*, pp. 154–170.

to mention in a speech "on the plutocracy" in 1937, that "Through circumstances which are well known a few rude workingmen, assisted by a lucky star, erected in years past considerable fortunes, the greater part in industry." The proletariat and the landed rich, each for their own reasons, considered them undeserving of their wealth. What defenses did the industrialists erect?[19]

The industrialists might have demonstrated more enthusiasm for charities. To have redistributed some of their wealth in social services might have persuaded the public of their civic pride, or at least of their aristocratic sense of responsibility for the poor. But in spite of frequent mention in the press of the charities of one industrialist or another, the donations or bequests to hospitals or orphanages, to the Italian school or the Mackenzie Institute, seem to have been quite modest and for the most part a matter of self-commemoration. Matarazzo's sizable gift to the Humberto I Hospital, for example, was in memory of his eldest son, and the faculty of business administration bestowed on the city by Francisco Matarazzo, Jr., is a bizarre monument to family pride. The interior was never completed, but from the front the public beheld an enormous marble façade, a broad, neatly trimmed lawn, and an immense statue of the Count gesturing grandly at the hollow building.

And yet, according to their public statements, neither did the entrepreneurs spend their wealth on themselves. At a testimonial dinner Matarazzo told his guests "of the extremely frugal life led by me and mine." His personal expenditures were very few, he said: "For me and for my personal comfort, I reserve and possess only this house, where I sleep at night, and a homestead where I dissipate the tedium of Sunday afternoons." Where, then, was the profit spent? "The profits, the fabulous profits that they talk so much about, are except for strictly necessary expenses . . . applied wholly to the realization of my ideal." He explained that "the preoccupation of enrichment was never the motive of any act of my life. Wealth I always regarded as a means of reaching an ideal: to enlarge, enlarge as much as possible, the industrial organism, already vast, to which I linked my name;

[19] *Folha de Manhã* (June 12, 1928); "Condições de trabalho . . ."; Armando Salles Oliveira, *Jornada democratica*, p. 51.

. . . to intensify all my effort in order to make more efficient the contribution, which I have imposed on myself as a duty, for the industrial emancipation of Brazil." In Matarazzo's case the claim that his profits were plowed back into his company was probably true, although the pose of extreme frugality is a trifle forced. In spite of the cost of the spectacular mansion on Avenida Paulista, which is supposed to contain two swimming pools, and of the mausoleum-like head office on the Chá Viaduct, which is faced with 170,000 tons of Carrara marble, the worth of IRFM continued to grow spectacularly under the guidance of Matarazzo's son. Reinvestment seems to have provided all the capital needed for expansion during the 1930's and 1940's, since windfall loans from the government were not available to IRFM. In order to achieve his continuous expansion, however, it was necessary for Francisco, Jr., to prevent the fragmentation of the Count's estate among his numerous heirs, a matter which displeased the rest of the family greatly.[20]

For the most part, the industrialists did not attempt to justify their wealth. They were able in some measure to ignore the criticism of the lower classes and even of the planters, because they did not fully recognize the ability of the latter to grant or withdraw status. Although the immigrant industrialists had been accepted readily enough by the plantation elite, and had even intermarried with it, these "few rude workingmen" were not willing to consider this acceptance the pinnacle of social grace. The attraction of their European homelands was still very strong, and those who could afford it frequently returned for vacations. Their children were sent back for schooling and learned to partake of their parents' nostalgia. A reporter who interviewed Siciliano's son discovered that after some years spent in Europe he had assumed, "without any pose, all the character of an English gentleman," that "he loves Italy as though he had never left, and says with a little pride that he cannot let a year pass without returning."[21]

When they could, if they were rich enough, they married European aristocrats, whose patents of nobility they no doubt considered to be

---

[20] *O Estado de São Paulo* (March 10, 1929); "Matarazzo's Mighty Empire," *Brazilian Business* (September 1953), pp. 24–30.

[21] A. d'Atri, *L'Etat de São Paulo*, pp. 140–141.

more genuine. Thus of the twelve Matarazzo children who married, three entered plantation families, but five married noble Italians, including two princes and a count. Titles and honors were more rapidly procured by a few industrialists by contributing to Italian or Papal charitable funds. Matarazzo and Crespi were made counts by Victor Emmanuel; Siciliano was a papal count; and many others were knights or commanders of various Italian orders: Ugliengo, Giorgi, di Camillis, Gamba, Briccola, Belli, and Scurrachio, among others. Puglisi Carbone's knight commander of the Crown of Italy was obtained by raising 700,000 lire ($35,000) for the victims of the Calabrian earthquakes. The Jafets displayed their strong sentimental ties to the homeland by, among other works, registering the local immigrant community for the Lebanese government, thus "zealously preventing the Lebanese from losing their true nationality." It is evident that the immigrant entrepreneurs deferred perhaps more readily to reference groups other than the planters.

A few of the industrialists expressed occasionally some fragmentary argument that is suggestive of an ideological justification of capitalism or of their own position in society. Nami Jafet, for example, who had once been a schoolteacher and was the patriarch of his family, attempted in a brief essay written in 1908 to expose the fallacies of socialism. Equality of fortune is impossible, he explained, because human abilities are unequal. This rudimentary proposition was not wholly satisfactory to him, since he acknowledged that some fortunes were not earned, but these he considered to be exceptional; besides, he added, inequality of income is socially useful because it creates capital stocks that are necessary for further progress. The contract between the capitalist and the worker is not a form of struggle but of social cooperation, since it is mutually advantageous. The theme of inherent inequality was quite often asserted by industrialists on commemorative occasions, and so was the thought that Brazilian society was incomparable with European, where socialist theory originated. In Brazil it was not a matter of redistributing wealth, but of creating it; Brazilian social conditions could not be compared with the injustices of Czarist Russia; and Brazil, especially São Paulo, was a land of opportunity. "Remember," said Matarazzo, "we live in a blessed land." Toward the end of the

1930's the industrialists found another reason to regard their privileges complacently. The regional differences in wage levels and the influx of workers from the depressed North proved that the Paulista worker was better off than the worker in other states. Simonsen gravely declared that wages elsewhere were "absolutely insufficient to assure the workers a decent and efficient existence." The cause was "an excess of labor," and the government would have to provide incentives to further industrialization in those areas.[22]

The origin of these arguments was, perhaps, liberal. Jafet's other concerns are typical of a classical liberal—secular education, religious toleration, women's rights, and the abolition of prostitution—but liberalism was not generally influential among Paulista industrialists during the 1920's and 1930's. It was associated, as an economic theory, with a no longer acceptable policy of free trade; it was supposed to be the root of Europe's social and political malaise and to be incapable of dealing with the menace of communism. It did not encourage men to accept their places in society; instead it fostered the uproar of the professional politicians and the wastefulness and grubby materialism of economic competition. In the 1920's one begins to find among the elites of São Paulo, but most particularly among the industrialists, a strong interest in the varieties of European fascism. They read O. Pupo Nogueira's translation of Manoilescu on corporativism, and they were stirred by the economic and political miracles wrought by Mussolini and Salazar in their homelands. According to R. C. Bastos—a Portuguese immigrant merchant and industrialist who knew the communities both of Rio de Janeiro and São Paulo—when a Portuguese merchant returned from a visit to Lisbon filled with praise for the dictator, only one or two fellow immigrants would contradict him in public.[23]

The conversion of Matarazzo began in 1923. He returned from a European voyage enormously impressed by the new regime. He found, he told the press, "An Italy in many ways new . . . The rhythm of

[22] Nâmi Jafet, *Ensaios e discursos*, pp. 223–230; Roberto Simonsen, *Níveis de vida e a economia nacional*, pp. 10–21; Matarazzo, *Scelta di discorsi e interviste*, p. 198.

[23] Stein, *Brazilian Cotton Manufacture*, p. 136; Raul Carvalho Bastos, *Homens e fatos*, p. 324.

life is absolutely changed. To begin with, the workers, in whom the consciousness of patriotic discipline has given birth to the just comprehension of their duties and their rights; then there are the trains that regularly run on time . . ." He went to see the *Duce* and was received twice. "I can have no motive for reticence regarding my admiration. . . . I say frankly that I came out of the Chigi Palace deeply enthusiastic. The impression one immediately gains is that of finding oneself before a man whose force of will has the gift of knowing how to penetrate everything to which it is directed. . . . The future is not only in the lap of Jove, but also in the hands of the Strong; he knows well that this is his motto." The leader of the Paulista Fascist Party immediately made contact with him.

He returned from trips made the following year and in 1925 with renewed enthusiasm. "I am a great admirer of Mussolini. Furthermore I am convinced that he is animated by an ardent patriotism and a strong sincerity." Matarazzo was not unaware of criticisms of the *Duce*. "And so they complain of his violence! But, *mio Dio*, it isn't possible to transform the mentality of an entire multitude without marking out with an iron rod the direction of the new road. A convinced ideologist cannot compromise either with the masses or with those who want to exploit them. And Mussolini, besides being a convinced ideologist, is also an extraordinary man of action." Nevertheless, Matarazzo preserved the same disinclination to involvement in organization that he had demonstrated before the CIFTSP.

The creation of the local Fascist Party, evidently subsidized by the Italian consulate, had provoked discord among the immigrants. The movement, to judge by the small number of *fasci* and the absence of any significant names on the roster of party secretaries, had not gained popular acceptance. Matarazzo therefore advised the Party emphatically that he opposed "any Fascist campaign or agitation whatsoever in Brazil. This would produce only a contrary result. Our attitude ought to be this: to work, to work hard, and only to work."[24]

It is evident that the Italian government regarded Matarazzo's opin-

[24] Vicenzo Blancato, *Conte Francesco Matarazzo*, pp. 375–378, 362; Matarazzo, *Scelta di discorsi e interviste*, pp. 82, 195–198; Salvatore Pisani, *Lo Stato di San Paolo*, pp. 1248–1251.

ions highly. He received the Order of the Crown of Italy with grand cross and cordon in 1926 and, the following year, the Gold Medal of Merit, accompanied by an autographed letter from the *Duce*. The latter honor was in recognition of a gift of a million lire ($51,000) for the Fascist Youth Movement. By the 1930's Matarazzo seems to have become wholly identified with Mussolini's aggressive foreign policy. Not only did he offer another million lire for the assistance of the expeditionary force sent to Ethiopia, he also participated in a social *cause célèbre* that was breathlessly related by the *Correio Paulistano* in telegraphic style: "A significant episode—We are in the period of sanctions in the campaign of East Africa. Count Matarazzo finds himself in Guarujá. The dining room. There are present various diplomats of the sanctioning powers. Matarazzo listens, observes, and is silent. Unexpectedly he makes an impetuous gesture. He arises. He calls the director of the orchestra and asks him to play 'Giovinezza.' Silence and stupor among those present. Matarazzo, superb, gives the Fascist salute and leaves the salon."[25]

It is probable that he became a member of the Party. When he died, in 1937, the obituaries noted a wreath that was sent to "Comrade Count F. Matarazzo" from the *fascio* of São Paulo. At the funeral a Fascist ceremony took place after the service in the chapel. Crespi was publicly identified with the cause of fascism even more strongly than Matarazzo. Mussolini's government presented him with the Order of Labor and made him a Commander of the Crown of Italy, and Crespi became a member of the Party. In his will he left 200 contos ($18,000) to Italian charities and 500 ($45,000) personally to Mussolini. He had also specified that he be buried in his uniform.[26]

It might be that a partiality toward authoritarian ideas on the part of industrial entrepreneurs ought to be considered a mere idiosyncracy, derived perhaps from the sense of nearly limitless power experienced in their daily lives and partly from a desire to arrogate the power of the state in order to extend the process of industrialization and suppress the workers' organizational efforts. On the other hand it might also be claimed that the fondness for the Fascist ideology was

[25] *In memoriam, Conde Francisco Matarazzo*, pp. 18, 181–185, 316, 467.
[26] *O Estado de São Paulo* (January 28, 1939).

symptomatic of a profound crisis in the development of Brazilian industrial capitalism. The authoritarian outlook at many points diverges from the structural requirements of a capitalist system. The turn of mind, for example, that relegates the worker to an unalterably inferior position in society and that sees his subsistence as the responsibility of the employer leaves open no possibility that the worker deserves more than a subsistence regime. What is given to him beyond the barest essentials is not conceivable as being his due. The worker is merely a poor man who has been rescued from starvation by the efforts of one of life's supermen, and whatever he obtains beyond a crust and a shirt and a roof over his head is the result either of thievery or the ineffable generosity of his employer. Bonuses, for example, were generally awarded on some occasion that reflected the grandeur of the entrepreneur: on Count Matarazzo's eightieth birthday the workers received gifts according to the number of years they had served IRFM, and special donations were passed out to those who married or who had children on the lucky day. His son's employees were treated to a holiday each year on Francisco Jr.'s birthday.[27]

The difficulty with this ideology is that it puts no money in the worker's pocket. The consumption by the worker of additional goods is not presented to the entrepreneur's mind as an opportunity to sell more. Instead he complains of the worker's profligacy, even if he has not increased his wage payments. If the rural workers did not eat so much, he feels, more beef and sugar might be exported and more foreign exchange be earned. It is quite possible that this attitude was a principle cause of the retarded development of an internal market in Brazil and of that absence of interest, so often remarked upon by observers, in mass production and narrow profit margins. Monteiro Lobato, a writer and publisher who was a strenuous advocate of industrial development, complained in the preface of his translation of Henry Ford's *Today and Tomorrow* that up to then (1927) industrialization in Brazil had created "magnates in return for the perpetuation or aggravation of human misery." The "genial ideas" of Ford of-

---

[27] *O Conde Matarazzo aos oitenta annos*, p. 271; "Matarazzo's Mighty Empire."

fered a solution. In Lobato's opinion "no country more than ours needs to understand and practice Fordism."[28]

The social abyss which separated the industrialist from his workers could give rise to ideas even more bizarre than the opinion that consumption beyond subsistence was profligacy. Eduardo Jafet, in a thesis presented to a conference on industry in 1944, foresaw a constant condition of "overproduction" in Brazilian industry. "The present state of Brazilian consumption imposes a pessimistic orientation concerning the future of our industrialization, and, if urgent measures are not taken, with a directing plan, we do not believe in the possibility of a more prosperous and progressive future for the nation." Although he recognized that purchasing power was low, this was not the main difficulty. Rather it was that the worker "doesn't want to consume; the problem consists, not in raising remuneration, but in creating social wants . . ." The families of the interior, he explained, generally bought only one change of clothing a year, not because prices were high; on the contrary: because of "over-production" they were *irrisórios*—"ridiculous." But the workers had neither the social desire nor the knowledge of hygiene, therefore "another piece of clothing is an extravagance." In the circumstances, "It would be useless to force high levels of remuneration, if the means to apply them has a minimum limit." Jafet's solution was to provide the masses more schooling, not in order to increase their productivity but to increase their desire for goods, which would make them work harder and stay on the job. At the same time, however, the cost of this effort ought not to fall on industry. "The lowering of costs of production also being necessary for the strengthening of internal markets, national productive activity ought not to be burdened by taxation and other legislative measures beyond those levels now in effect."[29]

Evidently the authoritarian system of beliefs did not allow the industrialists to take account of the potentialities of everyman. In turn, an industrial capitalism founded on such a system could never engage

[28] *Hoje e Amanhã*, p. 6; see Fernando Henrique Cardoso, *Empresário industrial e desenvolvimento econômico*, p. 154, for attitudes toward mass consumption.

[29] Eduardo Jafet, "Fortalecimento . . . ," pp. 10–15.

the sympathies of the masses. As Souza Martins has pointed out in his biographical study of Matarazzo, the Count's self-image of success through inherent qualities, or rather *quality*, turned the Italian community against him. In this formulation wealth and power are not commodities within the reach of any Horatio Alger hero: acquired skills or diligence are not recognized as means of achieving success, hence the ordinary worker cannot hope to improve his station. The ideal society would be that which provided the proletarian with security in his fated role and at the same time discouraged him from futile aspirations. But the authoritarian ideology has this defect: the worker cannot be engaged in that thralldom characteristic of the open society, in which success is each man's interiorized goal and failure is merely a personal and private disgrace. Still more disastrous, it is likely that the industrialists' pretensions were too bogus to be believed by former neighbors (the Italian consul assiduously spread the story of Matarazzo's aristocratic origins, to no avail). The Fascist myth, therefore, was not merely inappropriate, it was a self-deception practiced by an elite constantly more isolated from a cynical and uncooperative working class.[30]

The authoritarian attitude toward society may have been the cause of another peculiarity of industrialization in São Paulo. Until the middle of World War II, the entrepreneurs demonstrated almost no interest in the technical training of their manpower pool. It is true that the state possessed the Polytechnical School, but this was an institution that produced mainly civil and construction engineers, and it was an invention of the plantation elite. The Polytechnic and Mackenzie Institute by 1945 produced a total of only four hundred engineers whose degrees were applicable to industrial occupations. Only one training school for skilled workers existed, the *Liceu de Artes e Ofícios*; its courses were principally in crafts such as woodworking. The industrialists did not demand that the government provide additional courses in technical subjects; nor did they create private institutions for the purpose, because they found it cheaper to hire skilled workers and en-

---

[30] José de Souza Martins, *Empresário e emprêsa na biografia do Conde Matarazzo*, pp. 56–57.

gineers in Europe and the United States and because their own children, whom they expected to assume control of their businesses, were usually sent abroad to study.

A visitor to São Paulo in 1930 found foreign technicians "very numerous; one sees them everywhere . . ." Matarazzo kept "hordes of high salaried technicians, mostly German or Italian," according to another reporter who visited IRFM after the war. Because certain skills could not be found locally, the Center of Industries opposed Vargas' decree of 1930 that limited to one-third of the work force the number of foreigners a company might hire. Simonsen suggested that an exception be made in behalf of Portuguese technicians. Another manufacturer, quoting him, told an industrial conference in 1944 that "It is necessary to import technicians who have already been trained; it is much cheaper, and enriches the country, because it means an additional man, and an additional economic value."[31]

It was not until the middle of World War II that the manufacturers, faced with the total disappearance of their overseas reserve of manpower, founded and promoted a training program for Paulista workers. Of course, both for the entrepreneur and for the government it was true in a narrow sense that importing technicians was cheaper than training them. And yet of how little use to Brazil was an industrial system that condemned its citizens to unskilled labor. Not only were they excluded from jobs that offered better wages and a chance to use more of their talents and intelligence, but they also began to be filled with self-doubt. A sensitive French observer suggested that the "susceptibility" of the Paulistas to the condescension of the Europeans "is constantly kept lively by the contact with foreigners, who are only too ready to deprecate a country they get rich in, and whose inhabitants they find useful for some purposes. Their presence provokes perpetual comparisons." He found that urban Brazilians were "obsessed with the idea of race—and of racial inequality." Perhaps this "susceptibility" was a cause, as well as a result, of the employment of foreigners.

[31] *Revista Industrial de São Paulo* (July 1945), pp. 19–23; Louis Mouralis, *Un séjour*, p. 123; "Matarazzo's Mighty Empire"; Federação das Industrias do Estado de São Paulo, *Relatorio*, 1938, 78; Congresso Brasileiro de Indústria, *Atas*, Segunda Comissão, December, 1944, 7.

There were perhaps more devious reasons behind the "cheapness" of the already trained foreigner. He came for a stated period of time, under a visa that the employer had obtained for him; at the end of the contract he was not likely to set up a competing company. Meanwhile, the Brazilian worker without a diploma or formal education, who had obtained skills on the job, could not command a high salary and did not find it so easy to transfer his skills to some other employer.[32]

It is possible that the industrialists ignored another potential development of the industrial structure because of their commitment to an ordered and authoritarian society. Observers of the Brazilian economy frequently remarked how useful would be the organization of a stock market capable of mobilizing industrial capital. In São Paulo, however, the dealings there were principally in public securities. Various explanations have been advanced to account for the fact that the industrialists did not seek additional venture capital from the public. It has been said that the middle class was not interested in purchasing shares because it was so unsophisticated that it regarded urban real estate a better hedge against inflation or so hungry for consumer goods that it saved only a negligible proportion of its income. These difficulties might increase the cost of public sales of stock, but they are not insuperable obstacles. The first large offering of the stock of a private concern, for example, that of Panair do Brasil in 1944, was quite successful; four million dollars worth of shares, representing 40 per cent of its capital, were easily sold. Another sort of explanation admitted the existence of potential buyers but objected that the entrepreneur was faced with institutional obstacles, such as the tax on capital, which made it imprudent for him to declare the true amount of his assets. But the truly enterprising industrialists, as we have seen, exercised sufficient influence over activities of the government to resolve difficulties of this order. If the industrialists had desired it, the taxes on capital and on excess profits might have been transformed so that public revelation of their balances would not have compromised them.[33]

[32] Mouralis, *Un séjour*, p. 99; see also an anonymous engineer's letter in *Direção* (October 1962), p. 6.

[33] The problem is discussed in George Wythe, *Brazil, an Expanding Econo-*

A third explanation, admittedly somewhat risky because the evidence for it is wholly negative, is that the entrepreneur did not sell his stock publicly because he did not want to. The sale of stocks to the public was sometimes called "the democratization of capital," a euphemism that carried connotations of economic reformism along the same lines as profit sharing, with what disgusted reaction among the industrialists may well be imagined. The untapped reserve of capital was available at a cost they were not willing to pay: they would have to become legally accountable, not merely to the government but to people who were their social inferiors, for the management of their firms. It is entirely possible that the manufacturers also sensed that their attitude of disdain was reciprocated by the middle class, whose interests they had combatted in the tariff struggle, and that as a consequence it would be only with great difficulty that the middle class would allow them to manage its savings.[34]

The increasing consumption of consumer goods by the masses, the recruitment of great numbers of workers into a technical middle class, and the participation of large numbers of people in share ownership are all structural consequences of capitalistic industrial development. Yet there is evidence to suggest that Paulista entrepreneurs did not regard these transformations as desirable. It is true that alternative resolutions, such as the importation of technicians on contract, are viable for continued development of the individual firm, but if he relies upon them, is the entrepreneur still the prime mover of economic development that Schumpeter conceived him to be? The industrialists, along with the merchants and large landowners, were often referred to, and referred to themselves, as the "conservative classes," an interesting

my, p. 158; Henri van Deursen, "L'Émancipation industrielle . . . ," pp. 287–288; Cardoso, *Empresário*, pp. 108–110; Alexandre Kafka, "Brazil," in Benjamin H. Beckhart, ed., *Banking Systems*, pp. 81–82; Geraldo Banas, *Anuário Banas: bancos, investimentos e bolsas, 1964.*

[34] Supporting opinions in H. Jorge Müller Carioba, "Investidores versus empresários," in *Ibid.*; Constantino Ianni, "Formação de capital e desenvolvimento industrial," in *Problemas da economia industrial.* See also Constantino Ianni, *Poupança, investimentos, e mercado de capital no Brasil.*

definition because it acknowledges an attitude common to the industrialists' ruthlessness toward the workers, their admiration for hierarchy, and their indifference toward social development: once their factories were built, they were concerned not with enterprise but with hanging on to their property.

CHAPTER X

The Industrialists and the Liberal State

The collapse of international trade in 1930 nearly paralyzed São Paulo's industries. The value of coffee shipments declined 675,000 contos ($80,000,000) from the year before, or almost 40 per cent. The consequent failure of demand in the rural areas obliged many factory owners to suspend production. In the capital the unemployed were said to number 70,000 in July and 100,000 four months later. The state Department of Labor told the press that it had sent 40,000 jobless workers out of the city, "directing them to the countryside." The CIFTSP reported to its membership in November that twenty-four cotton mills were shut and that the textile, paper, and metalworking industries were operating at 25 to 40 per cent of capacity.[1]

Even though the immediate consequences of the trade depression were severe, they did not affect the industrialization of the state as profoundly as another event of that year, the overthrow of the old Republic. The revolution, carried out in October by a varied opposition, did not lack an occasion that was purely political: the abrogation by Washington Luis of the gentlemen's agreement that called for a

[1] *O Estado de São Paulo* (April 4, July 10–19, 1930); CIFTSP, *Circulares* (November 7, 1930).

Mineiro to succeed him. Nevertheless, the crisis transmuted this mis-
step into a cause worth disputing. The effective power of the government in Rio de Janeiro began to weaken as revenues declined and as
diverging opinions arose concerning countermeasures. Washington
Luis's unusual decision to maintain Paulista control of the presidency
had been determined, at least in part, by his feeling that only a Paulista
would continue his financial policy. Yet he alienated state planters and
industrialists when he persisted in a deflationary program that he had
initiated before the crisis. The disgruntled leadership in Minas Gerais
and Rio Grande do Sul rallied dissident elements in the other states,
including São Paulo's Democratic Party, to a "Liberal Alliance" in
behalf of the candidacy of Getúlio Vargas, governor of Rio Grande do
Sul. The support of the urban middle class and the workers was cultivated, and it was attempted to identify the Alliance with the revolutionary movements of the Bernardes era. In spite of the popular
enthusiasm, the political machines of the state Republican parties produced faithfully the electoral majorities that Washington Luis required
of them. The election justified the complaints of the urban liberals: no
matter what the crisis, or how great the opposition, the fraud of the
professional politicians would maintain the regime.

As the crisis deepened in the months following the election in
March 1930, the leaders of the Liberal Alliance determined upon a
rebellion against the government. The planters and industrialists of São
Paulo did not actively oppose the movement, although its purpose was
to forestall the inauguration of a second Paulista term of office. The
soldiers of Rio Grande do Sul swept through a shuttered and apathetic
capital, and on to Rio de Janeiro, only to find that the army had already
deposed Washington Luis. Vargas planned at first to serve provisionally and, after having remedied its defects by revolutionary decree, to
become president under the 1891 Constitution. But the failure of the
export economy had sapped the legitimizing force of the existing constitutional arrangements. The demands for radical reform were dis-
cordant, but they were almost universal. Vargas, therefore, had to
re-evaluate the Brazilian political system and its relationship to the
economy.

At first this re-evaluation was decidedly hostile to the industrialists.

Vargas came from a state in which manufacturing was politically of little significance, and nothing in his economic education had suggested to him that the industrialization of Brazil was an urgent matter. The deputy he sent to São Paulo, who was also from Rio Grande do Sul, was so unaware of the size of São Paulo's industrial park that he considered resolving labor troubles by inviting the owner and one worker from each firm to a meeting. He didn't realize the audience would have numbered eleven thousand. The industrialists in São Paulo, and apparently in other states, had defended the "situation" to the last. Far from having aligned themselves with the revolutionaries and the "progressive elements," they were its adversaries.[2]

On the other hand, the Liberal Alliance had made appeals to the urban middle class which obliged the acceptance of its invective against the supposed incompetence and corruption of the industrialists who burdened Brazil with high tariffs. Vargas' platform favored the protection only of industries that used domestic raw materials and repeated the planters' complaint against "artificial industries that manufacture with imported raw materials, increasing the cost of living for the benefit of privileged industries." Shortly after the revolution the British Chamber of Commerce reported to its members, evidently with satisfaction, that it could "be gathered from pronouncements made by many of the new rulers that there is a general recognition of the fact that Brazil's general and future well-being lies in the development of agricultural, pastoral, and mineral exploitation, and not in the setting up of an industrial structure which can exist only under cover of an outrageous tariff . . . ."[3] Nevertheless, the commitment to industries that transformed native raw materials implied, if it were carried out, an enormous economic transformation in a country so bountifully endowed with natural resources. Vargas limited his interpretation of this commitment, however, to a defense of existing interests such as growers of cotton and sugar and the gatherers of rubber, who desired an

[2] Paulo Nogueira Filho, *Ideias e lutas de um burguês progressista; o Partido Democrático e a Revolução de 1930*, II, 591.

[3] Getúlio Vargas, *As diretrizes da nova política do Brasil*, p. 153; Stanley Stein, *The Brazilian Cotton Manufacture*, p. 130; *Monthly Journal of the British Chamber of Commerce* (January 1931), p. 21.

assured market. Economic forces that were merely potential, and therefore not yet political, received promises that were correspondingly
conditional. He sensed, for example, the desires of the Mineiros for
the development of their iron ore deposits. The future of Brazil depended on the exploitation of Minas ore; he told them in 1931: ". . .
the task is arduous, make it your ideal." But his promises of federal
aid were elusive and abstract.[4]

Although Vargas was able to recount to his audience in Minas
Gerais the new styles of consumption which the domestic production
of iron and steel would make possible, he was not able to foresee the
transformations in society which heavy industry would inevitably bring.
Indeed those changes that had already occurred he looked on with
misgiving. Too many people had come to the cities—the poor, because their livelihood in the rural areas had been cut off; the rich, because they had been seduced by the comforts of the metropolis. "We
must encourage, in every way possible, the return to the good road. The
paths that may lead us there are many, but there is only one direction,
the return to the country. Once the means have been found of fostering
this return, one of the greatest of Brazil's present problems will be
solved."[5]

The provisional government began immediately to sustain its political and ideological commitments. Roberto Simonsen, by then president of the Center of Industries, was thrown in jail during the first
weeks of the revolution for being "a member of one of the firms that
contributed to the state of crisis in Brazil" and was not released until
the general amnesty. He emerged decrying the developing "class struggle" between planters and industrialists. "There are planters who
dream, as a remedy, of offering in the holocaust of coffee all the other
productive classes in Brazil, which would thus be transformed into a
vast coffee grove," in the hope that the industrialized countries would
buy more coffee if the Brazilians were to lower their tariffs—an illu-
sion, Simonsen warned. The further diversion of resources to coffee
would merely lead to the amassing of more unsalable stocks, and then

[4] José Pereira da Silva, *As melhores páginas de Getulio Vargas*, pp. 27–29.
[5] *Ibid.*, pp. 63–65.

the lower class would know whom to blame. There would be a "re-edition of Russia."[6]

Already it was evident that Vargas favored the restoration of credits to the coffee planters. The buying up of stocks, resumed during 1931, cost the Bank of Brazil 150,000 contos ($11,000,000). The government continued to view Brazil's difficulties not as a matter of pursuing autarkical goals but of rebuilding the external market. Vargas received warmly the Niemeyer Mission, a delegation of English bankers who counseled deflation in order to preserve Brazil's credit. He assured the country that "the measures suggested [by Niemeyer] are, in general terms, the same that constitute the program of the provisional government," and he assumed that acquiescence to the international bankers would cause an inflow of new investment from abroad. All that was needed to attract the "indispensable capital" was "firmness, direction, tranquillity, and equilibrium." The industrialists, on the other hand, probably agreed with Simonsen's opinion of the mission—that it "sought principally to organize in Brazil a tax collecting apparatus designed to better assure the service of the debt and the amortization of foreign capital invested here."[7]

Although their political position was unfavorable, the manufacturers' association began to petition the revolutionary government for relief before it was a week old. They asked for cash payments for requisitions, warrants against their inventories, easier credit, a reduction in taxes, the total prohibition of cloth imports, an exemption from duties on the importation of raw materials, and government contracts for public works. Vargas was disposed to withdraw favors rather than grant them. He sought to resolve the crisis by containing government expenses and increasing its revenues; therefore he paid no attention to inflationary requests for credit or tax relief. Instead of lowering the tariffs on imported wool, jute, and silk fibers, he totally prohibited their importation! The proprietors of the "artificial industries" were stunned, but Vargas was obliged almost immediately to rescind his drastic decree. He had discovered that closing factories put Brazilian

[6] Roberto Simonsen, *As crises no Brasil*, pp. 3–5.

[7] Simonsen, *A industria em face da economia nacional*, pp. 6, 117; Vargas, *Primeiro aniversario da Revolução de Outubro*, pp. 6–8, 25–28, 36.

workers on the street, an outcome to be avoided at all costs. Meanwhile
his ministers of finance and labor began to bombard the industrialists
with dozens of projects, decrees, and regulations designed to thwart
some activity or other which the middle class and the planters had
perennially complained about, to bring their associations under government control, or to curtail their exploitation of the work force. The
"Circulars" of the CIFTSP for 1931 numbered more than seven hundred pages of protests, counterproposals, and warnings to members,
most of them ineffective.[8]

One of the arbitrary dispositions of the provisional government was
a levy of 8 per cent on profits remitted abroad. The decree was intended
to appeal to the nationalistic sentiments of the middle class, who believed that foreign firms had intensified the crisis by withdrawing their
profits at an accelerated rate and who made no nice distinctions between
foreigners and resident aliens like Matarazzo and Jafets. Evidently the
measure embarrassed mills like Brasital which were controlled by foreign capitalists; the CIFTSP took up the matter with such alacrity,
however, that it appears possible that silent partnerships, mortgages,
and other forms of indebtedness to foreign bankers and merchants
were still widespread in São Paulo in the 1930's. The animus of the
middle class was also evident in a decree which required the identification of all domestic fabrics with an indelible label. The middle-class
consumers of foreign textiles did not like to be hoodwinked with
inferior Brazilian stuffs, a rather remarkable instance of wounded snob-
bery outweighing patriotism. Besides these measures, the manufacturers also confronted the threat of higher taxes on profits, output, and
real estate; of higher tariffs for imported raw materials; and of increased government inspection of their premises and products.[9]

Another of the early measures of the Vargas regime which affected
the industrialists was the decree issued on March 19, 1931, which

[8] CIFTSP, *Circulares* (October 24, December 9, 1930); *As crises,* p. 29;
Monthly Journal of the British Chamber of Commerce (November–December 1930), pp. 421–423; CIFTSP, *Relatorio* (1930); Sindicato Patronal das
Industrias Textis do Estado de São Paulo, [hereafter SPITESP] *Relatorio*
(1931); *Primeiro aniversario,* pp. 11, 24–25, 89–90.

[9] CIFTSP, *Circulares* (January 14, 1931); SPITESP, *Relatorio* (1931).

turned manufacturers' associations as well as trade unions into officially recognized syndicates. This decree pleased the young army lieutenants and others who were attracted to corporative theories and had come to regard a lack of discipline as Brazil's greatest problem. Although the manufacturers, who for the most part shared these views, were quick to reorganize themselves as the government demanded and raised no complaint over the edict, its intent was to a degree punitive. The authoritarians among the revolutionaries agreed with manufacturers when they insisted that Brazilian industry suffered from overproduction, unchecked individualism, and disorganization. But they assumed that cartelization carried out without government control would benefit no one except the industrialists. The syndicalization decree therefore implied something more than an official seal upon private activities. Nevertheless, the manufacturers may have felt some increased sense of power at the transformation of their associations. The CIFTSP, restyled the Employers' Syndicate of the Textile Industries of the State of São Paulo, nearly doubled in size and federated under the Center of Industries, which was renamed the Federation of Industries of the State of São Paulo. The syndicates acquired further prestige because they were eligible to participate directly in newly created government commissions like the Tax-payers' Council and the Advisory Economic Council of the State of São Paulo.

It might appear that the clearest threat facing the industrialists was the intention of the Vargas government to carry out the promises made to labor by the Liberal Alliance. Within a month of taking power it set up the labor ministry long demanded by the trade unions; significantly, the departments of industry and commerce were separated from the Ministry of Agriculture and attached to it as though as an afterthought. In December a decree was issued that attempted to protect the jobs of Brazilian workers by restricting further immigration and requiring employers to produce evidence that at least two-thirds of their work force was native-born. In March 1931 the syndicalization decree granted the unions the legal recognition they had long sought. Another decree reaffirmed the Law on Holidays. The number of government-sponsored pension funds was increased, and mixed arbitration commissions were created. By the middle of 1932 the labor ministry promulgated decrees that regulated the employment of women in industry, guaranteed work contracts, and limited the workday to eight hours. Although these measures were not enforced with any rigor and contained loopholes that made them rather easy to evade, as a whole they left the unions in a far better position to bargain with their employers.[10]

It did not follow, however, that the workers were grateful for these benefits or that the employers were particularly displeased. The manner in which the labor ministry dispensed and implemented the new regulations demonstrated to both sides that their purpose was to maintain the existing social order by trading concessions to the workers in return for political quiescence. The intention of the new government was clear even in the first of its decrees on the labor problem. The Two-Thirds Laws, on the surface a major victory in the cause of protecting the standard of living of the domestic worker, was promulgated for quite different reasons at the request of the employers themselves. Its preamble discloses the preoccupation of its authors with the cost of feeding and providing public services for the unemployed and the desire to avoid "the disorderly entrance of foreigners" who "frequently contribute to the increase in economic disorder and social insecurity." The law not only limited the entrance of third-class passengers and required that two-thirds of each firm's payroll be composed of Brazilian-born workers, thereby striking a blow for nativism; it also required the unemployed to register with the Ministry of Labor, which was to try to find them jobs on the plantations, thereby dragooning the work force in behalf of the official physiocracy.[11]

The regulation of the Law on Holidays bestowed upon the employers the most powerful implement they had ever had for the control of union organizers. In order to claim his vacation pay, the worker had to present a passbook showing that he had not claimed his yearly holiday from some other employer. However, the passbook was also useful

[10] On enforcement see Dudley Maynard Phelps, *Migration*, p. 219; Azis Simão, *Sindicato*, pp. 86–87.

[11] Decree 19482, December 12, 1930, articles 1, 3, 4, 7. Opposition to syndicalization in Leôncio Basbaum, *História sincera do Brasil*, III, 33; *Circulares* (August 21, 1931). Simonsen, *As crises no Brasil*, p. 29, on immigration.

as a method of identification. No longer would O. Pupo Nogueira have to maintain his fallible and incomplete card files in the offices of the CIFTSP. Now the worker would carry his security clearance, complete with a photograph stamped by the police, in his own wallet. The passbook would clearly show why he had left his last place of employment. Nogueira did not lose much time congratulating himself that "agitators from outside" would no longer disturb the workers; he petitioned the government to make out the passbooks during the worker's off-duty hours, so that the employers need not be put to any expense. Mass identification came to absorb the efforts of growing numbers of the middle-class bureaucracy. By the end of 1932 the workers were required to possess four different pass cards.[12]

In São Paulo the trade union movement was at a disadvantage in its struggle to gain a hearing before the new government. The industrialists enjoyed a special representative within the Ministry of Labor, Jorge Street, who had been invited to direct the Ministry's Department of Industry. Furthermore, the minister, Lindolfo Collor, an associate of Vargas from Rio Grande do Sul, remained almost constantly in the federal capital. His only visit to São Paulo ended in a fiasco. At the union hall he delivered a speech full of complacent appeals for "class collaboration" which he had used to good effect at the Rotary Club in Rio de Janeiro. Jeered by the workers, he panicked and had the meeting closed with police nightsticks. The Ministry lacked offices in São Paulo—it counted on the state Department of Labor to administer its new regulations—but the state government was continuously in the hands of politicians hostile to labor, or willing to trade off its support for more negotiable kinds of power. The first message the CIFTSP sent its membership after the overthrow said: "Esteemed Gentlemen: The provisional government has elements to suppress alterations in the order of the factories. In the case of agitation by the workers, for whatever reason, Your Excellencies can communicate with this Center, which will take immediate precautions."[13]

João Alberto, the young army lieutenant who served as "Interventor"

---

[12] SPITESP, *Relatorio* (1931); *Circulares* (April 1, 1931).

[13] Nogueira Filho, II, 751; Everardo Dias, *História*, pp. 180–181; CIFTSP, Letter, O. Pupo Nogueira to membership, October 28, 1930.

from November 1930 to the following July, maintained a repressive policy toward the unions perhaps from ideological conviction or because he found it expedient to widen his local political support by accommodating the industrialists. His few gestures toward the workers were inconsequential. In November, in order to draw attention from demonstrations favoring Democratic Party heroes, he called some of its leaders to form a committee "to resolve the question of the workers." They turned out a rhetorical appeal to labor rather than a program of action; nevertheless he thanked them profusely and dismissed them after the demonstrations had taken place. In December he countered Collor's instruction to apply at once the Law on Holidays passed in 1925. Collor insisted that back pay was due the workers for all the vacations unpaid since the law went into effect, but João Alberto suspended execution until, he explained, a labor code could be formulated nationwide. It is likely that the publication of a new decree the following March was intended to set aside the workers' suits for compensation for their lost vacations. The interventor continued the attempts of the state Department of Labor to rid the capital of the unemployed by putting them to work on the plantations. By the middle of 1931, he reported, sixty thousand had been sent to the countryside.[14]

On several occasions he used the police to break strikes. The strikes against the utility companies and the São Paulo Railway in April were put down, it was believed, because they embarrassed Vargas in his dealings with Brazil's foreign creditors. In July, João Alberto tried to end a strike in the textile industry with repeated promises of an eventual labor code, but he ended his exhortation with a threat: "To insure tranquility, the Government will take rigorous measures, in favor of those who work, impeding any groups or manifestations attempting to lead them to strike." Nogueira commented to the mill owners, "as you see, the public power is assuring in a formal manner the freedom to work." It is clear from the "Circulars" of the CIFTSP that the employers were continuing to fire labor leaders even though they now represented official syndicates. Nogueira indignantly complained to

[14] Maurício de Lacerda, *Segunda República*, pp. 281–283, 294; Leôncio Basbaum, *História sincera*, III, 34; Everardo Dias, *História*, pp. 177–178.

Collor that workers he was dealing with were "professional agitators" and "evil elements infiltrated in the midst of our honest workers."[15]

The civilian governments that followed João Alberto's resignation continued the same policy toward labor conflict. In January 1932 the members of the Federation of Industries and the CIFTSP were told confidentially that the state police were sending secret agents to mix with the workers and that they should be provided meals and lodging. To some degree this identification of the public powers with the interests of the manufacturers was attenuated after Lindolfo Collor left the labor ministry in March 1932. The new minister, Pedro Salgado Filho, resumed the promulgation of welfare measures. His first was a decree limiting the workday to eight hours; its effect, however, was lessened by a clause that permitted an extra two hours of work if both parties agreed. The CIFTSP evidently considered it a simple matter to get the workers' consent; they passed out sample forms the employers might use to record agreements. Decrees published simultaneously limiting the employment of women and setting up arbitration boards were more difficult to evade. The employers, at that moment in the midst of a strike movement, attempted to establish a connection in a complaint that they hurriedly wired to the labor ministry: "taking into account the grave agitations occurred in midst Paulista workers considering that serenity still not returned to spirits, . . . we make an appeal to patriotism Your Excellency in the sense of provisionally suspending in São Paulo execution of the social laws . . . Although of high humanitarian and patriotic objectives will require essential modifications . . . Your Excellency will have contributed strongly to the suppression of the political and social crisis the present Paulista Intervention . . . trying to resolve." Salgado Filho's reply to their curious message was decidedly unsympathetic. "Believe you labor grave error judging execution laws referred can contribute whatever worker agitation, to the contrary . . . will dissipate malaise reigning . . . do not comprehend how possible suspend them." This was the first time in twenty months that the industrialists had been dealt an absolute refusal in labor mat-

[15] *Circulares* (July 21, August 21, 1931).

ters. Possibly it contributed to the attitude they assumed in the rebellion that broke out a month later.[16]

The leaders of the Paulista rebellion of July 9, 1932, expressed their grievances in terms that were mainly political and nationalistic. They insisted that they sought to compel Vargas to recognize the liberal goals of the 1930 revolution: constitutional government and local autonomy. Their justifications of the rebellion tend to show, however, that the Paulistas desired a restoration of their autonomy principally for the control that they would thereby regain over the economy of the state. Although Vargas' program of coffee purchases had rescued the planters from ruin, almost all of his subsequent economic measures displeased them greatly. The taxes Vargas had decreed in order to balance his budget appeared to them to be a kind of confiscation. It was clear to the Paulista planters that the federal government was capable of making further demands on their income. The land survey promoted by the young army lieutenants was preparatory to an increase in the state land tax, to encourage its more intensive use. Before he resigned João Alberto raised the ad valorem rates from 0.5 to 1.0 per cent. The planters were probably most annoyed, however, by Vargas' imposition of exchange controls in September 1931. Required to sell their foreign exchange to the Bank of Brazil at a confiscatory rate, they chose to believe that the purpose of the measure was to support a horde of bureaucrats in idleness at Rio de Janeiro. In fact the government was using the money to pay off foreign loans that were largely incurred by Paulista presidents.[17]

The impact of Vargas' fiscal policy is reflected in a striking change in the flow of goods through the port of Santos (see Table X-1). Although the state began in 1931 to recoup its export losses, the value of its imports continued to decline. In 1928 and 1929 São Paulo received 69 per cent of the value of its exports in foreign goods; in 1931 and 1932 it retained only 39 per cent. Meanwhile, an extraordinary reverse had appeared in its coastal trade (see Table X-2). Since

[16] Everardo Dias, *História*, p. 184; *Circulares* (January 19, May 10, June 6, 23, 1932).

[17] São Paulo (state), Assembleia Legislativa, *Annaes da Constituinte, 1935*, II, 405; Great Britain, Board of Overseas Trade, *Economic Conditions in Brazil, 1932*, p. 20.

TABLE X-1. Trade Balance of the State of São Paulo, Foreign Trade

	Exports	Imports	Credit or Deficit
	(thousands of contos)		
1928	2,095	1,479	+616
1929	2,097	1,407	+690
1930	1,428	794	+634
1931	1,751	696	+1,055
1932	1,120	444	+656
1933	1,564	800	+764

SOURCE: São Paulo (state), Secretaria de Agricultura, Industria e Commercio, *Estatistica do porto de Santos com os paizes estrangeiros, 1927–1928 to 1933–1934.*

TABLE X-2. Trade Balance of the State of São Paulo, Coastwise Trade

	Exports	Imports	Credit or Deficit
	(thousands of contos)		
1928	418	601	−183
1929	378	514	−136
1930	314	354	− 40
1931	393	325	+ 68
1932	348	284	+ 64
1933	442	299	+143

SOURCE: São Paulo (state), *Commercio de cabotagem pelo porto de Santos, 1927–1928 to 1933–1934.*

the first statistics were gathered in 1907, São Paulo had always been able to afford to buy more from the other states than it sold. From 1921 to 1930 only 64 per cent of its purchases from other states were paid for with trade goods. But in 1931 and 1932 the Paulistas were obliged to ship 132,000 contos ($9,500,000) more than they bought. This change proved to be an enduring one. Through the 1930's and 1940's

São Paulo sold more than it bought from other states. It seems likely that this surplus came to be offset by an inflow of capital, but in the short run it represented a serious wrench in the state's usual pattern of trade.

It might seem that the curtailment of imports offered the industrialists an opportunity for which they would be grateful to Vargas. There is some evidence that production did increase in 1931 and might have been greater in 1932 had it not been for the rebellion. On the other hand, it became almost impossible, during the exchange crisis, for factories dependent on imported raw materials to continue to function. The importation of iron and steel, for example, declined from an average 59,000 tons a year from 1927 to 1929 to just 9,352 tons in 1932. The replacement or repair of machinery became extremely difficult as imports of iron and steel products and machinery declined from 157,000 to 22,732 tons during the same period.

Taken all together, the policies of the new government must have discouraged the manufacturers, especially since they seemed to be draining money from the coffee sector and from São Paulo as a whole. There is no doubt that they participated in the rebellion of 1932 through their associations, and quite possibly they helped prepare it. Simonsen wrote five years afterward that he had no role "of any significance" in planning it. The "Circulars" of the CIFTSP in May and June contained mysterious invitations to meetings in which "delicate and confidential matters" were to be discussed. Nogueira, who was still the syndicate's general secretary, later took part in mobilizing resources for the rebel government. The Federation of Industries, led by Simonsen, made an inventory of strategic materials, requisitioned them, and rationed their use. It encouraged production by mobilizing credit, and it regulated the use of ersatz materials. Young engineers from the Polytechnic experimented with the production of trench mortars, grenades, flame throwers, and bombs. They were unable to produce rifles or cannon only for lack of steel forges.[18]

Among the industrialists who contributed to Simonsen's work were Alexandre Siciliano, Jr., A. Dumont Villares, Paulo Álvaro de As-

[18] Simonsen, *A industria em face da economia nacional*, pp. 9–13; SPITESP, *Circulares* (May–July 12, 1932).

sumpção, Mário Whately, Jorge de Rezende, Anhaia Melo, Anibal Mendes Gonçalves, and Henrique Jorge Guedes. The memoirs of the political leaders of the rebellion fail to mention the names of the more important immigrant industrialists; it may be that the latter were indifferent to the movement, which was so evidently fated to fail and appealed so much more strongly to the exaltation of the old plantation families than to the recently arrived, or it may be that their participation was more circumspect. The office copies of the CIFTSP's "Circulars" from July 21 to October 10 are missing, and no records of meetings can be found in the syndicate's archive for the same period. They may have contained the names of factories that responded to the syndicate's early calls for contributions of uniforms, cloth, and canvas. The engineering and metallurgical production was carried out for the most part in government arsenals and in the repair yards of the railroad companies. At a meeting of the Federation of Industries held just as the rebel government capitulated, Simonsen recounted the achievements of his Industrial Survey and Mobilization Service and received a standing ovation.[19]

Although the leaders of the rebellion, including Simonsen, had to go into exile in order to escape imprisonment, Vargas soon allowed them to return and accepted the resumption of their direction of state politics. The rapprochement was completed in 1933 by the election of a "Single Slate" to the Constituent Assembly composed of elements of the former Republican and Democratic parties and by Vargas' appointment of a new interventor agreeable to them. Meanwhile, the industrialists were regaining positions of influence within the state political structure. The Federation of Industries recreated the Center of Industries as an unofficial trade association. The parallel organization would be able to act without government supervision, while the Federation preserved the right to represent the industrialists before the government. The new interventor, Armando Salles Oliveira, although identified with the liberalism of the city middle class, praised the manufacturers for supplying the state with goods it had not been able

---

[19] Clovis de Oliveira, *A indústria e o movimento constitucionalista de 1932*, pp. 31–33; Herculano de Carvalho e Silva, *A revolução constitucionalista*, p. 70.

to afford during the trade depression and seemed well disposed toward them. The restoration of their local base of power could not be immediately transformed, however, into increased leverage in Rio de Janeiro. The defeat of São Paulo had temporarily lessened its influence upon federal policies.

From the suppression of the Paulista rebellion until the coup d'état of November 1937, Vargas founded his economic policy upon an expectation that free international trade might somehow be restored. The Ministry of the Treasury was almost totally preoccupied with the deteriorating balance of trade, which compressed the flow of imports and embarrassed its efforts to service the external debt. Although the European countries had been following a course constantly more autarkical since 1918, and although all of Brazil's trading partners had raised their tariffs in a frightened response to the depression, Vargas continued to believe that some formula might be found that would restore the means of buying goods abroad. The interests of the industrialists were subordinated, and even sacrificed, to this hope.

Tariff policy during this period ceased to be a gentlemanly game of small favors arranged clandestinely. Because Vargas had to offer some kind of bait in his efforts to persuade the Americans and the Europeans to lower their duties on coffee and the rest of Brazil's commodities, the tariff schedule had to be mobilized for national purposes. This implied not only the possible sacrifice of certain manufacturing firms; it also demolished the stability of protection upon which all the manufacturers utterly depended. The strategy employed was to decree a general increase in the tariff and then to bargain with each trading partner for the reduction of individual rates. This was first attempted in 1931, when a new tariff established two schedules, a "general" rate, which was 24 per cent higher than before, and a "minimum" rate, which was 20 per cent lower. At first the revision provided increased protection, but as new trade agreements were signed the lower rates were put into effect and domestic manufacturing suffered. This phenomenon recurred in 1933 when the government abandoned collection of the tariff according to the fictitious gold milreis. The immediate effect of the decree was protective, because the value of the gold milreis, for the purpose of conversion into paper, was set 29 per cent higher than before. But the value of the paper milreis eroded during the following two years by 37 per cent. In 1934 another tariff was published. The general rates were set somewhat higher than before, but other coun-tries were invited to bargain for "minimum" rates, set 20 per cent lower, or for "most-favored-nation" rates, which might be lower still.[20]

Brazil was at a decided disadvantage in this game because the Europeans and even the Americans could survive without coffee more easily than could Brazil without fuels or machinery. Furthermore, they were pursuing a course that was much more aggressive and self-seek-ing. The Germans abandoned any attachment to the principle of multilateral trade and pressed Vargas to accept bilateral deals that would enable them to set the terms of trade to their own advantage. The other European countries agreeably signed most-favored-nation clauses but evaded their purpose by setting import quotas and man-aging the exchange rate. The United States threatened Brazil with an import duty on coffee unless it promised not to imitate the Europeans and agreed to lower its tariff on certain manufactured goods. Never-theless, Vargas persisted. In 1935 he denounced all of the commercial agreements he had signed since 1931, in the hope that further con-cessions might persuade the Europeans to forego their quotas and im-port licenses. In the United States his ambassador, Oswaldo Aranha, achieved nothing more in a new agreement than the promise that quotas would not be established in the future without prior consultation. In return he had to lower the rates on almost a hundred items, of which at least twenty were already being produced in São Paulo.[21]

The industrialists' representatives in the Chamber of Deputies fought hard to prevent the passage of the agreement, but Vargas was convinced that the Americans would retaliate against coffee if the Chamber did not act. The Federation of Industries reacted bitterly to

[20] Afonso de Toledo Bandeira de Mello, *Politique Commerciale du Brésil*, pp. 96–102; U.S. Tariff Commission, pp. 8–10; Jayme de Barros, *A política externa do Brasil*, pp. 46–48.

[21] A detailed discussion of the trade policies of Vargas during this period in John D. Wirth, "Brazilian Economic Nationalism, Trade and Steel Under Vargas." U.S. Department of State, "Reciprocal Trade Agreement . . . Ef-fective January 1, 1936" (Executive Agreement Series, No. 82).

the government's indifference. A memorandum sent to Vargas soon after the treaty took effect denounced the "animus of certain persons" against industry. It was instigated, the Federation complained, by foreign interests who wanted to conquer Brazilian markets and by a general ignorance of the interconnectedness of economic activities. More than anything else, the memorandum insisted, industry needed a set of directives, free of "indecision," "instability," and "brusque alterations of monetary and tariff policy," and based on the understanding that industry creates wealth and deserves support. Simonsen charged that the agreement had sold not one single sack more of coffee, but it had ruined several manufacturers. He also complained of the abolition of the fictitious gold quota, which had served to compensate for the depreciation of the paper milreis. The new tariffs, stated in paper money, were certain to lose their potency.[22]

Although the industrialists demanded protection for themselves, they readily approved of Vargas' intentions. They continued to look upon the resuscitation of the export trade as indispensable to their own prosperity. Simonsen was willing to spend much of his time devising new ways of promoting exports and prefaced many of his speeches with an appreciation of the wealth that coffee had bestowed on São Paulo. Furthermore, it seemed as though Vargas' policies were achieving a certain measure of success. Even though the price of coffee failed to respond, it was possible to ship a great deal more, and the demand for other commodities, especially cotton, began to grow. The value of goods shipped from Santos more than doubled, therefore, between 1932 and 1935.

The manufacturers succeeded in extracting an advantage or two from the government's drive to compress imports. They managed, for example, to convince Vargas that a state of overproduction existed in the textile, shoe, hat, and paper industries. He was persuaded, therefore, to ban the importation of machinery in these lines for three years, beginning in March 1931. This measure, later extended for another three years, was of course antidevelopmentalist in intent, but it did

[22] Wirth, "Brazilian Economic Nationalism . . .," pp. 63–68; "Exposição enviada ao Presidente da Republica," in Simonsen, *A industria em face da economia nacional*, pp. 41, 58–69.

reduce the volume of Brazil's imports during a critical period, thereby helping to solve the treasury ministry's major problem. A similar coup was arranged for Santa Catarina's mines, when the government obliged all coal dealers to mix at least 10 per cent domestic coal with imports. In December 1933 the export of scrap iron and steel was prohibited, thereby assuring the domestic metallurgical industry a part of their supply of raw materials, but also reducing the need to buy the same raw materials abroad.[23]

Meanwhile Vargas managed to reduce the pressure of the debt service. By 1929 the federal and local governments had contracted loans that cost $100,000,000 each year to service. This burden was offset, during the ebullient 1920's, with an inflow of new capital. When this money was cut off by the onset of the depression, Brazil was quite unable to keep up its payments. Vargas' first solution was a funding loan in the conventional style of the old Republic. When the principal came due in 1934, however, it turned out to be impossible to arrange another, and the government had to announce that in future only partial payments would be made on the interest and principal of the numerous outstanding foreign loans. This partial repudiation of the debt, which was alleged to be temporary, was the regime's most unorthodox action before 1937. Vargas was subjected to a great deal of criticism on account of it, not only from foreign bondholders but also from domestic proponents of free trade, who lamented the effect that it would have on Brazil's credit. Aranha had not even attempted to bargain for trade concessions in return for higher scales of repayment, as he might have, so anxious was the government to maintain its credit rating and avoid the suspicion of opportunism. Nevertheless, it was the first time that the government had had to admit its inability to play according to the rules. And it was a success. The debt service was reduced, first by the funding loan and then by the partial repudiation, to a third of the level of 1930.[24]

The effect of the export drive and the lightening of the debt service

---

[23] Simonsen, *Aspectos da política economica nacional*, pp. 20–23; *A indústria em face da economia nacional*, pp. 54–55. A full account of the ban on machinery in Stanley Stein, *The Brazilian Cotton Manufacture*, pp. 140–153.

[24] Valentim Bouças, *História da dívida externa da União*, pp. 253–281; Ar-

was to make possible a considerable increase in the flow of imports. It is here that the government's indifference to the necessities of the manufacturers is most evident, and the reaction of the manufacturers was most bitter. Had Vargas been willing to contain the consumption patterns of the middle class and had he been more sympathetic to industry, he would have lowered tariffs or licensed imports according to criteria that Simonsen suggested: priorities for fuel, raw materials, and spare parts. Such a move, however, would have antagonized the United States, which was seeking, through commercial agreements like the one it had signed with Brazil, to counter the aggressive bilateral policies of Germany and other European countries. The failure to apply priorities, however, led to what Simonsen called "an orgy of imports," most of it food products and other consumer goods. Between 1932 and 1936 the flow of goods into Santos almost quadrupled in value. In 1937 it rose another 400,000 contos ($25,000,000) even though the value of exports had fallen off somewhat. It was the first time since 1920 that Brazil had experienced a negative balance of trade.

Vargas' insistence on the abolition of interstate tariffs obeyed the same imperative need to encourage exports, although it has often been regarded as evidence of his commitment to the development of domestic manufacture. In an indirect fashion the final abolition of the interstate duties benefited industry, because trade across state boundaries was thereby simplified and encouraged. But it should be noted that manufactured products were rarely subject to these taxes. Most of the interstate tariffs were really undifferentiated export taxes. The Constitution of 1891 had granted the states the right to tax their exports but did not distinguish between exports to foreign countries and exports to other states. Because these duties were convenient and relatively painless to collect, there were hundreds in effect before World War I, some as high as 25 per cent, and they were the major source of revenue for each of the states. But they were usually applied only to commodities. São Paulo, for example, taxed coffee and tobacco. It is true that the Paulista manufacturers reacted favorably to the first de-

---

thur da Souza Costa, *Panorama financeiro e economico da Republica*, pp. 35–38.

crees on the subject in 1931 and 1932, since they promised to reduce the cost of raw cotton from the north, but they lost interest as local production began to increase shortly afterward. The industrialists might have reasoned that the abolition of interstate tariffs on foodstuffs would lower the cost of living of their workers, but they did not do so; possibly they were indifferent. They may have been more concerned with the incidence of the taxes that would replace the coffee duty. When São Paulo became the first state to abolish its export tax in 1936, in order to encourage the sale of coffee, the legislature chose to levy additional taxes, not on land but on industrial production and retail sales.

Menaced by Vargas' application of liberal economic doctrine in the sphere of foreign trade, and already attracted by European corporativism, the Paulista manufacturers began to consider ways in which the government might promote industrialization beyond inflation and application of high tariffs. Even Roberto Simonsen, who did not dissociate himself from liberal political doctrine, elaborated during this time several proposals that embodied the principles of economic planning and a total reorientation of government policy toward industry. In 1935 he called for a national conference of industry that was to have discussed trade policy and its relation to the internal market and was to have considered ways of determining "optimum conditions for the installation of industries." In the Chamber he pointed out that internally the economy was sound. Unemployment had declined, tax receipts were increasing, and price levels were no longer falling. The only difficulty was the government's inability to pay the foreign debt. Although it was essential for Brazil to expand foreign trade, the outlook was not favorable: the value of Brazil's exports had remained almost stationary over the past three decades, while population increased. In view of the growing tendency toward protection in Europe and the United States, the inescapable conclusion was that Brazil had to develop its internal markets. This would require the limitation of reciprocity to raw materials and machines, not to finished goods.[25]

In 1937, just before the coup, Simonsen expounded a more com-

[25] Humberto Bastos, *A conquista siderúrgica*, p. 146; Simonsen, *Aspectos da politica economica nacional*, pp. 18–20, 35, 37–50.

plete argument before the Federal Foreign Trade Council, in a report ostensibly devoted to the encouragement of exports. He employed the concept of per capita income to demonstrate that the Brazilian internal market was very small. He calculated individual income at 500 milreis, or $30 (most likely a considerable underevaluation), and compared it with a per capita income of $740 in the United States. He did not imagine the possibility of reaching such a level, but thought it reasonable to aspire to 1,650 milreis, or $4,400,000,000 for the economy as a whole. It would be impossible, he thought, to attain this goal by increasing exports; they accounted for only one-ninth of that figure and European commercial policies made it unlikely that they would increase. Although much of Simonsen's discussion of how to arrive at a strong internal market remained within the range of the solutions of the 1920's, including high tariffs, "elasticity" in the money supply, and the encouragement of the production of raw materials, he also displayed an interest in new techniques. He repeated the need for priority lists for machinery; he requested an improvement in mail services, so that products might be sold through the mails; and he suggested that capital might be mobilized for industry through the industrial bank that had been authorized but not organized and through postal savings and savings stamps. Simonsen was aware of the growing trade between São Paulo and other states. Governor Salles Oliveira had mentioned the favorable balance of the state's coastwise trade at a banquet of the "conservative classes" earlier in the year. It is likely that the possibilities of the trade were being noticed generally among the industrialists and merchants. Salles Oliveira had been unable to estimate the movement of goods by rail, yet it is probable that it had been growing rapidly since 1936. Simonsen's suggestions for the improvement of transportation therefore included a demand to solve the "crisis" of the Central Railroad that linked São Paulo to Rio de Janeiro.[26]

It might be held that Vargas failed to attend to the entreaties of Simonsen not because he was indifferent to the future industrialization

[26] Simonsen, *A industria em face da economia nacional*, pp. 28–30, 34–38; Armando Salles Oliveira, *Jornada democratica*, p. 48; Brazil, Ministério de Viação e Obras Publicas, *Estatistica das estradas de ferro do Brasil* (1936–1939), table 18.

of Brazil but because he sensed a more immediate crisis in foreign trade. It is a difficult matter to determine to what degree the subjective perceptions of Vargas and his ministers influenced their decision to deal with the external rather than the internal market, but there is evidence that those perceptions continued to be those of the planters and the urban middle class. The tariff of 1934, for example, contained clauses that permitted a temporary increase in rates to protect domestic factories against dumping or a temporary reduction if it was determined that domestic production was controlled by a monopoly. Before two years had passed the latter provision was invoked against Brazilian wheat millers. It was not until 1944, however, that the government discovered the first case of discriminatory price reductions by foreigners.[27]

Vargas rarely mentioned industry in his public speeches during that period, and the writings of his advisers display little interest in domestic manufacturing. Afonso de Toledo Bandeira de Mello, who was director-general of the Ministry of Labor and a participant in several international economic conferences, wrote a book explaining Vargas' tariff policy in which he conceded that protection was necessary, since it affected 600,000 workers and numberless merchants. But he was not ready to admit that its role was more dynamic than this, in fact, "It is possible that the artificial creation of national industry, thanks to tariff protection, was in the beginning an economic error, a burden on the public treasury, onerous for the consumer, and ruinous to the importing business." In other words, unfortunate, but a *fait accompli*. Although protection was necessary, he thought, it would be an error to forget that the consumer and the national economy must also be protected from the tendency of the industrialist to raise his prices without restraint. Factories that were unable to survive except with high tariffs, "positively and notoriously artificial," would be given a choice of reequipping or liquidating.[28]

A similar attitude was to be found in the Constituent Assembly that

[27] U.S. Tariff Commission, p. 11.

[28] Bandeira de Mello, *Politique commerciale*, pp. 89–94; see also Paulo Martins, *Problemas nacionais*, p. 162. Aluísio Fragoso de Lima Campos, *O imperativo economico brasileiro*.

began to deliberate in November 1933. Corporative representation was grafted onto the usual state delegations, thereby permitting the employers a direct hearing there. Of the forty "class representatives" three were Paulista industrialists, and among the twenty-two delegates from the state of São Paulo there were four more who owned factories. Nevertheless, these few spokesmen were beleaguered amid the hostility of the rest. Simonsen, who participated, struggled to delete from Article 115, which was supposed to define the relationship of the state and the economy, a clause stating that economic liberty was to be conditionally guaranteed according to principles that would "establish throughout the country a standard of living compatible with the dignity of man." He did not object to government intervention but strongly dissented from an attitude copied from Europe, in this case from the Weimar Constitution, that was to "redistribute wealth that had not yet been created." The clause was corrected, perhaps because the phrase "throughout the country" reflected on the higher standards of living of other states besides São Paulo.[29]

Simonsen also recorded a furious exchange with a delegate from Pernambuco, who insisted that tariff protection without price controls and minimum wages was an invitation to "sack the nation." Simonsen easily demonstrated, at least in the case of matches, that industry was not as "artificial" as the northeasterner supposed, but he was unable to deny that there was a cartel in match production, and he was embarrassed by the mention of others in beer, milling, and sewing thread. The Constitution drawn up by this assembly reaffirmed Vargas' blending of liberal and corporativist ideas. It ratified all the benefits that had been conferred on labor since 1930 (in the meantime the labor ministry had also decreed the prohibition of factory employment for children under fourteen and cash compensation for vacations refused by employers), and foreshadowed still more. On the other hand, it did not refer to the employers, except to guarantee, within broad limits, economic liberty and to regulate certain aspects of government contracts. For the rest, the Constituent had considered economic mat-

[29] Simonsen, *Ordem econômica, padrão de vida, e algumas realidades brasileiras*, pp. 24–26.

ters only in a nationalistic context. The government was to reassume control of subsoil rights and progressively to nationalize insurance companies and banks. The Two-Thirds Law was reaffirmed, and restrictions were placed on immigration which hinted at ethnic discrimination.[30]

It was very difficult to admit to monopolies and speak of industrial development in the same breath. The northern deputies had hit upon a principal flaw in the manufacturers' arguments: how could people who fix prices and restrict production be regarded as the vanguard of Brazil's economic future? Simonsen had similar difficulties in explaining matters to a fellow Paulista. Since 1930 he had exhorted the planters of the state to transfer their capital from agriculture to industry. Indignantly, Deputy Martinho Prado insisted that Simonsen stop proposing the reimposition of the ban on machine imports. The prohibition had made it very difficult for planters to enter new lines of production and had preserved the markets for existing manufacturers, who had been permitted to replace old machines. Prado, himself a planter who wanted to invest in industry, was subjected by Simonsen to a discourse on the crisis of overproduction. Clearly, Simonsen had been thinking of portfolio investment when he called for capital from the agricultural sector, and he was ready to use the government to prevent new investment that threatened competition.[31]

The most striking change in the economic environment of the 1930's was the increasing intervention of the government. But this intervention was not designed to accelerate the process of industrialization; the alternatives of the export economy had not yet been played out. During the provisional and constitutional phases of the Vargas years the government continued to believe that the world of 1913 might somehow be put back together again. The controls placed on the economy were measures of desperation, a constant rearguard action to save an existing system rather than an attempt to bring a new one into being. The major innovation of the period, a paternalistic sort of social reformism, had its origins in the meliorism of the middle class and was

[30] *Ibid.*, pp. 6–15, 42–46.
[31] Simonsen, *A industria em face da economia nacional*, pp. 121–122.

intended to stave off a political crisis, not to enlarge the market for manufactured goods or improve the quality of labor inputs. A variety of circumstances hindered the reorientation of government policy; not the least among them, perhaps, was the attitude of the industrialists, who were not able to convince the planters, the middle class, or the bureaucracy that in pursuing their private interests they were advancing the interests of Brazil.

CHAPTER XI

The Industrialists and the Estado Nôvo

The coup d'état of November 10, 1937, is usually explained in merely political terms. Vargas wished to remain in power. According to the constitution he could not succeed himself; therefore he had been obliged to preside over an electoral campaign. His distate for abandoning the presidency grew as he saw that even the candidate whom he had sponsored was unlikely to be a cat's-paw. The army had always been hostile to liberal democratic politics, and its upper echelons, personally loyal to Vargas, had long been urging him to install an arbitrary regime. Furthermore, the civilian political elites were dismayed by their creation. The promise of honest elections had encouraged many politicians to appeal to a broader electorate. Politics had become embittered and polarized, and many were ready to see an end to the experiment. Vargas could therefore justify the coup publicly as the disinterested act of a statesman who wished only to forestall a greater disaster. Privately, he could congratulate himself that he, not the Integralists, had made the coup.

It should be noticed, however, that the imposition of the Estado Nôvo coincided with a formidable economic crisis that Vargas probably could not have confronted within the democratic framework. Not only was he obliged to employ means antithetical to those he had been pursuing, he also showed, through his subsequent public statements and actions, that these new means were more than mere emergency measures.

Vargas mentioned, in the speech in which he justified the imposition of the new regime, a financial crisis brought on by a sudden decline in the price of coffee. Faced with an imminent reduction in the amount of foreign exchange available to cover vital imports and to maintain payments on the external debt, the new government would, he announced, be obliged to take stern measures. It is true that the price of coffee had fallen by two cents, but the total value of exports did not decline on that account. The loss was made good by other export crops that had either improved in price or had been sold in greater quantity. The crisis occurred not specifically because the price of coffee had fallen, but because Brazilian importers, influenced by the rise in the price of coffee the year before and encouraged by the attitude of the government, had bought 1,000,000 contos' ($84,000,000) worth of goods beyond their purchases of 1936. Santos' share of this "orgy of imports" was 400,000 contos ($32,000,000), an increase of 25 per cent over the year before. Vargas' insistence on the significance of the price of coffee is understandable; it was a variable beyond his control and therefore politically neutral. To have admitted, or to have it called to his attention, that his government's permissive attitude toward imports was to blame would have been extremely embarrassing. The consequences of that policy accelerated during August, September, and October. The value of the milreis in the free market declined from 15.08 to 17.23 to the dollar, and the Ministry of the Treasury, which had never shown a deficit before in its exchange transactions, was to lose 90,000 contos ($5,600,000).[1]

The moment called for Draconian measures, yet it could be foreseen that the constitutional regime could neither carry them out quickly nor survive the criticism of the press and Congress if it did. Only by dramatizing the political crisis could the government be made to appear less

[1] Vargas' speech transcribed in *Boletim do Ministerio de Trabalho, Industria e Commercio* (November 1937), pp. v–xvii; Valentim Bouças, *História da dívida externa,* I, 281; Arthur da Souza Costa, *Discurso,* pp. 38–39.

culpable and the necessary emergency powers be arrogated without a loss of confidence. Ten days after assuming dictatorial powers, Vargas issued a decree law suspending all payments on the external debt. Late in December, when it became clear that this measure and another that had lowered the surcharge on coffee exports were not sufficient to stem the crisis, the government declared a monopoly in the sale of foreign exchange and imposed a tax on all exchange transactions. This time, however, there was to be no leakage of gold. Throughout 1937 and 1938 the government held on to its reserves and refused to commit them to cover its debts.

Even more significant than these unorthodox methods of dealing with the emergency was the fundamental change in outlook that had preceded them. The Estado Nôvo abandoned economic, as well as political, liberalism. Fundamentally, Vargas had finally drawn the conclusion that Simonsen and others had been urging upon him. In a speech pronounced in April 1938 he noted that the value per ton of Brazil's exports was constantly declining, while the prices of imports remained the same. It followed that the country would have to begin to substitute domestic manufactures for foreign. His Minister of the Treasury, Souza Costa, pointed out another significant relationship. The crisis of late 1937 would not have occurred if the inflow of foreign capital had not ceased. This was the closest the government came to a recognition that the collapse in the coffee price and the tightening of credit were related to the deflationary policy pursued in the United States from the middle of 1937. The responsibility was at least implicitly affirmed. In implementing the exchange monopoly the Bank of Brazil was directed to allocate funds for the remission of profits only after imports had been covered. Vargas began to notice in his speeches the growth of the domestic market and the increasing diversification of industry "that have allowed us a perceptible respite and an improvement in the standard of living of ever wider groups of the population." Even though Vargas continued to search for ways of stimulating exports, the conception of priorities had dramatically altered.[2]

The balance of political forces shifted accordingly. In São Paulo

[2] Souza Costa, *Discurso*, p. 38; Getúlio Vargas, *O Estado Novo e o momento brasileiro*, pp. 10–11, 14–15.

the Democratic Party, still the representative of urban middle-class interests, was eliminated from the governing coalition. Members of the Republican Party were restored to full power, and with them the industrialists. Although Simonsen had attempted earlier to dissociate the "lamentable interdependence that they try to establish out of doctrinaire preoccupations, between political liberalism and free-trade theories," he could not be successful. The liberal middle class was not yet ready to abandon either the ballot, through which they might yet attain power, or free trade, which supported their style of consumption. Azevedo Amaral, one of the theorists of the Estado Nôvo, mocked the liberals' defense of "promiscuous suffrage." To him they were parasites who had never played a significant role in the development of Brazil but had always thwarted "the productive element," that is, the landowners. The planters did not suffer the ideological and political defeat of the middle class, but they were to find the government less concerned with maintaining their privileges and more preoccupied with increasing their productivity. Vargas was even ready to speculate upon the breaking up of coffee estates that had gone irremediably into debt, because small holders paid more attention to quality.[3]

These changed attitudes and alignments profoundly affected Paulista industrialization. First of all, the Estado Nôvo pressed forward with corporative theories that implied a new relationship between state and industry. The new constitution went far beyond the document of 1934, which had merely guaranteed "economic liberty." Now the state was to have the right to intervene in the economy "in order to supply the deficiencies of individual initiative and coordinate the factors of production so that conflicts may be avoided or resolved and a consideration of the interests of the Nation, represented by the State, may be introduced." Yet this was a limited intervention, as Azevedo Amaral explained: there was a difference between authoritarianism and totalitarianism. In the latter, all interests are subordinate to the state; in the former, the state merely coordinates and adjusts. Francisco Campos, who wrote the draft constitution, believed that enterprise would be

---

[3] Roberto Simonsen, *Aspectos da politica economica nacional*, p. 8; Azevedo Amaral, *O estado autoritario e a realidade nacional*, pp. 20–27; Vargas, *O Estado Novo*, pp. 36–39.

fostered by the decentralization of government, because the state would delegate the authority to the corporation to regulate itself and would exercise only the role of an arbiter of the public interest. In this way what had been a clandestine and corrupting process under liberal democracy would come to have legal expression and responsibilities. The advantages to the industrialists of this new system seemed evident, especially since the ultimate responsibility for economic affairs was also to be in their hands. The constitution created a separate legislative body, to be called the National Economic Council, with functional representation, in the style of Italian corporativism. This organization, Azevedo Amaral wrote, was not necessarily fascistic; although it would be "dissonant" in a liberal-democratic state, it was merely an expression of capitalism that had matured into a stage of trusts.[4]

In a sense, the need for the Estado Nôvo was wholly derived by its architect, Campos, from the economic transformation that had already occurred and had to be still further encouraged. He believed that a legislature elected through universal suffrage could function effectively only in a very simple society. The problems of government had grown so complex that it was no longer possible to educate the mass of the people to understand them. Their resolution had become more a matter of intervention than prevention; therefore parliamentary debates and the passage of laws were no longer relevant or effectual. The Estado Nôvo would manage all questions through consultation with the sectors affected and through the constant attention of a capable and responsible bureaucracy.

Another sort of transformation also preoccupied Campos: the growth of the urban proletariat. Reflecting the alarm of all sectors of the Brazilian elite, he doubted that the issues of the "social question," that is, the class struggle, could be debated in a legislature without undermining society. He wrote contemptuously of demagogic regimes that become "the distributor of the goods acquired and accumulated through the effort of individuals and the spirit of modesty, foresight and sacrifice of poor and Christian families." The solution devised by

[4] Amaral, *O estado*, pp. 156–157, 203–204, and his earlier book, *A aventura política do Brasil*, pp. 223–236; Francisco Campos, *O estado nacional, sua estrutura, seu conteudo ideologico*, pp. 62–64.

Campos was to resolve labor conflicts before special courts and to declare both strikes and lockouts "antisocial" and "harmful to labor and
capital."[5]

The technocratic and authoritarian content of the Estado Nôvo
strongly appealed to the bureaucracy and the military, and so did its
economic goals. The federal bureaucrats, who had observed the world
economic crisis most directly, were also convinced of the necessity for
self-sufficiency. They were ready to assume a wider degree of intervention in the economy, not only out of careerism but also because they
had become convinced that the experiments in *dirigisme* in Europe
and the United States were successful .The "cycle of economic em-
piricism" had past, according to J. M. de Lacerda and Eloy de
Moura, who were staff members of the Foreign Trade Council and
the Department of Industry and Commerce. The Estado Nôvo signi-
fied to them a commitment to "economic evolution, . . . that is, a more
rational consciousness in working, producing, and distributing." The
military was even more emphatic in regarding the dictatorship as an
instrument of economic development. For a long time they had operated government-owned enterprises such as railroads, shipyards, and
ammunition plants. Some of the officers had acquired technical skills
beyond the traditional mathematics and civil engineering and were
ready to take up more complex managerial tasks. For these officers national security demanded the implantation of steel, petroleum, and
coal industries in order to make the domestic production of munitions
self-sufficient.[6]

The November coup, unlike the crises of 1930 and 1932, evoked
no opposition from the industrialists. It can be imagined that many
found the program of the Estado Nôvo agreeable in an ideological
sense, but even those who were loyal to the liberalism of the 1934
constitution found much in the new order with which to console themselves. Simonsen, for example, expressed no opinions in public concerning the coup, although he had his first opportunity three days

[5] *Ibid.,* pp. 40–41.

[6] *O Estado Novo, democracia e corporativismo,* pp. 28–29; see also Waldyr
Niemeyer, *O Brasil e seu mercado interno;* Osorio da Rocha Diniz, *A politica
que convém ao Brasil.*

later at the Automobile Club. Regarding Vargas' new economic policies, however, he was, with only one exception, fully in agreement.
This is not surprising, because even the politically liberal Simonsen
had defined in the 1933 Constituent the acceptable forms of government economic intervention in the broadest possible terms: "Through
the execution of public works; through the operation of public services;
through the institution of credit organizations; through the regulation
of commerce; through its intervention in the administration of economic enterprises; as an industrial producer; through engaging in
trade; . . ." All this, and by less direct means as well, as long as the
object was to "promote the creation of wealth."[7]

Only the labor laws seemed to Simonsen a threat to individual
initiative, but in this matter he was willing to admit "that an excessive
individualism leads to the creation of the class struggle . . ." Besides,
the new regime offered a guarantee of labor tranquility. The regimentation of labor, in the words of José Maria Bello, another liberal critic
of the regime, although theoretically a diminution of its corporate
liberties, was permissible considering the state of society. "The incor-
poration of the proletariat," that is, the raising of its living standards,
"must never serve as an instrument of political maneuvres." And he
pointed to Spain as an unhappy example. In June 1939 the right of
workers to organize "parallel," that is, unofficial, unions was extin-
guished.[8]

Although it may be that none of the other industrialists had been
any more party to the coup than Simonsen, Vargas had certainly felt
the drift of their aspirations and knew that the new order would
strongly appeal to them. Even during the constitutional phase he repeatedly discussed the need for state intervention in behalf of industry and had remarked that "in not a few cases, it was solicited by private
enterprise itself."[9]

[7] *A industria em face da economia nacional,* p. 125; *Ordem economica,
padrão de vida, e algumas realidades brasileiras,* p. 13.

[8] *A questão social e a realidade brasileira,* p. 23.

[9] Rubens Rosa, "O plano quinquenal brasileiro," *Boletim do Ministerio de
Trabalho, Industria e Commercio* (June 1939), p. 204; José Pereira da Silva,
As melhores páginas, pp. 211–212.

The dictatorship soon fulfilled its promise. In the matter of trade policy its partiality toward domestic manufacture was at first obscured by the immediate crisis. During the first year imports rose relative to exports, yet the total amount was still $35,000,000 less than in 1937. At the same time the devaluation of the milreis, carried out in order to eliminate the free market, had increased the cost of imports by 10 per cent. By this time the manufacturers were probably less concerned with foreign competition than with acquiring exchange cover to pay for raw materials and equipment. As early as January 1938 it can be seen that the recently imposed monopoly on exchange was acting in such a way as to increase the flow of metals, machinery, and fuels at the expense of other kinds of imports. Then, late in the year, Vargas announced that he would inaugurate the policy that Simonsen had put forward so vigorously in the Foreign Trade Council in 1937. The government would license imports according to a scale of priorities. Transportation equipment and machinery would be favored; consumer goods would be discouraged. The planters and importers were extended the promise of equal treatment—the new policy did not imply a decline in the volume of imports; there would merely be a change in their composition. Since food products and vegetable raw materials drained so much of Brazil's foreign exchange, Vargas could assure the landowners that they would obtain government assistance to produce domestic substitutes. By means of this "constructive" formula, Vargas was able to promise all sectors of the economic elite simultaneously "excellent applications for capital" which were, nevertheless, destined for the "greater development of our industrial plant."

The Estado Nôvo opened up extensive new sources of public financing. During the constitutional phase it had been frequently suggested, without effect, that the social security institutes organized for workers in various trades use their reserves to finance agriculture and industry. By 1937 these funds amounted to 500,000 contos ($31,000,000), but they were invested, for the most part, in treasury bonds. Just two months after the coup a new Department of Agricultural and Industrial Credit was added to the Bank of Brazil, funded with special bonds that insurance companies and the social security institutes were authorized to purchase. The number of loans emitted by this department rapidly increased after the manufacturers were permitted to list their machinery as collateral. By the end of 1941 they had received 500,000 contos in long-term loans. Nevertheless, the planters received a larger amount of direct assistance from this source than industry. Vargas used the department to diversify agricultural exports and to supply the cities with food. The loans were, at least theoretically, accorded to planters who had rationalized production. Indirectly, they probably benefited the manufacturers, too. Besides holding down the prices of commodities, the additional production was destined partly to replace imported raw materials like jute. The social security institutes, along with the state and federal savings banks, were also authorized to make loans directly to farmers and builders. The new regime had shown businessmen how the "exigencies of the social policy" could, as Souza Costa, Minister of the Treasury, phrased it, "revert, in part, directly to the benefit of the increase in the production of wealth."[10]

The loans made to industry, like those made to agriculture, seem to have been directed toward increasing Brazil's self-sufficiency. In order to stanch the drain of foreign exchange for newsprint and paper pulp, Vargas was ready personally to shop about for an entrepreneur to build a new paper mill. Assis Chateaubriand, owner of the largest newspaper chain, was approached first, but he declined the opportunity. Then Vargas, according to Chateaubriand's recollection, asked his opinion concerning the suitability of several Paulista industrialists. Chateaubriand recommended the Klabin family. The Klabins had operated a paper mill since the early 1900's, had shared in setting up the Companhia Nitroquímica, and owned extensive pine forests at Monte Alegre, in the state of Paraná. The choice was acceptable to the dictator, and he commissioned Chateaubriand to go to São Paulo to offer them a loan and the necessary exchange cover, along with a monopoly, if they would build the mill. The conservative older generation refused, but Vargas himself later convinced the younger members of the family to accept.

[10] Brazil, Ministério de Trabalho, Indústria e Comércio, *Seus serviços, orientação e attitude deante dos problemas da nossa economia nacional*, p. 8; Humberto Bastos, *A conquista siderúrgica*, p. 145; Souza Costa, *Discurso*, pp. 121–126.

The Klabins could hardly have refused; Vargas also promised a railroad spur and a guaranteed market. This reminiscence is quite revealing. It demonstrates that Vargas, after setting out a rational developmental goal, avoided the alternative of creating a wholly new firm, which would have antagonized existing interests. By approaching the largest consumer of newsprint and obtaining a waiver from him, he made certain that there would be no difficulty in selling the newsprint to a vested interest that had formerly insisted on a low tariff for its principal raw material. Furthermore, as Chateaubriand himself must have realized, his representation to the Klabins effectively convinced them of this favorable circumstance.[11]

The reorientation of foreign trade policy and the more generous offers of credit were signs of the government's awakening interest in the development of manufacturing. The most significant action of the Estado Nôvo, however, was the construction of an integrated steel mill at Volta Redonda, in the state of Rio de Janeiro. The history of state-supported schemes to found a steel industry in Brazil is long and complicated. By the time Vargas came into power in 1930, there already were several small mills in Minas Gerais, but their potential expansion was limited by their dependence on charcoal to make coke. A large-scale, integrated mill that would employ coal for the coking process was an immense technical and financial problem, and yet it was the key to future industrial development. Since the mid-1920's there had been no substantial hope of building such a plant with foreign capital, because iron and steel producers in Europe and the United States wished to avoid increasing world capacity and feared the loss of overseas markets. Furthermore, the task seemed to be beyond the capacities of the government or private entrepreneurs.[12]

This drift ceased with the imposition of the dictatorship. In February 1938 Vargas declared a steel industry to be an urgent necessity.

[11] Assis Chateaubriand, transcription of a speech at a banquet honoring the Klabins, in *A Provincial do Pará* (February 10, 1967); Morris L. Cooke, *Brazil on the March*, p. 222.

[12] Most of this and the following paragraphs are derived from John D. Wirth, "Brazilian Economic Nationalism . . . ," pp. 99–149, and Humberto Bastos, *A conquista siderúrgica*, pp. 159–181.

He stood ready, he said, to accept any reasonable proposal, whether it involved public or private ownership. Two considerations had aroused Vargas to make so strong a commitment to a project that had languished for seven years. The first was his determination to reduce Brazil's dependence on imports. Iron and steel, he pointed out, had cost 220,000 contos' ($13,000,000) worth of foreign currencies in 1936. The second was a growing, vehement demand by the army that basic industries be created in order to make Brazil powerful and militarily secure. Both of these preoccupations were, of course, peculiarly those of the Estado Nôvo and its nationalistic bureaucracy. Paradoxically, the determined autarky of the new regime was to be matched by a reawakened interest on the part of foreign steel producers to obtain Brazilian ore. The rearmament programs of the United States and Europe caused the price of ore to remain high while agricultural prices were falling. Vargas believed that the sale of ore might pay for coal imports if the coal of Santa Catarina proved unsuitable, and he sensed that the rivalry of the Europeans and the Americans was severe enough that one might be played against the other in order to obtain the necessary foreign exchange to build the mill.

Throughout 1938 he allowed numerous proposals to be aired. There was a variety of opinion concerning the best location, the methods of production, the utility of domestic coal, and especially the source of capital. The combinations of these elements were nearly infinite, and competing economic interest groups had a more than technical interest in one solution or another. This controversy awakened a response among Paulista industrialists. In the past they had felt somewhat threatened by the prospect of a domestic steel industry based on the ores of Minas Gerais. Those who used iron and steel as raw materials were afraid that the building of a large mill would involve the prohibition of lower-priced imported steel. Those who operated small furnaces that converted scrap were afraid that such a mill would put them out of business. Furthermore, the exploitation of Minas ores on a large scale implied a shift of the industrial heartland away from São Paulo. There was no Paulista capital present in any of the mills already in existence in Minas Gerais, a circumstance that increased their feeling of alienation from the project.

Now that a solution appeared imminent that might exclude them from so promising a field, however, several entrepreneurs came forward with suggestions. Olavo Egydio de Souza Aranha, who had interests in banking, importing, and construction firms, proposed that the government sponsor the kind of enterprise that importers had so frequently organized in São Paulo. He wished to create a steel mill in partnership with Krupp, whom he represented in Brazil. Krupp was not the only German firm that expressed some willingness to invest in such a project, and for a time the German government encouraged proposals that might increase its political influence in Brazil. Another Paulista, Alexandre Siciliano, Jr., reminded Vargas in a confidential memorandum that "the creation in the country of a great steel mill (using coke), without connections among any of the firms now in existence may signify the complete ruin of those who have been the pioneers in small-scale steel production employing charcoal." Seconded by Trajano de Medeiros, who owned a small mill in Minas Gerais, he requested Vargas to permit the proposed mill to be incorporated by all the existing steel producers, so that their "legitimate and perfectly justifiable" opposition might be avoided.

The deal that Vargas had come to favor was neither of these. In February 1939 his emissary, Oswaldo Aranha, managed to convince Washington that if the United States did not extend credit for a mill, Germany would. With a commitment from the Export-Import Bank, he invited United States Steel to build the plant. The whole of 1939 was consumed in arranging and carrying out a field survey. In spite of a favorable report by their engineers, the company's directors decided not to carry out the investment, perhaps because they feared that Vargas' government was not stable enough to carry out their end of the bargain.

The denouement was tremendously disappointing to Vargas, but he had gone too far to drop the matter. United States Steel, with its own mills located on the Atlantic sea coast, had been the most likely partner for an investment that carried, as a principal inducement, the export of Brazilian ores. Nevertheless, there was an alternative. Vargas announced defiantly that the government would itself build the mill in association with domestic capitalists. Then, still faced with the need for a long-term loan of foreign currency to pay for equipment, he once again used American fears of German influence in their hemisphere to regain the commitment of funds from the Export-Import Bank. The National Steel Company had finally taken shape.

Although it took almost two and one-half years for the Estado Nôvo to settle upon a formula for the steel industry, the project appeared to be well conceived. The government and private sources would participate equally in the common stock. The financial problem was to be handled by Guilherme Guinle, a banker from Rio de Janeiro who had a major interest in the Santos Docks. The construction itself was to be managed by an army officer, Edmundo de Macedo Soares, who, besides being a *tenente* and a determined nationalist, was a trained metallurgist and a superb administrator. The plan employed was that recommended by the engineering team of United States Steel: an integrated plant between the markets of São Paulo and Rio de Janeiro, at Volta Redonda. The coal of Santa Catarina was found to be adequate for coking. The statist solution was rather better received than the original proposal of a controlling interest for United States Steel. The army had complained bitterly of foreign control; indeed it was reconciled only with difficulty to the prospect of the Export-Import loan. Even the industrialists may not have been unhappy with government ownership and control, since they would be a neutral presence, a threat to none of the existing consumers of steel. Siciliano, who had proposed a consortium of the existing firms, had earlier suggested that the government build the mill for precisely this reason and had supposed that the private firms could divert production to special steels.

It is therefore rather surprising that the manufacturers did not respond to Guinle's call for stock subscriptions with anything more than token donations. In fact, the "private" participation was composed almost wholly of contributions by the social security institutes and the federal savings banks. Simonsen was perhaps the most important subscriber among the Paulistas, yet he had only three thousand shares. In March 1943 Simonsen led a party of 120 Paulista entrepreneurs on a tour of the facilities still under construction. Apparently the businessmen of São Paulo were skeptical about the vast undertaking, and Simonsen and Macedo Soares designed an excursion that would elicit favorable statements from a group of eyewitnesses. Although Simonsen claimed that many had been turned away after the tour had been filled to capacity, the party represented not 120 but only 64 firms. Many of these were quite small companies, and industrialists like Matarazzo and Siciliano were not present. The visitors listened to a lengthy explanation of the work in progress by Macedo Soares, incisive and well-organized, but informed mainly by a geopolitical, not a capitalist, outlook. He compared the National Steel Company to the wartime efforts of the Americans to create a steel complex on the Pacific coast and asserted that the mill proved the validity of Rio Branco's vision of a grand alliance between Brazil and the United States. But he also sought to reassure them. The works were proceeding slowly, but this was because of the war and because Brazil was not as highly organized as the industrialized countries; the project, nevertheless, was halfway finished. The Company, even though a government enterprise, would have to compete, and it was organized like any other corporation.[13]

Then the businessmen went out to look at the construction. Perhaps other justifications were suggested to them as they observed the immense concrete structures, such as those that were included in the memorandum printed by the Federation of Industries. The Volta Redonda project would enrich the Paraíba Valley and reopen it to Paulista industry. The by-products of the coking process would be made available to São Paulo's chemical industry. The projected prices for rails, tinplate, and sheet steel would be less than the prices of imports. And besides all these advantages, the mill would cost less than had a political campaign under the old Republic![14]

The industrialists were asked afterward to write down their impressions of the trip. Although only a few of these responses were included in the memorandum, they provide some clue to the reaction of the Paulista entrepreneurs to the largest and most important initiative that had yet been made to implant basic industry in Brazil. The most frequent comment was nationalistic: "the emancipation of our industries."

[13] Federaçao das Indústrias do Estado de São Paulo, *A cidade do aço*, pp. 59–91.

[14] *Ibid.*, pp. 25–49.

The businessmen themselves were not immune to the sentiments that impelled the army. A second generalized feeling was awe before the size and technical perfection of the construction. The visitors, many of them also engineers, expressed the hope that the mill would set an example and perhaps train personnel for work in other sectors of industry. About half remarked that the mill's future output would be of great significance to Paulista industry, a few because they thought prices would be lower, but most because the supply would not be interrupted by the vicissitudes of the export sector. It appears that the Paulista industrialists, or at least those who thought the journey worth while, had been won over to the cause of a basic industrial sector outside their state borders.[15]

Clearly, the drive to self-sufficiency in the production of raw materials and manufactured goods was not entirely inspired by Vargas' disenchantment with the export economy. It was also a sign of growing apprehension that the European powers were heading for war. Before that happened Brazil had to make every effort to insulate its economy. After the invasion of Poland the importance of domestic industry loomed still larger. At first efforts were directed mainly toward suppressing the inflation consequent upon the breakdown of international trade by means of price and import controls. These activities were not wholly successful, yet they stimulated industrial production by holding down the cost of raw materials more effectively than wholesale or retail prices. The industrialists used the emergency to obtain a renewed ban on the importation of cotton textile machinery, this time on the grounds of excluding obsolete equipment, although the real purpose appears to have been, once again, the restriction of production. When Brazil entered the war in August 1942, the government took upon itself a pervasive supervision of the economy. The office of the Coordinator of Economic Mobilization absorbed an earlier price control agency and was empowered to allocate materials, control wages, assign transport, and stimulate the production of exports.

Manufacturers who were willing to try to relieve the shortage of

[15] *Ibid.*, pp. 112–211.

imports by producing ersatz were granted loans, subsidies, tax abate-
ments, embargoes of competitive imports, guarantees of wholesale
prices, and government contracts. These favors were strikingly successful in a few cases. Metal-working and automotive repair shops, with
the assistance of a state-employed engineering team, turned out fifteen
thousand "gasogênio" units by the middle of 1943, which, when
attached to automobiles, produced a usable motor fuel from the com-
bustion of charcoal. Industry was also significantly assisted by the
government's encouragement of agricultural raw materials. In São
Paulo, the production of sugar, cotton, vegetable oils, wool, and beef
increased enormously during the war. Other states supplied coal, rubber, and jute substitutes. At the same time investment in coffee and
staple commodities was discouraged by price controls and export
quotas.

The exigencies of war produced another considerable change in the
environment of industry. The United States, urgently in need of an
expanded list of Brazilian raw materials, had in return guaranteed the
delivery of manufactured goods to Brazil. Shipping space was strictly
rationed, however; it followed that it would be filled most efficiently
not with manufactures but with machinery, so that Brazilians might
produce the goods themselves. Throughout the war the Bank of Brazil
and the Office of Economic Warfare cooperated to this end. The
United States sent a mission, at the request of the Brazilian government, to recommend ways of increasing the production of raw materials and ersatz. So ebullient was the spirit of cooperation in the midst
of war that its leader, Morris L. Cooke, interpreted his commission as laying the foundation "for a long range strengthening of Brazil's whole industrial system." In the preliminary joint report,
published in the Brazilian press in December 1942, the American
mission even subscribed to a veiled attack on the privileges of the
industrialized nations. "The history of industrial civilization shows that
a great and prosperous international commerce develops between prosperous nations, but not between rich nations and poor, nor between
those that seek to increase their own prosperity by retarding that of
their neighbors." The contrast with the outlook of the Niemeyer Mis-

sion of 1931 was total. Never had the developed world bestowed so much prestige upon Brazilian efforts to industrialize.[16]

The shortage of ocean shipping stimulated manufactured exports at the same time that it discouraged manufactured imports. The consumer markets of Argentina, Uruguay, and other South American countries were opened to the Brazilians when the customary sources of supply for textiles were cut off. Exports of cotton cloth, by the middle of 1942, were second only to coffee in value, and canned and frozen meats were third. Woolens, cotton and rayon spinning threads, vegetable oils, and sugar provided additional exchange. Once again a considerable part of these sales were at the expense of the domestic market. Vargas made only halfhearted attempts to protect the consumer; it would appear that the "economic expansion of Brazil" was a more important goal. In this matter he greatly accommodated the manufacturers, who had never forgotten foreign demand for their products during World War I. For twenty years their trade associations repeatedly requested government aid to restore that market. Amazingly, Simonsen had thought that drawbacks and export credit would have made it possible. For some of the Paulista manufacturers the war marked the beginning of a new era. Nicolau Filizola, who owned a metal products firm, thought that 1940 marked the end of the cycle of internal market development; from that date forward Brazilian manufactures would be exported.[17]

It is difficult to understand why industrialists were so sanguine concerning the durability of a market that was so clearly temporary. Overseas buyers complained to Brazilian shippers that their prices were

[16] Frederick W. Ganzert, "Wartime Economic Conditions," in Lawrence F. Hill, ed., *Brazil*, pp. 313–314; Cooke, *Brazil*, p. viii; "Conclusões preliminares do trabalho conjunto da comissão técnica brasileira e da missão técnica americana," *Boletim do Ministerio das Relações Exteriores* (December 1942), p. 849. The original text of the Cooke report, not made public until 1948, and never published, is far more autarkist and *dirigiste* than the published version. American Technical Mission to Brazil, *Report*.

[17] CIFTSP *Circulares* (December 9, 1930); Stanley Stein, *The Braziiian Cotton Manufacture*, p. 155; Federação das Industrias do Estado de São Paulo, *Relatorio* (1940), pp. 140–141; *A cidade do aço*, pp. 136–137.

double those of the Americans or the English. Even the optimistic
Cooke had been shocked by the absence of inexpensive technical improvements in cotton mills. "There is so little that is really right about
the textile industry," he wrote, "that radical changes should be easy."
A team of engineers from the state government, sent to all factories
burning coal or diesel fuels, found so little attention paid to this basic
expenditure that they were easily able to reduce consumption by 40
per cent, without slowing production, by requiring improvements in
the fuel systems.[18]

It is likely that the emphasis on the external market was connected
to the concept of overproduction in the minds of the industrialists. "It
is the ideal that much be produced and much be sold at low prices,"
admitted Eduardo Jafet, in a speech inaugurating his company's welfare projects in 1949, but it is impossible unless the market is large
enough. "For reasons of all kinds of origin, the internal market of
Brazil cannot consume all the production of the textile industry, and
it reaches its saturation with a small increase in production." He did
not suggest lowering margins or reducing the costs of manufacture
or distribution. In his opinion there was "no other solution than the
export of the excess of production, to the point that the standard of
living of the consuming masses can account for all the product of the
national textile industry." The foreign market, in other words, was
conceived in teleological terms. The problem was not over-production
of cotton textiles but underconsumption itself. How strange it is to hear
this ingenuous witness of Lenin's critique of imperialism echoed so far
from the metropolis![19]

The need to exploit manpower resources to the fullest during the
emergency of war led the government to extend even further the advantages industrialists had been granted in dealing with workers. It
appears that during the first two years of the Estado Nôvo the Ministry of Labor had grown more diligent in enforcing the labor laws,
perhaps in order to mitigate the increased regimentation of the unions.
The annual report of the Federation of Industries in 1939 observed

[18] Cooke, *Brazil*, pp. 211, 276; Humberto Dantas, "Indústrias paulistas,"
Observador Economico e Financeiro (January 1944), p. 33.
[19] Antônio Jafet, *Vida e obra de Basílio Jafet*, p. 129.

that formerly laws were made in the legislature, with full opportunity for discussion; now they were made in bureaus, by "theoretical functionaries, who do not know the practical aspects of the matter and limit themselves to copying what is done in other countries." It complained in detail concerning the Law of Dismissals, the decisions of the labor courts, the Two-Thirds Law, and the proposed minimum wage. In the same year Simonsen sent the labor ministry a separate memorandum suggesting ways of permitting immigrants to engage in certain critical occupations, despite the Two-Thirds Law, and requesting trial contracts so that temporary workers and apprentices could be employed without protection of the labor laws. Morvan Dias de Figueiredo, vice-president of the Federation, sought reconsideration of child labor laws on what he considered to be humanitarian grounds. He asked the Minister of Labor to notice that in São Paulo children finished primary school when they were eleven or twelve. "Already we have a very grave problem, which is that the minor remains unemployed between this age and that at which he is permitted to work, which is fourteen years. The number of newsboys, of children who play football in the streets, of small thieves who are sometimes caught by the police, are formed during this interregnum." His remedy was earlier employment rather than more schooling. Yet he also maintained somewhat paradoxically that workers at eighteen were not mature enough to receive the full pay of an adult and requested that this legal age limit be raised to twenty.[20]

The war served to justify a more sympathetic hearing for these complaints. Indeed it was accompanied by an almost complete extinction of workers' rights. Union meetings, it was decreed, could not be held unless prior written permission had been obtained from the authorities. Enemy nationals were forbidden to attend union meetings or to vote in union elections. At the time 12 per cent of the Paulista industrial work force was foreign-born. The ten-hour workday was, in effect, restored and sanitary standards reduced. Workers in military plants, and in those plants designated as militarily essential, were forbidden to quit, or transfer to other jobs, or even absent themselves. They would,

[20] *Relatorio* (1939), pp. 70–71, 98; Simonsen, *Ensaios sociais, políticos e econômicos*, p. 107; see also *Boletim do Ministerio de Trabalho, Industria e Commercio* (April 1937), p. 134.

if Brazilian, be treated as deserters; if enemy aliens, they would be considered guilty of sabotage. The textile industrialists, who were fortunate enough to have their sector designated militarily essential for the purposes of these regulations, were given the right to enforce them. A Textile Executive Commission, created in 1944, was supposed to oversee the movements of workers and could also grant permission to suspend the laws on vacations, overtime pay, and nightwork for women. The Commission contained eight representatives from industry, five from government, but none from labor.[21]

The industrialists were deeply responsive to the government's efforts to control the workers and snuff out conflicts. Those who came to Volta Redonda repeatedly used the phrase "social tranquility" in describing the workers' village. It epitomized the paternalistic industrial society of their hopes. The workers, well fed and housed, looked after by a benevolent management, and earning more money because they were more productive, would cease to be troublesome and exigent. The visitors were no longer critical of the labor laws, but praised them extravagantly. Nevertheless, thought one engineer, laws do not resolve social questions. "Only good instruction and a sound physical and moral life can furnish the means of understanding and tolerance, which teach men cooperation, discipline, and the well-being of the collectivity. Social tranquility reposes on that sublime comprehension of the duties that each one has for his neighbor."[22]

While Vargas withdrew rights from the workers, he also bestowed, seemingly, further benefits. The chief of these was a minimum wage law, decreed in May 1940. The average monthly wage, according to the Census of 1940, was 205 milreis, compared to 115 in 1920, although the cost of living had doubled. The minimum wage, which varied within the state according to the cost of living, seems to have been set at a level unrealistically high, if it was really intended to be applied to all workers. The scale decreed in December 1943 for the capital was 360 cruzeiros, higher than the average wage at the time. It is likely that the minimum wage did exert some official pressure in

[21] U.S. Office of the Coordinator of Inter-American Affairs, *Industrial Labor in Brazil*, p. 20.

[22] *A cidade do aço*, pp. 159–160.

behalf of higher pay, but it also seemed likely to observers that wages and salaries lagged behind the cost of living during the war.[23]

The Estado Nôvo had greatly increased the amount of interference in the operations of private businesses, yet the attitude of industrialists, it can be seen, was increasingly favorable to the dictatorship. Not only was it providing them with a whole new range of incentives and favors, but it also assured them a docile pool of cheap labor and permitted them a considerable sphere of influence in the formation of economic policy. The trade associations had been transformed into technical and consultative organs that had, with rare exceptions, collaborated in writing the decrees that affected them. There were seventy syndicates like the textile mill owners syndicate affiliated with the state Federation of Industries of the State of São Paulo (FIESP). The Federation represented 1,465 firms in 1938, only 10 per cent of the total, but by 1944 more than 5,000 were members. The state Federations were brought together in a National Confederation of Industry in April 1943. The significance of this institutionalized form of lobbying can be read in the industrial censuses. In spite of all the benefits heaped on labor since 1931, the manufacturing firms of São Paulo reported total costs of wages and salaries lower proportionate to sales in 1940 than in 1920 (11.3 compared to 11.6 per cent). The tax load on Paulista industry, despite the relative decline in import revenues, was also lower than it had been in 1920 (2.1 compared to 2.7 per cent).[24]

It is likely that there is some truth in very common rumors among Paulista businessmen concerning another form of reciprocal interest. The Estado Nôvo, it is claimed, obtained political complicity and even kickbacks from firms it permitted to evade wartime production controls. An example of this kind of activity was reported in a polemic written against João Alberto, once interventor in São Paulo and during the war Coordinator of Economic Mobilization. During the war the ceiling price of three-sixteenths-inch construction steel was 3.20 cruzeiros per kilo unless it had been rolled by a separate finishing mill,

[23] *Industrial Labor in Brazil*, pp. 25–32; *Economic Conditions in Brazil* (1944), pp. 26–27.

[24] Humberto Dantas, "Indústrias paulistas," p. 37; *Industrial Labor in Brazil*, p. 35.

in which case 6.50 cruzeiros was the maximum price permitted. It was claimed that a Paulista steel producer constructed or bought up thirteen local "rolling mills" that were little more than warehouses. The steel, already reduced to three-sixteenths, was transported to the subsidiary, stored there, and delivered to customers at the higher price. The author charged that João Alberto was the recipient of a bribe made the government in order to avoid prosecution. The source of the accusation is perhaps suspect, and it may be that the reputation of fraud and corruption that clings to the activities of the Estado Nôvo was wholly the creation of its liberal enemies. Yet the absence of press criticism or open congressional inquiry may have made it easier for businessmen to engage in illegal activities.[25]

World War II, like the earlier war, caused enormous difficulties for Paulista industry. It is possible, however, that the wartime shortages and dislocations had in the second instance the salutary effects often attributed to the first. The industrial census of 1950 shows an increase of 7 per cent a year in value added for the decade since 1940. The years immediately following the war cannot account for much more than half that gain, because, in spite of rapid growth in 1948 and 1949, the two previous years were quite unfavorable. It follows, then, that industrial output increased at least as fast during the war as before, and probably faster. But the war itself probably ought not to be considered the cause of this growth. Clearly, the efforts of the Vargas government to counter the dislocations of war had some effect. They secured a flow of credit, raw materials, and spare parts and kept the workers on their jobs. It is also likely that the industrial plant was better able to meet the challenge in 1939 than it had been in 1914. It was far more diversified and sophisticated. There were firms capable of producing special steels, steel forgings, machinery, and industrial chemicals. The hydroelectric output of the state had been greatly augmented shortly before the war. Finally, the United States was committed to supplying technical assistance and equipment to keep the Brazilian economy running.

Even though many of the companies founded under these conditions

[25] Brasílio Machado Neto, *Em defesa das classes produtoras*; Carlos Telles, *História secreta da Fundação Brasil Central*, pp. 52–53, 60–61.

were craft shops operating on a small and inefficient scale or repair shops not engaged in production at all, the list of new or expanded enterprises is quite long. It included cement, plate glass, canning, automobile tires and rubber products, machine tools, inorganic chemicals, electric motors, plastics, explosives, and office machines. The plant for producing tires was installed providentially just before the outbreak of war. The manufacture of automobile parts was much expanded; it was calculated in 1944 that parts makers could supply more than two thousand different parts, including radiators, pistons, and springs. Three new companies were organized to produce railroad rolling stock. On the other hand, it can be seen that the government incentives were in some cases ineffective. Volta Redonda, the Klabin paper mill, an aluminum smelter, and many other plants could not begin production until after the war. It is likely that the installation of new plants in petroleum refining, organic chemicals, and pharmaceuticals was also delayed by wartime shortages.

As the war drew to a close, Paulista manufacturers began to wonder what role they would be given to play in the peacetime economy. Vargas seemed ready to continue the partnership. He expressed concern over the return of foreign competition and spoke of creating an industrial "reconstruction" bank to permit the re-equipment of Brazilian firms. It was to be funded by a surtax on profits, so that industrial gains would not be diverted to other sectors. In January 1944 a tax was levied on excess profits in order to drain off some of the inflationary pressure caused by the shortage of goods formerly imported and by the prepayment in cruzeiros of dollar balances frozen in the United States. An exemption was allowed, however, to firms that banked twice the amount of the profits subject to tax or that used the profits to buy a special re-equipment bond. The bond paid only 3 per cent interest, but it represented a prior claim on the use of Brazil's frozen balances at the end of the war. The latter alternative was more than an emergency measure; it committed the government to spend the vast reserves accumulated in wartime, not for consumer goods but for another round of industrialization.[26]

[26] Ganzert, "Wartime Economic Conditions," p. 320; Souza Costa, *Discurso*, pp. 13–16.

Furthermore, a multifarious bureaucracy had arisen in the meantime, not only to administer emergency controls and to develop specific projects like Volta Redonda but also to intervene continuously in areas such as industrial credit and imports and to plan the development of petroleum and electric power. In order to maintain its momentum, further industrialization was necessary. Eventually, the cumulative impact of these activities might be heightened through the institution of an over-all economic plan. In fact, Vargas had decreed a plan of sorts a year before the outbreak of the war. This "Special Plan of Public Works and Equipment for National Defense" was allotted a total of 3,000,000 contos ($150,000,000), including 1,000,000 contos' worth of foreign exchange. These funds, nearly 10 per cent of the government's resources, were obtained from profits on exchange transactions and other special sources. Evidently, the plan was inspired by the rearmament programs of the European powers and the United States; half of the money was allocated to the military ministries. Much of this portion, in the form of contracts for construction, shipbuilding, and so forth, reverted to local industries. Most of the rest of the funds were used to import oil field equipment, road building machinery, railroad stock, and other kinds of capital goods. The rapid growth after 1938 of companies in São Paulo that produced parts for rolling stock may be attributed to the sudden availability of funds from the Five Year Plan. The first plan was completed at the end of 1943 and another was immediately instituted. Although they were not programs for controlling the growth of the economy, but merely special accounts for development purposes, a rationale had been found for transferring money from the export sector to domestic industrial development.[27]

The Cooke Mission inspired Roberto Simonsen to urge the government to draw up a plan for postwar industrialization. Simonsen had not been privy to the work of the mission, but he had read its recom-

[27] Ganzert, "Wartime Economic Conditions," p. 311; Rosa, "O plano . . . ," pp. 197–208; Brazil, Ministério da Fazenda, *Relatório* (1943), pp. 45–46. On the structural transformation of Paulista industry during the war see also Lucila Herrmann, "Características da evolução do parque industrial do Estado de São Paulo," *Revista de Administração* (December 1947), pp. 87–114.

mendatiòns as a member of the advisory council of the Economic Mobilization Coordinator. His suggestions were presented to the National Council for Commercial and Industrial Policy, a study group under the Minister of Labor, Industry and Commerce, in September 1944. The proposal reveals a considerable evolution in Simonsen's understanding of economic development. As before, he started off with a fairly sophisticated discussion of income per capita, the world commodity market, and the interrelatedness of industrial and agricultural development. But this time he did not limit himself to demanding the containment of imports. He adopted the premise of the Cooke report that directed capital inputs were necessary in transport, energy, basic metals, and chemicals. Explicitly, Simonsen accepted the necessity of planning as a government function in order to carry out these investments. It seemed to him that the United States would be willing to make a long-term loan available to cover half the costs of an industrial plan. Apparently, he wanted the Brazilian government to lend these funds in turn to private Brazilian manufacturers. The government, however, would consult with private interests on the advisable degree of state intervention and would avoid creating firms that might compete with existing plant. Finally, "it would not be conceivable" during this "full constructive period" to permit the internal market to be "disturbed" by foreign competition.[28]

These thoughts surely represented an advanced attitude of permissiveness regarding governmental tutelage of the industrial sector, even though they were hedged with the expectation that the planners would tolerate unlimited profits for the entrepreneurs. Nevertheless, Simonsen was not regarded sympathetically by the technocrats of the National Council. For them he was already an obsolescent phenomenon, a self-taught eclectic, marginalized by the Estado Nôvo, with visions that were tendentious and secondhand. Several members of the Council had participated in the work of the Cooke Mission and were impatient with Simonsen's justifications of measures they were already convinced of. The minutes of the Council sessions show that the president of the

---

[28] *A planificação da economia brasileira*, pp. 13–15. An earlier version of Simonsen's forecasting may be found in his *Alguns aspectos da política mais conveniente ao Brasil no período do após-guerra*.

Federation of Industries, probably the most enlightened spirit of
Paulista entrepreneurship, was an irrelevance. He did not have the
grounding in economics possessed by the professional bureaucrats, and,
since they had little concern for the opinions of the industrialists or the
public, his evident talents as a sounding board and a publicist were lost
to them.[29]

Simonsen, undismayed, continued to agitate publicly for a postwar
industrial development plan. He noted that a conference on economic
affairs sponsored by the Commercial Association in Rio de Janeiro
was well attended, and he persuaded the National Confederation of
Industry to organize a similar conference in São Paulo. This first
Brazilian Congress of Industry took place in December 1944 during
an industrial exposition. Its several sections were supposed to examine
theses concerning aspects of postwar planning, including transport,
energy, basic industry, the industrialization of the north, and the relationship of industry to agriculture and government. On the whole,
the theses were disappointingly narrow in scope and lacking in foresight. Many were produced by engineers who dwelt on technical matters; the few written by industrialists seem perfunctory, written more
for the occasion than for any serious purpose. Their recommendations
generally involved government assistance or the creation of a new
government bureau, but there was also evidence of their real worries
concerning the postwar world. Somehow they would have to adjust
to an economy of mass production and low profit margins; they would
have to accept the spread of industry to hitherto backward areas of
Brazil; and they would have to call upon foreigners for part of the
funds for continued development, even though this posed the question
of competition.[30]

The government's disposition to carry out the recommendations of
the industrialists lasted only one more year. As the war came to an end,
the Estado Nôvo gradually lost the support of the political elite. Its

[29] Conselho Nacional de Política Industrial e Comercial, Minutes of Sessions, August 18–October 10, 1944.

[30] Congresso Brasileiro de Indústria, Atas (December 1944); "Congresso
Brasileiro de Indústria," *Observador Econômico e Financeiro* (January 1945),
pp. 133–138.

Fascist constitution was an embarrassment and annoyed the United States, once the crisis had passed. Within the country the liberal democratic opposition to the dictator took heart from the attitude of the Allies and found that even the army was ready to renounce its earlier commitment to the authoritarian state. Vargas was therefore pressured into calling elections. The military, considering that it would be risky to allow him to preside over them, removed him from office on October 29, 1945. With the fall of Vargas the industrialists fell, too.

Conclusion

E conomic liberalism was restored to power, and most of the decisions of the Estado Nôvo were at least temporarily reversed. The urban middle class had not been the only sector dissatisfied with the drive to industrialization. Even within the government there had remained spokesmen for the view that free trade was the only theoretically justifiable policy. Arthur da Souza Costa, who as Minister of Finance carried out the highly autarkical policies of the Estado Nôvo, had always been at pains to justify them as temporary measures. The breakdown of the "stability reigning until 1913," an "agreeable memory," was a direct cause of World War I, in his opinion, and he was equally certain that in the postwar world the Allies would restore that perfect interdependence that had disappeared thirty years before. Even Vargas betrayed occasionally a nostalgia for the rural society that was more real to him, and perhaps to most Brazilians, than the industrial cities. "We must not forget the countryside, the land, that feeds us all," he said in 1940. He thought it important to avoid the "dangers" of "excessive" urbanism which would depopulate the countryside. The favoritism shown the industrialists had reaffirmed the beliefs of the middle class that their profits were exaggerated and undeserved. Simonsen complained of "elements ignorant of economic problems" or, "more unfortunately, at the service of foreign imperialisms," but it was likely that the feeling was widespread. Simonsen's proposed industrial plan was attacked by Eugênio Gudin, an associate of Souza Costa in the Ministry of Finance, and a delegate to Bretton Woods, who opposed not only the concept of *dirigisme*, but even industrialism itself. He considered agriculture "the only economic activity for which we demonstrate a capacity."[1]

The interim government began immediately to redress the grievances of middle-class consumers. The prices of textiles, hitherto uncontrolled, were subjected to a 10 per cent cut, and textile exports were embargoed. The entire system of import licensing was done away with, so that the middle class might enjoy once again the imported goods it had been deprived of. This measure had the most unhappy consequences for postwar industrialization, because it diverted the immense reserves of foreign exchange accumulated during the war from the task of re-equipping antiquated Brazilian factories.

The liberal middle class of the cities did not emerge the winners in the presidential election that followed the coup against Vargas. The party that most closely approximated their interests, the National Democratic Union (UDN), was defeated by the rural political boss-ism that had survived the crises of 1930, 1937, and 1945 nearly intact. Nevertheless, the influence of the UDN in the new administration was strong, and its attitudes of economic and political liberalism shaped the 1946 Constitution. Industrialists of São Paulo, confronted with a new alignment of political forces, did not hesitate to choose membership in the party of the rural bosses, the Social Democratic Party (PSD). The UDN, hostile to the creation of domestic industry, was an inconceivable ally. Nor was the urban middle class capable of turning its party into an expression of more popular aspirations, so fearful was it of lowering the barriers of class to a mass of factory workers. It became ever more isolated, therefore, and bitter in its sense of moral superiority. Within the PSD, on the other hand, the grand alliance of the Paulista Republican Party could be restored. The industrialists

[1] Arthur da Souza Costa, *Panorama financeiro e economico*, pp. 18–31; Getúlio Vargas, *As diretrizes da nova política do Brasil*, pp. 153–156; *Diario de São Paulo* (September 1, 1945).

still shared most of the attitudes and interests of the planters, and when they did not, they were still willing to defer. Simonsen's campaign for the federal Senate in 1947 demonstrates the nature of the alliance the industrialists returned to. Running with a PSD label, he was the most popular candidate in rural areas, but lost the election because he ran next-to-last in the capital. At any rate, the PSD was clearly the party of the "situation." It would accommodate every disparate element, even the more docile elements of the labor movement, if an electoral victory might be gained thereby. The critical matter of individual lobbying for one's own interest would therefore most readily be solved within its ranks.

Vargas returned to the presidency in 1951. He had discovered in the urban and rural workers a political base broad enough to elect him to office constitutionally. Unfortunately his appeal to the masses caused the industrial bourgeoisie to join the city middle class in the opposition. The game of electoral politics, even though limited to the literate, was clearly laden with hazard for the liberal middle class when it was played by someone who did not scruple an appeal, no matter how bogus, to the overwhelming mass of minimum wage earners. Again the military overthrew Vargas, but not before several other politicians had learned his style and his technique. In São Paulo after 1950 the PSD was splintered by several personalistic "populist" leaders, all competing for the confidence of the masses, most of them for sale to potential backers. The industrialists, of course, grasped the opportunity for personal representatives in the federal and state legislatures. A new sort of articulation had been found for state politics, but not a long-lasting one. The politician was incapable of delivering his promises, and the industrialists were once again absolved of the necessity of evolving a program.[2]

Meanwhile, the economic situation grew more and more unstable. The postwar world did not work out to anyone's satisfaction. The manufacturers discovered that the United States was not at all interested in promoting the industrialization of Brazil. The urban middle

---

[2] The politics of the postwar period are analyzed in Octavio Ianni, ed., *Política e revolução social no Brasil*, and Thomas Skidmore, *Politics in Brazil*, 1930–1964.

class discovered that the world economy was to be little more favorable to a restoration of free trade than before. The bureaucracy, struggling with the immense problem of Brazil's balance of payments, was finally forced to reimpose the controls of the Estado Nôvo and then to surpass them. The government did not cease acquiring industrial holdings. Instead, pressed by political or economic necessity, it began to produce electric power, petroleum, motor vehicles, special steels, and chemicals.

In the meantime, industrialization in the private sector had taken a wholly new direction. Foreign corporations, attracted by the size of the Brazilian market, began to transform their sales agencies into branch manufacturing operations. In many cases they were responding to government decrees designed to solve the balance of payments problem with an increased flow of foreign capital. In order to take advantage of these incentives they had to engage Brazilian associates or buy out Brazilian firms. The effect of this movement was overwhelming. By the early 1960's perhaps half of the industrial capital in São Paulo's private sector, excluding craft shops, was foreign-owned or controlled. Few of the largest Paulista firms had succumbed, but whole new lines had arisen in foreign hands: automobiles, pharmaceuticals, tobacco, construction equipment, tires, and electronics. In other lines one or two foreign companies attained a dominant position.

The postwar industrialization of São Paulo has therefore been, in political and social terms, very different from the earlier period. It has also been more complex economically, because the foreigners introduced more complicated patterns of distribution and finance and called forth an underbrush of parts suppliers and dealers. On the whole the Paulista industrialists favored these developments or, at least, accommodated themselves. A few, angered by the prospect of competition, waged political battles against foreign capital, but the rest were pleased to receive new capital resources and new markets.

It may be that only a narrow parochialism would condemn this transformation. Perhaps the increasing complexity of technique and the need for vast accumulations of capital will lead fatally to the absorption of all the world's industry into one unified and centralized system, from which all will derive greater benefits. It may be that the opposite is true, that the alienation of ownership of much of the industrial capacity of Brazil is a disaster for the Brazilians, to be paid for dearly, both economically and politically.

No matter which point of view is adopted, the history of industrialization before 1945 explains in good measure the ease of penetration by foreign capital and the need to resort to government enterprise. Beginning with cheaper and less-finished consumer goods, sometimes merely a last screwing together of imported goods, the end product sometimes covered with a false label, domestic industry always seemed a shoddy affair to the consumer, especially for the middle-class consumer who lost face when he couldn't afford to buy imports. The manufacturer of consumer goods seemed as reluctant as his customers to buy his own raw materials locally, thereby impeding the installation of basic industry. Furthermore, the manufacturer, with his monopolies, price-fixing, and other illegalities, his manipulation of political connections and his preference for inflation, never enjoyed a favorable "image." His success was not admired; nor did he embody the aspirations of the masses. Between the industrialist and his workers yawned a social abyss that would have made public relations an incongruous and unrewarding occupation. For these reasons the manufacturers were plainly disqualified from embarking their society upon a conscious policy of industrialization.

By 1950 the industrial plants of São Paulo were more than a generation behind Europe and the United States in technique. Until World War I only the newest equipment had been installed; then, in the 1920's and 1930's, the factories slowly became obsolescent, in part because of the difficulties of the coffee trade that could no longer pay for new machinery, but also because of decisions taken within the elite to spend foreign exchange on other imports, to restrict the importation of machines, and even to restrain credit for domestic machine producers. The entrepreneur, more eager to protect current profits than to prepare for the future, participated in these policies. In the meantime there was no mobilization of local savings, no training for a cadre of technicians and engineers. With the recurrence of economic crisis in 1937 and the coming of war, it is not surprising that the state seemed better prepared than the entrepreneurs to resolve the problem of stagnation and to encourage rapid industrialization. When a reapplication of liberal trade theory after the war proved to be mistaken, the controls were taken up again by a clearly reluctant government that was also obliged, for lack of an alternative, to call in foreign capital on its own terms. To some degree the industrialists had presented to Brazil not the solution for its economic crisis, but the crisis itself.

BIBLIOGRAPHY AND INDEX

BIBLIOGRAPHY

GOVERNMENT SOURCES

American Technical Mission to Brazil. *Report.* Mimeographed. 8 vols. Washington, 1948.

Boletim do Departamento Estadual de Trabalho. São Paulo, 1911–1930.

Boletim da Directoria de Industria e Commercio. São Paulo, 1910–1928.

Boletim do Ministério das Relações Exteriores. Rio de Janeiro, 1939–1945.

Boletim do Ministério do Trabalho, Industria e Comércio. Rio de Janeiro, 1934–1960.

Brazil. *Coleção das leis.* Rio de Janeiro, 1880–1946.

————. Conselho Nacional de Política Industrial e Comercial. Minutes of Sessions. Mimeographed. Rio de Janeiro, August 18–October 10, 1944.

————. Instituto Brasileiro de Geografia e Estatística. *Recenseamento geral do Brasil (10 de setembro de 1940).* Part XVII. 3 vols. Rio de Janeiro, 1950.

————. Instituto Brasileiro de Geografia e Estatística. Conselho Nacional de Estatística. *O Brasil em números.* Rio de Janeiro, 1960.

————. Instituto Brasileiro de Geografia e Estatística. Conselho Nacional de Estatística. Serviço Nacional de Recenseamento. *Recenseamento geral do Brasil, 1950.* 30 vols. Rio de Janeiro, 1954.

————. Ministério de Agricultura, Indústria e Comércio. Directoria Geral de Estatística. *Anuario estatistico do Brasil, 1908–1912.* Rio de Janeiro, 1917.

————. *Recenseamento geral do Brasil realizado em 1 de setembro de 1920.* 18 vols. Rio de Janeiro, 1922–1929.

————. Ministério de Trabalho, Indústria e Comércio. *Seus serviços, orientação e attitude deante dos problemas da nossa economia nacional.* Rio de Janeiro, 1937.

————. *Sociedades mercantis autorizadas a funcionar no Brasil, 1808–1946.* Rio de Janeiro, 1947.

————. Ministério de Viação e Obras Públicas. *Estatistica das estradas de ferro, 1936–1939.* Rio de Janeiro, 1937–1940.

Comissão Americana de Técnicos em Óleos Vegetais. *O Brasil e os óleos vegetais.* Rio de Janeiro, 1942.

Comissão Mista Brasil–Estados Unidos para Desenvolvimento Econômico. *Relatório geral.* 17 vols. Rio de Janeiro, 1954.

Great Britain. Department of Overseas Trade. *Economic Conditions in Brazil, 1929–1945.* London, 1929–1945.

São Paulo (state). *Anuario estatistico de São Paulo (Brazil), 1898–1929.* São Paulo, 1900–1935.

————. *Diário Oficial.* São Paulo, 1892–1945.

————. *Mensagens apresentados ao Congresso Legislativo de São Paulo pelos Presidentes do Estado e Vice-Presidentes em Exercicio desde a proclamação da Republica até ao anno de 1916.* São Paulo, 1916.

————. Assembleia Legislativa. *Annaes da Constituinte, 1935.* 2 vols. São Paulo, 1937.

————. Departamento Estadual de Estatística. *Dados gerais do Estado: 1890–1938.* São Paulo, 1940.

————. Junta Comercial de São Paulo [JCSP], 1891–1940.

————. Secretaria de Agricultura, Indústria e Comêrcio. *Estatistica do commercio do porto de Santos com os paizes estrangeiros, 1911–1912— 1934–1935.* São Paulo, 1912–1935.

————. *Commercio de cabotagem pelo Porto de Santos, 1907–1909— 1943–1944.* São Paulo, 1909–1944.

————. Secretaria de Agricultura, Indústria e Comêrcio. Directoria de Estatística, Indústria e Comêrcio. *Estatistica Industrial do Estado de São Paulo, 1928–1938.* São Paulo, 1929–1939.

————. Tribunal de Justiça. *Outros balanços do Conde Francisco Matarazzo Junior. Apelação Civil N. 46055.* São Paulo, 1949.

United Nations. Economic Commission for Latin America. *Problemas y perspectivas del desarrollo industrial latinoamericano.* Buenos Aires, 1964.

U.S. Department of Commerce. Bureau of Foreign and Domestic Commerce. *Banking and Credit in Argentina, Brazil, Chile, and Peru.* (Special Agents Series, No. 90), Washington, 1914.

————. *Boots and Shoes, Leather, and Supplies in Brazil.* (Special Agent Series, No. 179), Washington, 1911.

U.S. Office of the Coordinator of Inter-American Affairs. *Industrial Labor in Brazil.* Washington, 1944.

U.S. Department of State. "Reciprocal Trade Agreement . . . Effective January 1, 1936." Executive Agreement Series, No. 82.

U.S. National Archives. Department of State, Decimal Files, Rio de Janeiro, São Paulo, 1900–1929. [NA-DS]

————. Records Relating to the Internal Affairs of Brazil. Consular reports from São Paulo, 1910–1929. Microfilm. [RRIAB]

U.S. Tariff Commission. *Economic Controls and Commercial Policy in Brazil.* Washington, 1945.

TRADE ASSOCIATION SOURCES

Associação Comercial de São Paulo. Atas. Typewritten. 1926–1945.

————. *Relatorio da Directoria de 1923.* São Paulo, n.d.

————. *Relatorios das directorias de 1924 e 1925.* São Paulo, 1926.

Boletim Official da Associação Commercial. São Paulo, 1926–1928.

Brazilian Business [American Chambers of Commerce for Brazil]. Rio de Janeiro, 1921–1967.

British Chamber of Commerce of São Paulo and Southern Brazil. *Importers and Manufacturers in the State of São Paulo.* São Paulo, 1929.

————. *Personalidades no Brasil.* São Paulo, 1933.

Centro das Indústrias do Estado de São Paulo. *Relatorio.* São Paulo, 1929.

Centro de Commercio e Industria de São Paulo. "Relatorio de 1917." *Revista de Commercio e Industria,* January, 1918: 28.

Centro dos Industriaes de Fiação e Tecelagem de São Paulo [CIFTSP]. *A crise textil.* São Paulo, 1928.

————. *A vida das industrias textis do Estado de São Paulo durante um decennio: 1912–1921.* São Paulo, 1923.

————. Atas das sessões extraordinarias. Manuscript. 1919–1925.

————. *Circulares.* Mimeographed. São Paulo, 1921–1946.

————. *Relatorio.* Mimeographed. 1921–1930.

Centro Industrial do Brasil. *Annaes, 1926–1928.* Rio de Janeiro, 1928.

————. *Relatorio, 1912.* Rio de Janeiro, 1912.

Centro Industrial do Brasil. Commissão d'Expansão Economica do Brasil. *O Brasil.* 3 vols. Paris, 1910.

Congresso Brasileiro de Indústria. Atas. Mimeographed. São Paulo, December, 1944.

Federação das Indústrias do Estado de São Paulo. *A cidade do aço.* São Paulo, 1943.

————. "Exposição enviada ao Presidente da Republica." In Roberto Simonsen, *A industria em face da economia nacional*. São Paulo, 1937.

————. *Relatorio*, 1938–1941. São Paulo, 1939–1942.

Monthly Journal of the British Chamber of Commerce. São Paulo, 1918–1940.

Revista da Associação Commercial de São Paulo. São Paulo, 1915–1928.

Revista de Commercio e Industria [Centro de Commercio e Industria de São Paulo]. São Paulo, 1915–1919.

Revista Industrial de São Paulo [Federação e Centro das Industrias do Estado de São Paulo]. São Paulo, 1944–1949.

Sindicato Patronal das Industrias Textis do Estado de São Paulo. *Relatorio*. Mimeographed. 1931–1933.

OTHER SOURCES

A Gazeta. São Paulo, 1916–1918.

Abranches, Dunshee d'. *Governos e congressos da Republica dos Estados Unidos do Brasil. 1889 a 1917*. 2 vols. São Paulo, 1917.

Al conte Francesco Matarazzo, gloria dell'ingegno e del lavoro. São Paulo, 1954.

"Aliam a técnica ao comércio." *Visão* (October 16, 1964), 37–38.

Almeida, Aluísio de. "Biografias sorocabanas." *Revista do Arquivo Municipal*, October, 1952: 13–39.

————. "Notas para a história de São Paulo." *Revista do Arquivo Municipal*, July, 1952: 3–22.

Amaral, Azevedo, *A aventura política do Brasil*. Rio de Janeiro, 1935.

————. *O estado autoritario e a realidade nacional*. Rio de Janeiro, 1938.

"Anderson Clayton Celebrates 25 Years in Brazil." *Brazilian Business*, January, 1960: 24–25.

"As industrias paulistas." *Revista do Algodão*, July, 1935: 301–310.

Atri, A. d'. *L'État de São Paulo et le renouvellement économique de l'Europe*. Paris, 1926.

Baer, Werner. *Industrialization and Economic Development in Brazil*. Homewood, Ill., 1965.

Banas, Geraldo. *Anuário Banas: A indústria brasileira de máquinas, 1962*. São Paulo, 1962.

————. *Anuário Banas: bancos, investimentos e bôlsas, 1964*. São Paulo, 1964.

————. *Anuário Banas: máquinas e ferramentas, 1963*. São Paulo, 1963.

————. *Nos bastidores do setor bancário*. Mimeographed. São Paulo, 1959.

————. *Relatório industrial: indústria de bebidas.* São Paulo, 1956.

Bandeira, Jr., Antônio Francisco. *A industria de São Paulo em 1901.* São Paulo, 1901.

Barbour, Violet. *Capitalism in Amsterdam in the 17th Century.* Ann Arbor, Mich., 1963.

Barros, Jayme de. *A política externa do Brasil.* Rio de Janeiro, 1941.

Basbaum, Leôncio. *História sincera do Brasil.* 3 vols. 2d ed. São Paulo, 1962.

Bastos, Humberto. *A conquista siderúrgica no Brasil.* São Paulo, 1959.

————. *O pensamento industrial no Brasil.* São Paulo, 1952.

Bastos, Raul Carvalho. *Homens e fatos do meu tempo.* São Paulo, 1962.

Bell, Daniel. "The Break-up of Family Capitalism." *Partisan Review,* Spring, 1957: 317–320.

Bello, José Maria. *A questão social e a realidade brasileira.* Rio de Janeiro, 1936.

Bittencourt, A. M. *Os postulados da revolução.* Rio de Janeiro, 1931.

Blancato, Vicenzo. *Conte Francesco Matarazzo.* São Paulo, 1925.

Boletim Algodoeira. São Paulo, 1921–1923.

Bonardelli, Eugenio. *Lo stato di S. Paolo del Brasile e l'emigrazione italiana.* Turin, 1916.

Bouças, Valentim. *História da dívida externa da União.* Rio de Janeiro, 1946.

Brasil Economico. São Paulo, 1928–1929.

Brazilian Year Book, Second Issue, 1909. Rio de Janeiro, 1909.

"Brazil's Milling Industry." *Brazilian Business,* October, 1951: 39.

Bürger, Otto. *Brasilien, Eine Landes- und Wirtschaftskunde für Handel, Industrie und Einwanderung.* Leipzig, 1926.

Calmon, Pedro. *História do Brasil.* 5 vols. São Paulo, 1939–1956.

Campos, Aluísio Fragoso de Lima. *O imperativo economico brasileiro.* Rio de Janeiro, 1937.

Campos, Francisco. *O estado nacional, sua estrutura, seu conteudo ideologico.* Rio de Janeiro, 1940.

Canabrava, Alice P. *O desenvolvimento da cultura de algodão na Província de São Paulo, 1861–1875.* São Paulo, 1951.

Capri, Roberto. *Album comemorativa, Companhia Vidraria Santa Marina.* São Paulo, 1919.

————. *O Estado de São Paulo e seus municipios.* São Paulo, 1913.

Cardoso, Fernando Henrique. "A estrutura da indústria em São Paulo." *Educação e Ciências Sociais,* February, 1960: 29–42.

————. "As condições sociais da industrialização de São Paulo," *Revista Brasiliense,* March–April, 1960: 31–46.

————. *Empresário industrial e desenvolvimento econômico.* São Paulo, 1964.

————. "The Industrial Elite." In *Elites in Latin America,* edited by Seymour Martin Lipset and Aldo Solari. New York, 1967.

Chandler, Alfred. "The Beginnings of 'Big Business' in American Industry." *Business History Review,* Spring, 1959: 1–31.

Chateaubriand, Assis. Speech published in *A Provincial do Pará,* February 10, 1967.

50 anos de vidro, 1903–1953. São Paulo, 1954.

Commercial Encyclopedia, Third Sectional Issue, South America. London, 1922.

Commercial Encyclopedia, Fourth Sectional Issue, South America. London, 1924.

"Conclusões preliminares do trabalho conjunto da commissão técnica brasileira e da missão técnica americana," *Boletim do Ministério das Relações Exteriores,* December, 1942: 846–849.

"Condições do trabalho na indústria textil no Estado de São Paulo." *Boletim do Departamento Estadual de Trabalho,* 1911: 35–77.

"Congresso Brasileiro de Indústria." *Observador Econômico e Financeiro,* January, 1945: 133–138.

Cooke, Morris Llewellyn. *Brazil on the March.* New York, 1944.

"Côres e corantes," *Revista Paulista de Indústria,* January, 1955: 5–18.

Correio Paulistano. São Paulo, 1910–1930.

Costa, Aguinaldo. "Monopólio da indústria e do comêrcio do vidro." *Revista Brasiliense,* November–December, 1955: 132–145.

Costa, Arthur da Souza. *Discurso proferido no banquete do Teatro Municipal do Rio de Janeiro.* Rio de Janeiro, 1944.

————. *Panorama financeiro e economico da Republica.* Rio de Janeiro, 1941.

Costa, Isaltino. "As origens da cultura do algodão em São Paulo," *Revista do Algodão,* February, 1935: 5–11.

Coutinho, Afrânio. *Brasil e os brasileiros de hoje.* 2 vols. Rio de Janeiro, 1961.

Cusano, Alfredo. *Il Brasile, gl'italiani, e la guerra.* Rome, 1921.

————. *Italia d'oltre mare.* Milan, 1911.

Dantas, Humberto. "Indústrias paulistas." *Observador Econômico e Financeiro,* January, 1944: 33–42.

Denis, Pierre. *Le Brésil au XXe siècle.* Paris, 1909.

Dettman, Eduard. *Das moderne Brasilien.* Berlin, 1912.

Deursen, Henri van. "L'Émancipation industrielle du Brésil." *Revue Economique Internationale,* August, 1934: 275–335.

Diario de São Paulo. São Paulo, 1929–1946.

Dias, Everardo. *História das lutas sociais no Brasil.* São Paulo, 1962.

Direção. São Paulo, 1962–1963.

Diniz, Osório da Rocha. *A politica que convém ao Brasil.* São Paulo, 1937.

Economist. London, 1897.

Egas, Eugenio. *Galeria dos Presidentes de São Paulo.* 3 vols. São Paulo, 1926–1927.

Empreza Editora. *São Paulo moderno.* Porto Alegre, 1919.

Erstes Jahrbuch für die deutschsprechende Kolonie im Staate São Paulo, 1905. São Paulo, n.d.

F. Upton e Cia. "Catalog A." São Paulo, 1904.

Feis, Herbert. *Europe, The World's Banker.* 2d ed. New York, 1965.

Folha de Manhã. São Paulo, 1928–1929.

Finocchi, Lino. *In memoria* [Count Alexeandro Siciliano]. São Paulo, 1924.

Ford, Henry. *Hoje e amanhã.* Translated by Monteiro Lobato. São Paulo, 1927.

Frankenstein, Herbert. *Brasilien als Aufnahmeland der jüdischen Auswanderung aus Deutschland.* Berlin, 1936.

Furtado, Celso. *Diagnosis of the Brazilian Crisis.* Berkeley, Calif., 1965.

———. *Economic Growth of Brazil.* Berkeley, 1963.

Ganzert, Frederick W. "Wartime Economic Conditions." In *Brazil,* edited by Lawrence F. Hill. Berkeley, Calif., 1947.

Gauld, Charles. *The Last Titan.* Stanford, Calif., 1965.

Gerschenkron, Alexander. *Economic Backwardness in Historical Perspective.* Cambridge, Mass., 1962.

Grossi, Vicenzo. "Gl'italiani a São Paulo." *Nuova Antologia,* September 16, 1896: 231–260.

"Há sessenta anos faz-se ouvir nos acontecimentos de maior relevância para a vida do estado e do pais," in *Ensaios paulistas,* São Paulo, 1958.

Hagen, Everett E. *On the Theory of Social Change.* Homewood, Ill., 1962.

Herrmann, Lucila. "Características da evolução do parque industrial do Estado de São Paulo." *Revista de Administração,* December, 1947: 87–114.

———. "Evolução da estrutura social de Guaratinguetá num período de trezentos anos." *Revista de Administração,* March–June, 1948: 1–326.

Hilton, Ronald. *Who's Who in Latin America*, Part IV, Brazil. 3d ed. Stanford, Calif., 1948.

Hirschmeier, Johannes. *The Origins of Entrepreneurship in Meiji Japan.* Cambridge, Mass., 1964.

Hoselitz, Bert F. "Entrepreneurship and Economic Growth." *American Journal of Economics and Sociology*, October, 1952: 97–110.

Ianni, Constantino. "Formação de capital e desenvolvimento industrial." In *Problemas da economia industrial.* São Paulo [1962].

————. *Poupança, investimentos, e mercado de capital.* São Paulo, n.d.

Ianni, Octavio, ed. *Política e revolução social no Brasil.* São Paulo, 1965.

In memoriam, Conde Francisco Matarazzo. São Paulo, 1937.

Jafet, Antônio. *Vida e obra de Basílio Jafet.* São Paulo, 1957.

Jafet, Eduardo. "Fortalecimento dos mercados internos." Mimeographed. Thesis presented to the Congresso Brasileiro de Industria. São Paulo, December, 1944.

Jafet, Nâmi. *Ensaios e discursos.* Translated by Taufik Daúd Kurban. São Paulo, 1947.

James, Preston E. "Industrial Development in São Paulo State, Brazil." *Economic Geography*, July, 1935: 258–266.

Jornal do Commercio. *Retrospecto Commercial.* Rio de Janeiro, 1889–1930.

Jornal do Commercio (São Paulo). São Paulo, 1917–1929.

Joslin, David A. *A Century of Banking in Latin America.* London, 1963.

Kafka, Alexandre. "Brazil." In *Banking Systems*, edited by Benjamin H. Beckhart. New York, 1954.

Knowlton, Clark. "Spacial and Social Mobility of the Syrians and Lebanese in the City of São Paulo, Brazil." Unpublished Ph.D. dissertation, Vanderbilt University, 1955.

Kriesberg, Louis. "Entrepreneurs in Latin America and the Role of Cultural and Situational Processes." *International Social Sciences Journal*, 1963: 581–596.

Lacerda, José M. de, and Moura, Eloy de. *O Estado Novo, democracia e corporativismo.* Rio de Janeiro, 1938.

Lacerda, Maurício de. *Segunda Republica.* 2d ed. Rio de Janeiro, 1931.

Lafer, Horácio. "Brazil's Paper Industry." *The Commercial.* Published by the *Manchester Guardian*, June 27, 1929: 24.

LaFond, Georges. "Les raisons économiques de l'agitation politique au Brésil." *La Vie des Peuples*, 1924: 539–553.

Leal, Victor Nunes. *Coronelismo, enxada e voto.* Rio de Janeiro, 1948.

Leão, Antônio Carneiro. *S. Paulo em 1920.* Rio de Janeiro, 1920.

LeClerc, Max. *Cartas do Brasil.* Translated by Sergio Milliet. São Paulo, 1942.

Leite, Aureliano. *Subsídios para a história da civilização paulista.* São Paulo, 1954.

L'Empire du Brésil. L'Exposition universelle de 1876 à Philadelphie. Rio de Janeiro, 1876.

Lima, Heitor Ferreira. *Mauá e Roberto Simonsen.* São Paulo, 1963.

"Lion SA Keeps Pace with São Paulo's Industrial Growth." *Brazilian Business,* August, 1961: 26–27, 64.

Lopes, Juárez Rubens Brandão. "Relações industriais na sociedade tradicional brasileira." Mimeographed. Unpublished thesis, University of São Paulo, 1964.

Lowrie, Samuel H. "O elemento negro na população de São Paulo." *Revista do Arquivo Municipal,* 1938: 5–56.

Luz, Nícia Vilela. "A administração provincial de São Paulo em face do movimento abolicionista." *Revista de Administração,* December, 1948: 80–100.

———. *A luta pela industrialização do Brasil.* São Paulo, 1961.

Machado Neto, Brasílio. *Em defesa das classes produtoras.* São Paulo, 1948.

Mantoux, Paul. *The Industrial Revolution in the Eighteenth Century.* Rev. ed. New York, 1961.

"Máquinas para tecelagem." *Revista Paulista de Indústria,* September, 1955: 8–21.

Martin, Percy Alvin. *Latin America and the War.* Baltimore, 1925.

Martins, José de Souza. *Empresário e emprêsa na biografia do Conde Matarazzo.* Rio de Janeiro, 1967.

Martins, Luciano. "Formação do impresario industrial." *Revista Civilização Brasileira,* No. 13, May, 1967: 91–132.

Martins, Paulo. *Problemas nacionais.* São Paulo, 1935.

Matarazzo, Francesco. *Scelta di discorsi e interviste.* São Paulo, 1926.

"Matarazzo's Mighty Empire." *Brazilian Business,* September, 1953: 24–30.

Mattos, Dirceu Lino de. "O parque industrial paulistano," in Associação dos Geógrafos Brasileiros, Secção Regional de São Paulo, *A cidade de São Paulo,* vol. 3. São Paulo, 1958.

Maurette, Fernand. *Alguns aspectos sociais do desenvolvimento actual e futuro da economia brasileira.* Geneva, 1937.

Mello, Afonso de Toledo Bandeira de. *Politique commerciale du Brésil.* Rio de Janeiro, 1935.

Memorial historico da industria de 1933. São Paulo, 1933.

Moacyr, Primitivo. *A instrucção pública no Estado de São Paulo.* 2 vols. São Paulo, 1942.

Momsen, Richard P. *Legal Requirements for Operations of Foreign and Domestic Corporations in Brazil.* Rio de Janeiro, 1919.

Monbeig, Pierre. *La croissance de la ville de São Paulo.* Grenoble, 1953.

————. *Pionniers et planteurs de São Paulo.* Paris, 1952.

Monte Domecq' et Cie., Société de Publicité Sud-Américaine. *O Estado de São Paulo.* Barcelona, 1918.

Morse, Richard M. *From Community to Metropolis.* Gainesville, Fla., 1958.

Mosconi, Ferrucio. "Le classi sociali al Brasile e loro funzioni." *La Riforma Sociale,* 1897: 581–594.

Mouralis, Louis. *Un séjour aux États-Unis du Brésil.* Paris, 1934.

Müller Caravellas, Oscar Reinaldo. *História de uma indústria.* São Paulo, 1949.

Müller Carioba, H. Jorge. "Investidores versus empresários." In *Anuário Banas: bancos, investimentos e bolsas, 1964,* edited by Geraldo Banas. São Paulo, 1964.

Mulqueen, Frederick. "A Canadian Enterprise Abroad." *Canadian Banker,* Winter, 1952: 34–55.

Nash, Manning. *Primitive and Peasant Economic Systems.* San Francisco, 1966.

Niemeyer, Waldyr. *O Brasil e seu mercado interno.* Rio de Janeiro, 1948.

Nogueira, O. Pupo. "Em torno de uma estatística industrial." *Observador Economico e Financeiro,* January, 1937: 19–21.

Nogueira Filho, Paulo. *Ideias e lutas de um burguês progressista: o Partido Democrático e a Revolução de 1930.* 2 vols. São Paulo, 1958.

O Conde Matarazzo aos oitenta annos. São Paulo, 1934

O Estado de São Paulo. São Paulo, 1890–1945.

O Estado de São Paulo. Suplemento Comercial e Industrial. São Paulo, 1948–1963.

Observador Econômico e Financeiro. Rio de Janeiro, 1937–1945.

Oliveira, Armando Salles. *Jornada democratica.* Rio de Janeiro, 1937.

Oliveira, Clovis de. *A indústria e o movimento constitucionalista de 1932.* São Paulo, 1956.

"Organizações Nôvo Mundo-Vemag Enters Automobile Industry." *Brazilian Business,* May, 1957: 16–19.

Paláez, Carlos. "A balança comercial, a grande depressão, e a industrialização." *Revista Brasileira de Economia,* March, 1968: 15–47.

Park, Robert E. *Race and Culture.* Glencoe, Ill., 1950.

Pearse, Arno S. *Brazilian Cotton.* Manchester, 1921.

Pearse, N. S. *Cotton Progress in Brazil.* Manchester [1937].

Pestana, Paulo R. "A industria de banha." *Boletim da Directoria de Industria e Commercio,* October–November, 1914: 497–499.

———. "As industrias manufactureiras de São Paulo." *Revista da Associação Commercial de São Paulo,* March, 1923: 147–148.

———. "As nossas industrias durante a guerra." *Revista de Commercio e Industria,* November, 1918: 387–388.

Phelps, Dudley Maynard. *Migration of Industry to South America.* New York, 1936.

Piccarolo, Antonio, and Finocchi, Lino. *O desenvolvimento industrial de S. Paulo.* São Paulo, 1918.

Pinto, Adolfo Augusto. *Historia da viação publica de São Paulo.* São Paulo, 1903.

Pisani, Salvatore. *Lo stato di San Paolo nel cinquantenario dell'immigrazione.* São Paulo, 1937.

Piza, Antonio de Toledo. *Relatorio apresentado ao cidadão Dr. Alfredo Pujol Secretario de Negocios do Interior do Estado de S. Paulo.* São Paulo, 1896.

Pôrto, S. *Cia. Comêrcio Industria "Antonio Diederichsen," 1903–1953.* São Paulo: Riberão Prêto, 1953.

Prado, Caio. *Historia econômica do Brasil.* 7th ed. São Paulo, 1962.

Prado, Nazareth. *Antonio Prado no Imperio e na República.* Rio de Janeiro, 1929.

Queiroz, Maria Isaura Pereira de. "A estratificação e a mobilidade social nas comunidades do Vale do Paraíba." *Revista da História,* April–June, 1950: 195–218.

Quem é quem no Brasil. 1st–7th eds. São Paulo, 1948–1963.

Raffard, Henri. *A industria saccharifera no Brasil.* Rio de Janeiro, 1882.

Rangoni, Domenico. *Dopo un viaggio in Italia.* São Paulo, 1903.

Revista do Algodão. São Paulo, 1935–1937.

Revista Paulista de Indústria. São Paulo, 1952–1961.

Riesser, Jacob. *The Great German Banks.* Translated by Morris Jacobson. Washington, 1911.

Robertson, Ross. *History of the American Economy.* New York, 1964.

Rolfe, E. Lloyd. *Report on Brazil's Trade and Industry in 1918.* São Paulo, 1919.

Rosa, Rubens. "O plano quinquenal brasileiro." *Boletim do Ministerio de Trabalho, Industria e Commercio*, June, 1939: 197–208.

Ruotolo, Francesco, and Basile, Carlo. *Il libro d'oro degli italiani nel Brasile*. Rio de Janeiro, 1924.

Schlesinger, Hugo. *Enciclopédia da indústria brasileira*. 5 vols. São Paulo, 1959.

Schompré, Emile Quoniam. *La Bourse de São Paulo, 1911*. São Paulo, 1911.

Siciliano, Alexandre. *Valorisação do café; bases de contracto entre um syndicato e o governo federal apresentadas a Sociedade Paulista de Agricultura*. São Paulo, 1903.

Siciliano Jr., Alexandre. *Agricultura, comercio e industria no Brasil*. São Paulo, 1931.

Silva, Herculano de Carvalho e. *A revolução constitucionalista*. Rio de Janeiro, 1932.

Silva, José Pereira da. *As melhores páginas de Getulio Vargas*. Rio de Janeiro, 1940.

Silveira, Joel. *Grã-Finos em São Paulo e outras notícias do Brasil*. São Paulo, 1946.

Simão, Azis. *Sindicato e estado*. São Paulo, 1966.

Simmel, Georg. *The Sociology of Georg Simmel*. Glencoe, Ill., 1950.

✓ Simonsen, Roberto. *A evolução industrial do Brasil*. São Paulo, 1939.

———. *A industria em face da economia nacional*. São Paulo, 1937.

———. *À margem da profissão*. São Paulo, 1932.

———. *A planificação da economia brasileira*. São Paulo, 1944.

———. *Alguns aspectos da política econômica mais conveniente ao Brasil no período do após-guerra*. São Paulo, 1943.

———. *As crises no Brasil*. São Paulo, 1930.

———. *Aspectos da política economica nacional*. São Paulo, 1935.

———. *Brazil's Industrial Evolution*. São Paulo, 1939.

———. *Ensaios sociais, políticos e econômicos*. São Paulo, 1943.

———. *Niveis de vida e economia nacional*. São Paulo, 1940.

———. *Ordem econômica, padrão de vida, e algumas realidades brasileiras*. São Paulo, 1934.

———. *Rumo à verdade*. São Paulo, 1930.

Skidmore, Thomas. *Politics in Brazil, 1930–1964*. New York, 1967.

Spiegel, Henry W. *The Brazilian Economy, Chronic Inflation and Sporadic Industrialization*. Philadelphia, 1949.

Statuts de la Banque Brésilienne Italo-Belge, Société Anonyme. Antwerp, 1911.

Stein, Stanley. "Brazilian Cotton Textile Industry." In *Economic Growth: Brazil, India, Japan,* edited by Simon Kuznets, Wilbert E. Moore, and Joseph J. Spengler. Durham, N.C., 1955.

————. *The Brazilian Cotton Manufacture.* Cambridge, Mass., 1957.

————. *Vassouras, A Brazilian Coffee County.* Cambridge, Mass., 1957.

Strassman, W. P. "The Industrialist." In *Continuity and Change in Latin America,* edited by John J. Johnson. Stanford, Calif., 1964.

Street, Jorge. *Carta aberta ao exmo. sr. dr. Araujo Franco, presidente da Associação Commercial do Rio de Janeiro.* São Paulo, 1928.

Subiroff, Ivan [Nereu Rangel Pestana]. *A oligarchia paulista.* São Paulo, 1919.

Svennilson, Ingvar. *Growth and Stagnation in the European Economy.* Geneva, 1954.

"Sweden's Aga in Brazil." *Brazilian Business,* December, 1957: 26–28.

Telles, Carlos. *História secreta da Fundação Brasil Central.* Rio de Janeiro, 1946.

Twentieth Century Impressions of Brazil. London, 1913.

"Uma vida de animador." *Diario de São Paulo,* March 9, 1934.

Vargas, Getúlio. *As diretrizes da nova política do Brasil.* Rio de Janeiro, 1942.

————. *O Estado Novo e o momento brasileiro.* Rio de Janeiro, 1938.

————. *Primeiro aniversario da Revolução de Outubro.* Rio de Janeiro, 1931.

Vieira, Dorival Teixeira. "The industrialization of Brazil." In *Brazil, Portrait of Half a Continent,* edited by T. Lynn Smith. New York, 1951.

"Villares Four-Part Industrial Empire." *Brazilian Business,* December, 1957: 32–36.

Visão. São Paulo, 1958–1967.

Walle, Paul. *Au pays de l'or rouge.* Paris, 1921.

Wileman's Review. Rio de Janeiro, 1923–1926.

Wirth, John D. "Brazilian Economic Nationalism, Trade and Steel Under Vargas." Unpublished Ph.D. dissertation, Stanford University, 1966.

Witt, Lawrence W. "Brazilian Business Families," *American Universities Field Staff Reports,* East Coast South America Series (November 21, 1952).

Wythe, George. *Brazil, An Expanding Economy.* New York, 1949.

INDEX

abolition of slavery: 35

agricultural production: 9–10, 130–131, 145, 146. SEE ALSO coffee cultivation; cotton production; planters

Agro-Fabril, Companhia: tariff struggle of, 138–139

Alberto, João: 183, 189–191, 192, 227–228

Alberto Lion and Company: 30, 74, 100, 113

aluminumware manufacturers: oppose Matarazzo, 148

Amaral, Azevedo: on Estado Nôvo, 210

Andrighetti, Paulo: 116

army: supports intervention in economy, 212, 217, 219

"artificial industry": 69, 145, 146, 183, 185, 203

automobile production: 33

balance of payments (1904–1919): 88–89

Banco Francês e Italiano para América do Sul: 55, 57–58, 138

Banco União (Sorocaba): 103–104

Bank of Naples (São Paulo branch): 6

Barretos packing plant: 75, 96, 111

Belli, Bruno: 157, 164–165, 170

Bernardes, Arthur, President of Brazil: 131, 137, 159

blacklists of workers: 164–165, 166

Botucatu: 102

Brasilianische Bank für Deutschland: 55, 100

Brasital. SEE Belli, Bruno; Dell'Acqua, E., e Companhia

Brazilian Congress of Industry: 232

Brazilian Traction, Light and Power Company: 8. SEE ALSO São Paulo Traction, Light and Power Company

British interests: 24, 47, 55, 110–111

bureaucracy: supports industrialization, 212, 230; and Roberto Simonsen, 231–232

Caixa de Conversão: 87

capitalism: ideology of, 126, 170–171; and fascism, 174–176

cartels: listed, 121

Center for Spinning and Weaving Manufacturers of São Paulo (CIFTSP): 121; and cotton supply, 124; campaign for textile tariffs, 142–143; lobbies against labor legislation, 160, 191; represses union, 162–167, 189; membership, 165; petitions revolutionary government, 185, 186; syndicalized and renamed, 187; in 1932 rebellion, 194, 195

Center of Commerce and Industry of São Paulo: 100

Center of Industries of the State of São Paulo: 141; opposes labor legislation,